MATTHEW K. MINERD

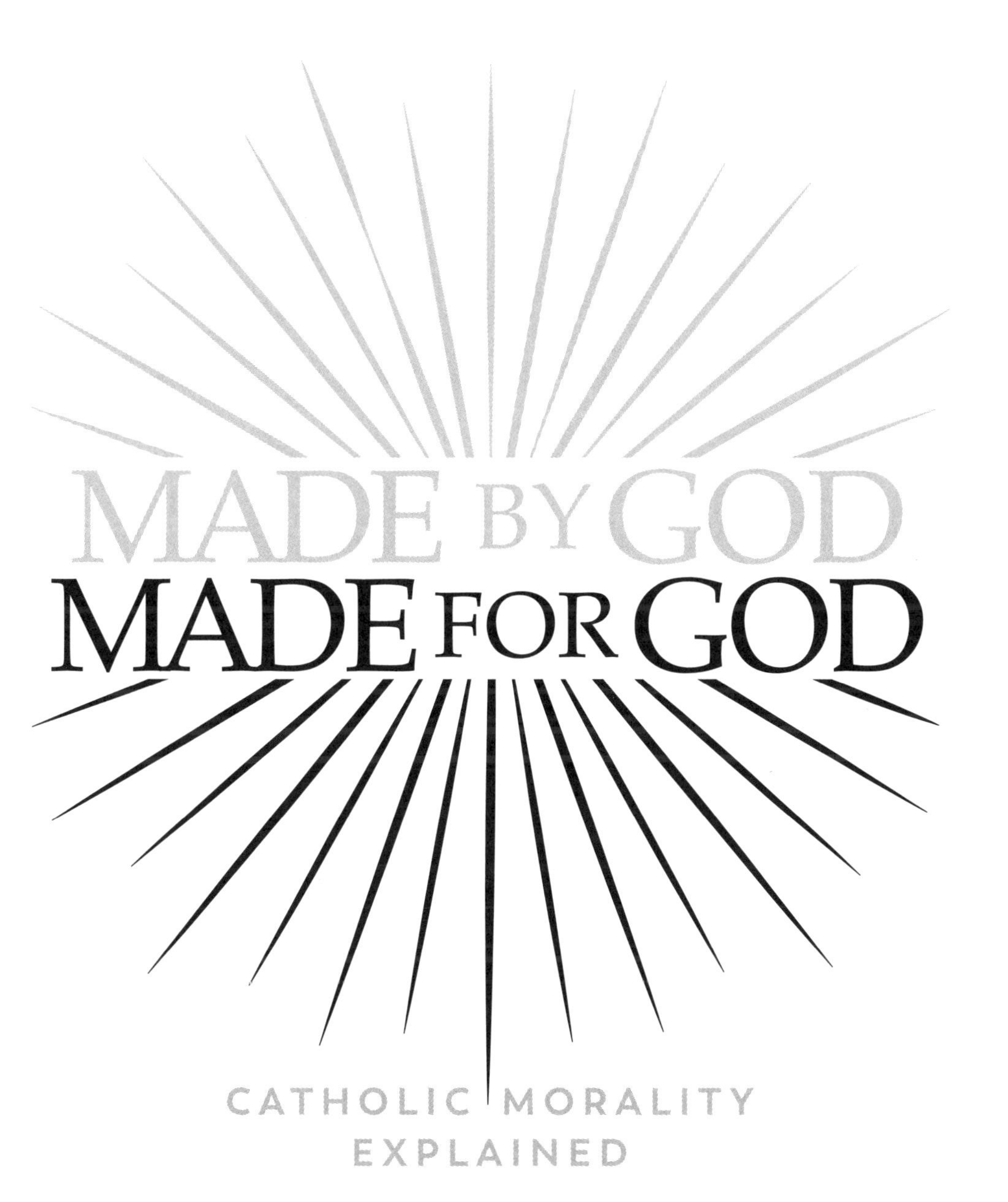

The publisher has applied for a *nihil obstat* and *imprimatur*. When they are granted, the details will be noted here.

Ascension
PO Box 1990
West Chester, PA 19380

1-800-376-0520
ascensionpress.com

Cover design: Rosemary Strohm

Printed in the United States of America
21 22 23 24 25 5 4 3 2 1

ISBN 978-1-950784-94-3 (hardcover), 978-1-950784-95-0 (ebook)

To Shirley Leiberger,
in love and appreciation for her humble, loving,
and holy witness to the Christian life.

CONTENTS

INTRODUCTION

We live in an age of immense division: within our families, within our communities, within our nations, and even within our Church. *Us versus them* ... Our human psychology readily seeks out such tribalism, and the marketplace is all too ready to capitalize on it. The world would have us believe that our primary alliance is to be found in some secondary factor: class, sex, gender, nationality, ethnicity, race, political affiliation, etc. ... But our true point of union goes much, much deeper: our fundamental dependence upon our Triune God, who has called us into existence and, through his grace, offers us a participation in his very life. There is but one *real* question concerning our "communion," our shared union, and it divides the heart of each one of us: Are you living in the old Adam, or have you been reborn in Christ? (See Romans 5:12-21.) And if we have received this new birth, we are called to pour forth Christ's own salvific love: "A new commandment I give to you, that you love one another; even as I have loved you, that you also love one another. By this all men will know that you are my disciples, if you have love for one another" (John 13:34-35).

In this book, I will write to you as a Catholic, specifically a Ruthenian Catholic, the member of a small, poor, Slavic Byzantine church in union with the pope of Rome. The theology that animates this volume attempts to be truly Catholic and "universal," putting down its roots into Sacred Scripture, though it is also animated by the theology of the Common Doctor of the Church, St. Thomas Aquinas, along with his later school. But fear not! I strive throughout to avoid technicality and scholarly tedium. You can go elsewhere to find a volume on "Thomistic ethics." That is *not* this volume's goal. It is meant to be a theologically informed meditation on our faith, expressed with a personal tone.

My dear and departed mother, Laura Szepesi, was a writer for our local newspaper, and seldom did she author a column without her heart somehow being expressed in her prose. Her favorite articles to write were personal stories, as she would say "to make someone famous, in his or her hometown, at least for a day." Her personal touches had only one goal: to help her interviewee shine forth in his or her own uniqueness. My aim is the same here. Please excuse my own eccentricities, which ultimately are but *instruments,* helping me to share with you the most important truths that we can know. The truths of faith, which animate our morality, are a *gift,* and like every gift, they call for admiration and love.

I have dedicated this book to Shirley Leiberger, who navigates life's joys and sufferings always with her hand firmly placed in Christ's. Such a dedication is but a small act of love, expressed for someone who has radiated over my little hometown what I think is a true example of Christian love: simple, quiet, dutiful, and among the most beautiful of all things I have experienced here below. However, I also hope that this volume, my first book in my own voice (and not a translation of someone else's work), would have made my mother proud. In every phrase, I could hear her say to me: *Don't use five words where two will do the work! Be plain, not pompous!* I hope I have succeeded in this task, for my only desire is to tell you, my reader, a little tale about this wonderful vocation to which we are all called, a vocation which is in fact a participation in the greatest gift ever given, the very life of God.

In affection as brothers and sisters, let us pray for each other and for our poor world, repeating today the words of St. Benedict of Nursia (d. 547):

> Just as there is a wicked zeal of bitterness that separates from God and leads to hell, so there is a good zeal which separates from evil and leads to God and everlasting life. This, then, is the good zeal which monks [indeed, all Christians] must foster with fervent love: "They should each try to be the first to show respect to [each] other" (Romans 12:10), supporting with the greatest patience one another's weaknesses of body or behavior, and earnestly competing in obedience to one another. No one is to pursue what he judges better for himself, but instead, what he judges better for someone else. ... *Let them prefer nothing whatever to Christ, and may he bring us all together to everlasting life.*[1]

Section I: The Divine Life of Grace

An old and wise maxim runs, "A small error at the beginning leads to a great one by the end." We must get our principles correct, for otherwise we will draw all sorts of wrong conclusions! Therefore, this opening section is devoted first and foremost to the principles of the Christian life. Above all, we will be concerned to show the amazing gift that God has given to us in grace: "The free gift of God is eternal life in Christ Jesus our Lord" (Romans 6:23). This section is *very* important for understanding everything else that will follow in this book, so I invite you to read it slowly and carefully. In its chapters, we will reflect on the great mystery of faith implied in these words of Christ: "No longer do I call you servants. ... I have called you friends, for all that I have heard from my Father I have made known to you. You did not choose me, but I chose you and appointed you that you should go and bear fruit and that your fruit should abide; so that whatever you ask the Father in my name, he may give it to you" (John 15:15-16).

CHAPTER ONE

The Christian Life: The Divine Life of the Children of God

What is "moral theology?" I recall a corny joke that an in-law always makes when he is reminded that I teach moral theology at the small Byzantine Catholic seminary in Pittsburgh: "Moral theology? Instead of *immoral* theology?" The man is a devout Christian himself, so the joke is not intentionally cynical. In any case, I think it contains a kind of lesson. These two words interact very interestingly with each other. If we take the time to reflect on them, we might learn something both about God and about our own destiny as Christians.

Let's begin with the word "theology." Its form is familiar, for we all know of many disciplines having similar sounding names: biology, sociology, endocrinology, zoology, meteorology, paleontology, and even enology (the study of wine). Some of the word roots here are a little bit hidden, but others are quite obvious: bio-logy (the study of life); socio-logy (the study of the nature of society and societies); and zoo-logy (no, not the study of zoos but rather of animals, from the Greek word *zōion*). So, isn't the question quite simple for theology? If "theo" comes from the Greek *theos*, meaning "God," then theology quite obviously is "the study of God." There we have it. Everything is quite clear, right?

Perhaps not. This phrase should stick in our throat a little bit. We can study the natures of plants, animals, societies, the organs of the body, and even the nature of galactic movements. But God? How can we study him? There is no microscope nor any telescope to give us information about him. What kinds of experiments can we run on the Creator in order to understand his nature? Therefore, it seems like a kind of paradox to say that theology is "the study of God." How can we study something—*Someone*, indeed, *three divine Someones*—who is invisible and unseen?

Maybe we can *trust* in God. Maybe we can have a kind of religious *sentiment and feeling*. However, the *study* of God? *That* seems impossible.

In a passage of Scripture that has been quoted many times in the history of Christianity, St. Paul wrote, "Ever since the creation of the world his invisible nature, namely, his eternal power and deity, *has been clearly perceived in the things that have been made*" (Romans 1:20, emphasis added). The great saint of the early Western Church, St. Augustine, perceived this fact so strongly that he thought that the whole world cried out, telling us that it was created: "Behold: the heavens and earth exist, crying out that they were made. ... In fact, they proclaim that they didn't make themselves, also crying out: 'Therefore, we exist only because we were made. Before we existed, we didn't exist, so we could not have created ourselves.'"[2] Or, in the poetic words of the psalms, "The heavens are telling the glory of God; and the firmament proclaims his handiwork," and their message is said to be unending: "Day to day pours forth speech, and night to night declares knowledge" (Psalm 19:1-2).

Our minds are made to know God. In fact, we technically do not need the Church to tell us that God exists and that we can know something about him, at least "indirectly," by reflecting on creation. This is something that the greatest philosophers understood and defended. And yet, what could be less certain? We look around and see a world full of doubt: How could God allow such suffering? Doesn't modern science disprove the existence of God? How could we mere humans know God, even if he does happen to exist? Moreover, life is busy and difficult: "I'm just trying to get by. How could I spend time staring at my belly button long enough to figure out whether or not God exists? I barely have time to clean the house and get the kids to bed!" Finally, there are all of our bad habits as well. How many things do we not know merely because we don't put down the television remote? "I need to unwind after a long and hard day." And then we binge the night away! Such are the weaknesses of human life ... !

And yet the truth remains: Our minds are made to know God. Thankfully, God has provided for us a great remedy: the gift of revelation, the Word of God. Through the whole of salvation history, he has spoken to us the Word of Life. In fact, in Jesus Christ, "the Word became flesh and dwelt among us" (John 1:14). Now, this doesn't merely mean "God came down to work some miracles, let us know he exists, and then disappear." Rather, in the same verse from St. John's Gospel, we are told that Jesus was "full of grace and truth." What God communicates, in Christ, is *himself*. The mystery of the Incarnation, the "enfleshment" of God, represents the greatest of all gifts and, as we will see in a future chapter, the greatest of all graces.

When we speak about "revelation," we are speaking about a message beyond our wildest imagining. By its *nature*, our mind is made to know God *the Creator*. However, through *grace*, new horizons open up before us. It is a repeated theme in the Gospels and in the letters found in the New Testament: Baptism brings about a *new birth*. And when St. Paul writes to the Christian community in Rome, "Do not be conformed to this world but be transformed by the renewal of your mind" (Romans 12:2), he is not proposing a self-help program. He is not merely giving us helpful advice as though he were saying, "You can only control your own thoughts." No! The profound reason that we must renew our minds is because our minds have been actively renewed by God himself, being given a kind of "mind transplant": "'For who has known the mind of the Lord so as to instruct him?' But we have the mind of Christ" (1 Corinthians 2:16).

What has been revealed in the Scriptures? What has the Church taught through the centuries? Nothing short of "the depths of God" (1 Corinthians 2:10)! We do not merely know God as the Creator. Creation did not need to occur, but it has taken place, like a kind of gift that is stamped on our very being. The Catholic Faith proclaims something much greater, however, than "God is Lord. God is the Creator." Our faith gives us a gift more precious than a beautiful pearl from the ocean depths (Matthew 13:45-46). God is much more than the Creator. *He is God.* "Wrapped up" in the words of the Creed, which we pray every Sunday as though it were something familiar and perhaps unremarkable (or at least unsurprising), there is a great mystery, the mystery of God: "I believe in God the Father ... in one Lord Jesus Christ ... and in the Holy Spirit." No philosopher ever imagined such a mystery, which only God himself by rights knows.

Therefore, theology is the study of *God precisely as God*. We could say "God in his inner mystery." However, God has not chosen to remain locked up within himself. He has created all things, and they reflect him like the refracted light in a prism. But as we have already said, his love did not limit itself to this great gift. No, this Love felt a great need: the need to freely give *himself, precisely as God*—the need to reveal, indeed to give to us, *the inner mystery of his very life*, "the depths of God." Theology not only studies God but also studies the great *gifts of God*, gifts which theologians call "supernatural" because they are completely above ("super-") everything ever possible in nature. The theologian must reflect on *God as supernaturally giving himself*, in Christ, through the Church, in the sacraments, in revelation, through grace, and so forth. In short, theology is one, unified story: God, his self-gift, and the return of all things to himself.

Thus we come to the adjective "moral" in "moral theology." Moral theology studies the image of God reflected in human action.[3] Don't be fooled by the word "reflected." We tend to think of reflections as being shadows, unimportant replacements for what is "really real." But this is not the whole story! Pictures, paintings, reflections, video calls, and all such things actually help to make something present, even when that thing or person is far away. In our actions as baptized believers, we truly make Christ present; in fact, we truly make God present as Father, Son, and Holy Spirit, for the Holy Trinity dwells in our souls through grace. Therefore, Catholic morality is not merely morality, mere "doing your duty, doing what is right." It is a divine life, the very life and love of God, "poured into our hearts through the Holy Spirit" (Romans 5:5).

Thus, moral theology is not some kind of list of rules and reasons to feel guilty. Yes, there are things that no child of God can do, things that no child of God would indeed ever wish to do. Some things are *always wrong*. Sin is real and failure quite possible. (Blessedly, too, God is patient and merciful!) However, moral theology first and foremost seeks to lay out a divine subject: the supernatural God, Father, Son, and Holy Spirit—the Holy Trinity, whose very life is given to us through the gift of grace. Its first concern is not with the shadows of sin but, rather, with the light that we are all called to be: "Let your light so shine before men, that they may see your good works and give glory to your Father who is in heaven" (Matthew 5:16).

Moral theology strives to lay out the great gift that is given to all of us through Baptism and continuously all our life long in grace, through prayer and the sacraments, and *in our very actions*. As Christians, we are all called to great holiness, to divine holiness. Jesus did not address only priests, monks, and nuns when he spoke in the Sermon on the Mount. Rather, he spoke to all, saying, "You, therefore, must be perfect, as your heavenly Father is perfect" (Matthew 5:48). All are implicated in this great divine proclamation, this divine calling: "All of you, have unity of spirit, sympathy, love of the brethren, a tender heart and a humble mind" (1 Peter 3:8).

Christian morality is more than anything that society could ever propose to us. It is something greater than what is found in the writings of any philosopher. It is greater than any moral duty that we could merely think up on our own. We are not called to human perfection. We are called to divine perfection, something that only God himself can give, and in this divine perfection we find our highest human perfection as well. Grace is *gratis*, a gift, something freely given: "For by grace you have been saved through faith; and this is not your own doing, it is the gift of God" (Ephesians 2:8). But St. Paul is quite clear that this gift calls for us to be transformed and active, a new creation that is brimming with life: "For we are his workmanship, created in Christ Jesus for good works, which God prepared beforehand, that we should walk in them" (Ephesians 2:10). Everything remains divine in this moral tale. God is at its source (through creation and grace), he is at work in our action (in and through grace), and he is its end and goal (loved above all things, with his own eternal love, in glory, which is the consummation of grace). God gives us himself so that we can have the greatest honor ever imaginable: to give God to God, through his love, which has been poured out into the depths of our hearts.[4] From top to bottom, from head to toe, indeed, to use a somewhat earthy metaphor, down to the tips of our toenails, we are called to be remade in Christ, to do all things in him: "So, whether you eat or drink, or whatever you do, do all to the glory of God" (1 Corinthians 10:31).[5]

Through the gift of grace, we receive a new light, a new vocation. Our eyes are opened to the glory of God, which we are called to manifest to the world. In the words of St. John Chrysostom, we are the light "not of one nation, nor of twenty states, but of the whole inhabited earth."[6] Christianity spreads most effectively in our action, as the well-worn line attributed to St. Francis of Assisi states: "Always preach the Gospel, but only use words if necessary." Indeed, it was Christ himself who said, "Let your light so shine before men, that they may see your good works and give glory to your Father who is in heaven" (Matthew 5:16). In short, your light is not for you but, rather, is meant to shine forth for others, so that we might be instruments of God's own self-gift, which we are all called to share in eternity: the divine life shared by all, even now here below. How marvelous a vocation! Love himself gives Love to us so that we might love with that Love.[7] The world was transformed by the light of this love. As St. John Chrysostom continues, "More vehemently than the sunbeam did they overrun the whole earth, sowing the light of godliness."[8]

Thus, as Christians, we have new eyes, a supernatural viewpoint, the "God's-eye" view of everything. This is the mystery of the gift of God given to us as our life as *brothers and sisters* of Christ. We are adopted not merely by a kind of "legal declaration," but rather we are really and truly born anew. "By his great mercy we have been born anew to a living hope through the resurrection of Jesus Christ from the dead" (1 Peter 1:3). And as the same St. Peter says in his second letter,

> His divine power has granted to us all things that pertain to life and godliness, through the knowledge of him who called us to his own glory and excellence, by which he has granted to us his precious and very great promises, that through these you may escape from the corruption that is in the world because of passion, and *become partakers of the divine nature.* (2 Peter 1:3-4, emphasis added)

This is what we will be studying in this book: moral theology, our re-creation in and through Christ. We will understand what we must *do* based on what we *are*. Action follows being. Our task will be to reflect on the supernatural gift of the divine life given to us. Then we will see the various kinds of actions that should be performed by children having so noble a birth. And when we discuss sin, as we indeed must do, we will see how horrible it is precisely because it blots out a divine light which should fill us entirely. "If your eye is sound"—that is, if you truly live your life *from the God's-eye perspective*—"your whole body will be full of light; but if your eye is not sound, your whole body will be full of darkness. If then the light in you is darkness, how great is the darkness" (Matthew 6:22-23). In short, we will be discussing the divine pathway which is illuminated by the Word of God and proclaimed by the Church's Tradition: "Your word is a lamp to my feet and a light to my path" (Psalm 119:105).

CHAPTER TWO

"This New Commandment I Give to You"

"Therefore every scribe who has been trained for the kingdom of heaven is like a householder who brings out of his treasure what is new and what is old" (Matthew 13:52). God has been working his salvation for ages, and he is faithful in his works. When he brings about something new, he has, in fact, already prepared for this new event. For him, the new is foreshadowed in the old, and the old is fulfilled, abundantly so, in the new. After his resurrection, Christ walked on the road toward Emmaus with two of his disciples. They did not recognize him while he laid out the Law and Prophets to them, telling them step by step how his death fulfilled all that had been written. And their hearts burned within them, for they sensed here the deepest meaning of their lives, both as men and as Jews (Luke 24:13-32).

The ancient people of Israel were given the Law. This was God's great revelation to them as they were formed into a people following their exodus from Egypt. We tend to think of law as being a burden: "Don't break the law." "He is in trouble with the law ..." Every year, when we pay our taxes, even when we are very careful not to do anything wrong, we perhaps have a small lump in our throats and think, "I hope that I don't get audited." The law seems to be a kind of limitation, a kind of harsh requirement and chain on our freedom.

We should not, however, confuse what merely *happens* to be the case with what is *essential*. The law seems so harsh because of sin: the sins of others who unjustly abuse the law to their own advantage and our own sinful attachment to our desires instead of to the rights of others. The ancient people of God often transgressed the Law; they often fell short of its "measure." Nonetheless, deep in their identity, they knew that the Law was their true joy. It enabled them to live their whole lives as a kind of offering to God. With all of its detailed requirements, it already was a kind of foreshadowing of the words of St. Paul which we cited in the previous chapter: "So, whether you eat or drink, or whatever you do, do all to the glory of God" (1 Corinthians 10:31). Words which many perhaps attribute to Christ were, in fact, proclaimed in the old law: "Hear, O Israel: The Lord our God is one Lord; and you shall love the Lord your God with all your heart, and with all your soul, and with all your might" (Deuteronomy 6:4-5).

Already, here in the desert following the Exodus, God has given his people *explosively powerful* words. *Every fiber* of our being should quiver with the desire to devote all things to him: "Bless the Lord, O my soul; and *all that is within me, bless his holy name!*" (Psalm 103:1, emphasis added). In fact, even in the desert, the children of Israel already were told that the Law should indeed be written upon their hearts: "And these words which I command you this day shall be upon your heart" (Deuteronomy 6:6). All of life, indeed every relationship, must be transformed: "And you shall teach them diligently to your children, and shall talk of them when you sit in your house, and when you walk by the way, and when you lie down, and when you rise" (Deuteronomy 6:7). We cannot help but think here of the psalmist's words: "From the rising of the sun to its setting the name of the Lord is to be praised" (Psalm 113:3). And all this devotion should imprint itself on our very appearances and homes: "And you shall bind them as a sign upon your hand, and they shall be as frontlets between your eyes. And you shall write them on the doorposts of your house and on your gates" (Deuteronomy 6:8-9).

This is the deep meaning of the Law in the Old Testament. It was what the prophets ardently desired: "I will put my law within them, and I will write it upon their hearts; and I will be their God, and they shall be my people" (Jeremiah 31:33); "A new heart I will give you, and a new spirit I will put within you; and I will take out of your flesh the heart of stone and give you a heart of flesh. And I will put my spirit within you, and cause you to walk in my statutes and be careful to observe my ordinances" (Ezekiel 36:26-27). Such was the great hope of the people of Israel, the chosen people whose *entire* identity was, like a beautiful tapestry, knit together by the Law given to them by God. Reflect on the lengthy text of Psalm 119, and you will see the endless and repeated joy that the Jewish person had in the Law.[9]

Yet law can become a burden, an encumbrance, and indeed much worse. The mere letter of the law is burdensome, a shell of words if we don't know its spirit. We must ask, "Why does this law exist? What is it trying to accomplish?" Using the Greek terms *epieikeia* (equity / fairness) and *oikonomia* (good household management), the Church speaks of the need to apply the law with a merciful awareness of its *purpose*. As we will discuss in detail in a later chapter, the Church (and sane philosophy too!) teaches that evil may *never* be done so that good may come about. However, it is also true that *left to itself* the letter of the law is a harsh taskmaster. In the succinct words of St. Thomas Aquinas, "To follow the letter of the law when it ought not to be followed is sinful."[10] And sin is a form of spiritual death! The words of St. Paul, written against those who would zealously follow merely the letter of the law, ring true: "The written code"—that is, *the letter alone*—"kills, but the Spirit gives life" (2 Corinthians 3:6).

During Jesus' own lifetime, we see an example of the letter of the law dealing its fatal blows. Members of the Jewish sect known as the Pharisees were extremely devoted to the Law. They were concerned to keep every detail of it, with inflexible devotion. And yet, in their zeal, they went overboard. How many times do we see the Pharisees coming to Jesus, angry that he has been lax with the Law. And how often do his words ring out in response to them with a very strong tone: "You brood of vipers" (Mathew 12:34); "Woe to you Pharisees! for you love the best seat in the synagogues and salutations in the market places" (Luke 11:43; see Matthew 23:2-12); "You are like whitewashed tombs" (Matthew 23:27). To the eyes of Christ, this was all wrongheaded. The Law was meant to be the means for arriving at a true and holy life, not a shackle and burden for the soul. We are complete fools if we merely pay attention to the road without ever asking, "Where is this road going?" Means only have their meaning in relation to the end, the goal!

But Christ did not come merely in order to do away with the Law. He came to fulfill it as the giver of the new law. Any Jewish person who reads the words of the Sermon on the Mount (Matthew 5–7) could not help but think of Moses receiving the Law on Mount Sinai. Here, God himself in the flesh, Christ, is present proclaiming the law to the people. Here, the deepest meaning of the law is being proclaimed: "Do not think that I have come to abolish the law and the prophets; I have come not to abolish them but to fulfil them" (Matthew 5:17). He even goes on to say that "not an iota, not a dot" of the law will pass away and that his followers must surpass the scribes and Pharisees in holiness (Matthew 5:18-20).

This seems crazy! The Jewish law contains many commandments that seem to make no sense. Merely skim through Leviticus chapter 11, and you will find a whole list of animals that are unclean to eat: swine, rock badgers, vultures, ravens, geckos, etc. ... Later theological teaching would come to distinguish between three kinds of commandments in the Law: ceremonial precepts, judicial precepts, and moral precepts.[11] The first group pertains to the worship offered by the Jewish people, something which has come to an end with Christ's sacrifice on the Cross. This worship is now taken over into the offering of the Eucharist and the other sacraments gathered around it, by which Christ's one sacrifice is offered until the end of time. The second group of precepts contains everything that *happened* to be proclaimed as necessary for the community of Israel and for the relationships formed among the Jewish people. Both of these types of precepts are not *necessarily right* in themselves but, instead, *are right because they are decreed and fixed by God's authority* for the sake of "fleshing out" the details of worship and communal justice. However, the third and final group of precepts, the moral precepts, are the unchanging aspect of the Law. They are reflected in the Ten Commandments but are also found throughout the Old Testament, in the wisdom literature, in the prophets, and in the words of the psalms. These moral precepts are what remain *unchanging*. The first two kinds of precepts are indeed necessary, but they serve this third kind (see Matthew 23:23). This is what St. Paul means when he writes, "'All things are lawful,' but not all things are helpful" (1 Corinthians 10:23). In short, the moral precepts are the inner soul of the others.

Now, the new law of Christ is an interior law, the "law of grace." It is *more* demanding than the old law. It requires us to sacrifice ourselves so that Christ may animate everything that we do, so that he may quite truly be our life (Galatians 2:20). Following the most ancient of insights by the Christian community (Romans 6:3-11), the Church's baptismal liturgies, in both East and West, repeatedly connect our Baptism to Christ's death and resurrection. Through Baptism, we become changed, sealed with what theologians call the "indelible character" of Baptism. We "put on Christ," or even, in a certain sense, as we will discuss more in the next chapter, ourselves become "Christified."

This idea was not invented by St. Paul or by the early Church. It was already present in Christ's own preaching. On several occasions, the Gospels present us with the story of a young adherent to the Law asking what he must do to attain eternal life (see Matthew 19:16-22; Mark 10:17-22; Luke 18:18-23). He keeps the commandments, but is there anything else to be done? Christ does not look at him and say, "You legalist. Stop getting tied up about the rules. Just chill out." No! Jesus is not a kind of indulgent parent, nor a reformer who throws the law away. Instead, he looks at the young man with a loving glance, sees his devotion, and tells him that there is merely one more thing to do. But how difficult a thing it is! The young man must sell everything and follow him, leaving behind family and friends. In short, Christ demands everything of him, every fiber of his being, every relationship. But in compensation, he gives all things. As St. Paul would later proclaim, "All things are yours ... and you are Christ's; and Christ is God's" (1 Corinthians 3:21, 23). God is indeed merciful to those who struggle to be holy, like a father who wishes for his children to become fully "grown up" in their new divine life. However, mercy is not laxity, and the Christ-conformed life requires us to be created anew, living the life of grace in all our actions, not merely looking for exceptions to the rules.

Thus, if you go back to the Sermon on the Mount, you will see the New Lawgiver proclaiming something which reaches far deeper than any external law. In a striking set of verses, Christ repeatedly says, "You have heard that it was said to the men of old, ... But I say to you ..." (Matthew 5:21-48). No longer is it merely adultery that is sinful, but even a lustful thought or look! And the fifth commandment, "Thou shalt not murder," seems easy in comparison with what Christ requires: "Whoever insults his brother shall be liable to the council, and whoever says, 'You fool!' shall be liable to the hell of fire." In short, we are called to be as perfect as our merciful Father in heaven! Are we truly merciful, forgiving others seventy times seven times for the faults that they commit against us (Matthew 18:21-22)? The bar has been set so high! The Law has been renewed, and the ancient words ring true, though even more profoundly:

"You shall love the Lord your God with *all* your heart, and with *all* your soul, and with *all* your mind ... You shall love your neighbor as yourself" (Matthew 22:37-39, emphasis added). How we would despair if we did not have the hope given to us by God's grace and the continual mercy extended to us in the sacrament of Reconciliation!

Yet none of this is presented as being burdensome: "My yoke is easy, and my burden is light" (Matthew 11:30). The new law is indeed a law of freedom, above all a freedom to pursue the most profound "thing" we are called to love: God himself. In fact, every creature can be said to love God more than it loves itself. The deepest fibers of all beings actually turn to God first and foremost. In him, the God who *is* goodness and love, our hearts find their true fulfillment, their true perfection, and their true joy.[12] In the beautiful words with which Dante closes the Divine Comedy, God is "the Love that moves the sun and the other stars."[13] One of the great pains of hell will be the fact that this fundamental inclination is eternally frustrated by the free creature's rejection of God.[14] This new law of Christ fulfills—in an infinite, unexpected, divine way—this deepest bent of our being. But we must put on a new nature, the nature of Christ, renewing in us the likeness of God which was (and is) lost through sin (Colossians 3:8-10).

Thus, we see the meaning of the well-known words of Christ, spoken after he washed his disciples' feet: "A new commandment I give to you, that you love one another; even as I have loved you, that you also love one another" (John 13:34). This is the sign of being Christ's disciple. It is a lofty bar, for we are called to love with that same love that impelled Christ to the Cross for our sake! As St. John writes elsewhere in one of his letters, "We love, because he first loved us" (1 John 4:19). We might rephrase this and say, "In your love, Christ, we see love" (see Psalm 36:9). We live a new life, not merely according to an external written code but, rather, "the new life of the Spirit" (Romans 7:6), impelled onward with a new point of view, the "divine point of view" (see 2 Corinthians 5:14-16). Therefore, in the next chapter let us reflect on the face of Christ, in whose image we are being refashioned.

CHAPTER THREE

"Putting on Christ": The True Meaning of Virtue

The words of St. Paul rang out to the church in Galatia: "My little children, with whom I am again in travail until Christ be formed in you!" (Galatians 4:19). How great was his desire for them, for he knew that he needed to help fulfill the great gift given to his spiritual children in Baptism. Through Baptism, we are like branches placed on the vine of Christ, from whom we draw life as from a new, eternal sap (John 15:1-8). We are given a new "character," a new abiding quality, a *new birth*. The merely human life which we had lived is now marked with his life, and his greatest act, his death and resurrection, becomes the greatest reality in our own lives as well: "I have been crucified with Christ; it is no longer I who live, but Christ who lives in me; and the life I now live in the flesh I live by faith in the Son of God, who loved me and gave himself for me" (Galatians 2:20).

This will mark the whole of our moral lives. It is tempting to think about these words as though they fit somewhere else in theology: in spiritual theology, in dogmatic theology, in Christology, in sacramental theology. And, yes, they do have their place there too. However, action flows from being. If we are a new kind of being, if we live a new life, then we will have new acts and, therefore, a new morality. Christian morality is a "Christic" morality, one which bears the divine mark of its divine "model." And if that new morality finds its root in something divine, in Someone divine, then we should understand something about that *Someone*, for otherwise we will fail to know what *we ourselves* are and must do!

I would like to return to words from our first chapter, for they contain everything that we will say in this chapter (and, in a sense, in this entire book): "The Word became flesh and dwelt among us, *full of grace* and truth

... And *from his fulness have we all received, grace upon grace*" (John 1:14, 16, emphasis added). All grace is "Christic," in three senses: it comes from Christ, it conforms us to him, and it gives us over to him, in whom and through whom all things were created (Colossians 1:16).[15] We receive the divine life—the very life of the Holy Trinity—by being "incorporated" into Christ, by being refashioned as members of his mystical body, the Church.

This is what was brought about through Christ's incarnation and death. In fact, theological language sometimes refers to the Incarnation as the *Redemptive Incarnation* in order to emphasize the unity of Christ's purpose, the motive for his incarnation, reflected in the words of the Creed: "For us men *and for our salvation*, he came down from heaven." Now, the very word "redemption" comes from a Latin root meaning "to buy back," from the same root that we see in the relatively well-known legal phrase *caveat emptor*, "Let the buyer beware!" But, when God "buys" humanity back after the fall of Adam, he does something much greater than pay the debt of sin. He gives us his very self.

Before the Fall, humanity lived a truly graced and supernatural life. Already, Adam and Eve lived *both* by nature and by grace. Before the Fall, they walked with God as with the truest friend of their souls. When our first parents sinned, we lost something immense. We lost the life that we were to share with God perpetually. We were created in the image and likeness of God (Genesis 1:26). However, a number of Church Fathers taught an important truth: by sinning, Adam and Eve were deprived of the grace by which they truly lived as God's likenesses. The dogma of original sin means that we receive this same loss, this same disfigurement. Certainly, we are not wholly corrupted. However, without the grace of divinization, we no longer reflect the light of God which we are created to radiate.[16] God is very merciful, however, and almost immediately after the first sin, the rescue effort begins. God proclaims to the serpent:

> I will put enmity between you and the woman,
> and between your seed and her seed;
> he shall bruise your head,
> and you shall bruise his heel. (Genesis 3:15)

This verse has been called the *proto-evangelium*, the first promise of the Gospel. From early in the Church's history, these words were interpreted as being concerned with something more than how people hate snakes. The "seed" spoken of here was Christ, who will overcome sin through his crucifixion, death, and resurrection.[17] However, the grace given in Christ is, in fact, greater than any gift Adam received and then lost: "But the free gift is not like the trespass. For if many died through one man's trespass, much more have the grace of God and the free gift in the grace of that one man Jesus Christ abounded for many" (Romans 5:15).

In fact, the entire notion of grace finds its highest expression in Christ himself. But let's be careful. Christ is not merely *the best man ever*. We must take care to search out the true meaning of being "brothers and sisters" in Christ. Jesus is not merely our brother, as though he were a human person who was most favored by God. Jesus is a divine person—"God from God, Light from Light, true God from true God." The eternal Word does not "reduce himself" to being human. Instead, he draws humanity to himself. He does not give up his divinity. Rather, he shoulders the burdens, difficulties, and griefs of human nature. Above all, without himself being sinful, he shoulders the burden of our greatest grief, sin, which separates us from the love of our life, the love of God: "For our sake he made him to be sin who knew no sin, so that in him we might become the righteousness of God" (2 Corinthians 5:21). Thus, he fulfills the prophecy: "He was despised and rejected by men; a man of sorrows, and acquainted with grief ... Surely he has borne our griefs and carried our sorrows" (Isaiah 53:3-4).

Every week, in the Creed, we pray that Christ is simultaneously God and man. His humanity isn't a kind of divine playacting, putting on the mere appearance of being human. (This was an ancient error condemned under the names of Docetism and modalism.) However, on the other extreme, he is not merely stitched together out of two parts, as though he were both a human person and a divine person. (This was an error condemned under the name of Nestorianism.) But neither does Christ's divinity completely "overshadow" his humanity. (This was an error condemned under the name Monophysitism, meaning "one-nature-ism," as though the divine nature ultimately "swallowed up" Christ's human nature.) No, Jesus Christ, our Lord and Savior in the flesh, is a divine person, the second Person of the three Persons who have been revealed to exist in the one God, who is Father, Son, and Holy Spirit. However, the incarnate Christ has two natures, human and divine.

Many great theological minds had to work all of this out during the first centuries of the Church's history. Great battles were fought over these matters. The answers ultimately given by the Church are very abstract, using very abstract notions: *hypostasis*, personhood, nature, subsistence, etc. But all of this was done in order to defend and define this basic truth of faith: Jesus Christ is "God in the flesh." This dogma of faith, the dogma of the "hypostatic union," the *union* of two natures in one person (or in the terminology used in Greek, *hypostasis*), merely wishes to give some explanation for the words of the angel Gabriel to Mary: "The child to be born will be called holy, the Son of God" (Luke 1:35). But let's repeat the point once again: this dogma only offers *some* explanation. No matter how long the books might be that are written about this dogma of the faith, the mystery remains, a very powerful and great mystery indeed: Jesus Christ is "God in the flesh." This mystery is so great that we must join Mary, who "kept all these things, pondering them in her heart" (Luke 2:19).

Our purpose here, however, is to show how all of this is relevant for our moral lives. In the mystery of the Incarnation, the enfleshing of the Word of God, we have the great fruit of God's salvific activity (1 Corinthians 15:23). Christ is said to be the new Adam (Romans 5:12-21), even in the crib of Bethlehem (and, indeed, in the womb of Mary[18]). This is why, in the Roman rite, it was traditional to kneel at the words of the Nicene Creed "and by the Holy Spirit [he] was incarnate of the Virgin Mary, and became man." These words recognize the greatest grace ever given to human nature: the "grace of union," the substantial gift of the eternal Word.

We are not saved merely because God says so. The theology of grace is quite "realistic"; it asserts something quite real for us. In the words of the Council of Trent, "Not only are we *considered* just" (as though redemption were a question of God merely saying we were righteous, giving us Christ's righteousness without changing us), "but indeed, we are *truly* called just and are so, with each person receiving within himself or herself, his or her own justice, according to the measure that 'the Holy Spirit apportions to each.'"[19] Christ's own grace radiates to us so that we really receive this grace as our own.

In traditional theological vocabulary, this "radiating" grace of Christ is called his "capital" grace. The term comes from the fact that Christ is the head of the Church (see Ephesians 1:22, 5:23; Colossians 1:18, 2:19), based on the Latin word for head, *caput*. From the "grace of union," Christ's human nature is carried to the heights of holiness, without ceasing to be human, and from these heights not only is he *personally* holy but, moreover, he radiates holiness to his whole body, through the sacraments and all of the means of grace which draw us together into this one body. How befitting! The mark of a truly wealthy person is generosity for others. Or as the old philosophical maxim runs: the good, by its very nature, is self-diffusive, *bonum est diffusivum sui*. In Christ, the divine image is restored, not merely for his own sake, but rather "for the life of the world" (John 6:51). In the words of St. John: "And from his fulness have we all received, grace upon grace" (John 1:16). Throughout all of history, his salvation radiates forth like a light which itself renews and changes us. Christ is not merely a moral example. He is the source of all our moral abilities, the wellspring of all grace.[20]

The whole Incarnation is motivated by this one desire: to give all things over to God, saving a world which cries out for redemption (Romans 8:19-25). This is why Baptism is presented as being "baptized into Christ's death" (see Romans 6:3), "being buried with Christ" (see Colossians 2:11-12). In short, Baptism enables us to take part in the great work of salvation, so that we might "complete what is lacking in Christ's afflictions for the sake of his body, that is, the Church" (Colossians 1:24), not as though the head were lacking something but, rather, inasmuch as the body must be permeated by the light of his grace, being refashioned in his image, through the gift of the life of the Holy Trinity. It is a regenerative light, for the light of God does not merely pass through us like glass, nor does it simply shine on us and allow us to remain who we are. No, as St. Benedict of Nursia, the great father of Western monasticism, writes in his rule, this is a God-forming or God-making light, *deificum lumen*.[21] It makes us (*-ficum*) divine (*dei-*). The gift of grace is not merely a new birth certificate. It is a new birth! We must return to this truth of faith over and over again, for it illuminates all of the various nooks and crannies of what we will discuss in later chapters about various, specific moral topics.

We are permeated with the light of Christ, even now. The kingdom of God is not a merely future reality. It has truly begun now because Christ has truly come and truly lives in us, often in the most hidden ways. The

Pharisees looked for a great outward show of the kingdom, but Christ responded to them, "The kingdom of God is not coming with signs to be observed; nor will they say, 'Behold, here it is!' or 'There!' for behold, *the kingdom of God is in your midst*" (Luke 17:20-21, emphasis added). The Christian life is hidden from the world, which does not know the Light which has come (John 1:10). Our life "is hidden with Christ in God" (Colossians 3:3). We do not build the city of God. Instead, it comes down from heaven from God (Revelation 21:2 and following). In fact, this living city already has come down, even in the silent womb of Mary. And we are to be built up like living stones into this spiritual abode (1 Peter 2:5), transformed from one glory to the next (2 Corinthians 3:18), so that when Christ appears in full glory, we too will appear with him (Colossians 3:4). But it will be a glory which already began, the kingdom already alive through the grace of Christ in the depths of our souls.

Indeed, as St. Thomas so tersely summarizes all of this, "Grace is nothing else than a beginning of Glory in us."[22] And as the great spiritual theologian Fr. Ambroise Gardeil so poetically expressed this point, "There is no disturbing hiatus at this solemn moment [of death], no dissolution of continuity. The last beating of our divinized heart on earth is merely one with the first great beating of this same heart amid the splendors of the saints."[23] The lines from the book of Revelation devoted to the end of time already begin today: "And the city has no need of sun or moon to shine upon it, for the glory of God is its light, and its lamp is the Lamb" (Revelation 21:23). And all of this is just a commentary on Christ's own words, to which we cannot return frequently enough, for they contain rich deposits of truth: "Let your light so shine before men, that they may see your good works and give glory to your Father who is in heaven" (Matthew 5:16).

Here we have an excellent example of the way that faith and morals are woven together into a single tapestry. At first glance, all of this seems very esoteric, very "highfalutin." If you have friends and family over for burgers and start talking about "the hypostatic union of two natures in the one Person of the Word," most people will say, "Please pass the ketchup," not, "Please tell me more." But if we understand how this mystery of faith is related to our lives, we will immediately see something vitally important for Christian morality. We will see that the Western term *divinization* and the Eastern term *theosis* are not pious words telling us that we are "like God." They are utterly powerful words, containing within themselves a kind of supernova-level strength, one that is already contained, if we know how to see it, in words which should take our breath away: "You, therefore, must be perfect, as your heavenly Father is perfect" (Matthew 5:48). Christ did not say, "Try it out." Nor did he say, "Be somewhat perfect. Give it a good shot." Nor, even, did he say, "Be moral to a human level." No! He calls us to a divine measure of holiness and thankfully communicates to us from the fullness that he himself has, giving us all the sap needed for living the divine life, giving us all the great strength needed in order to live this high calling: "I am the vine, you are the branches. He who abides in me, and I in him, he it is that bears much fruit, for apart from me you can do nothing" (John 15:5). Thus do we become, in a real sense, generous distributors of God's manifold grace (1 Peter 4:10). We will see this, in particular, when we come to discuss "fraternal charity."

Thus, from start to finish, in all of our actions, we must press on toward the perfection which St. Paul desired with all his heart: "Not that I have already obtained this or am already perfect; but I press on to make it my own, because Christ Jesus has made me his own" (Philippians 3:12). Our morality will require us to shine with the very light of Christ's grace, given to us by God, "who has shone in our hearts to give the light of the knowledge of the glory of God in the face of Christ" (2 Corinthians 4:6). Thus, the Lord's transfiguration on Mount Tabor, when the glory of his divinity shone through his face and clothes, becomes a kind of mystical image for the Christian life, one which has been held dear by many saints.[24] In Christ, we see, touch, and look upon the very Word of God (1 John 1:1-3). The people of Israel had to look upon Moses through a veil, for the glory of God reflected upon his face was too bright for them (2 Corinthians 3:7-16; Exodus 34:34-35). But working in our souls, through the activity of Christ's redemptive and adoptive grace, we see not a reflection but, rather, *his very likeness*, being fashioned within us: "And we all, with unveiled face, beholding the glory of the Lord, are being changed into his likeness from one degree of glory to another; for this comes from the Lord who is the Spirit" (2 Corinthians 3:18).

In short, the whole of the Christian life will be one long work which we undertake, animated by God's own love. Indeed, we will undertake the task of this Christian life with God *dwelling in us*: "If a man loves me, he will keep my word, and my Father will love him, and we will come to him and *make our home with him*" (John 14:23, emphasis added). Rephrasing the words with which we opened this chapter, for the Christian, the moral life involves God travailing within us, stamping upon us the face of Christ, illuminating us with his light, a light which remakes us (*deificum lumen*), so that we too may shine with the divine light. From the "grace of union" to the "capital grace" of Christ our head to the grace which we receive, being remade as sons and daughters of the heavenly Father, we have the spring of water welling up from the Son's "eternal life which was with the Father" (1 John 1:2) and flowing back to eternal life (John 4:14). Thus, we return to the moral-spiritual meaning of the words from Christology which guided our reflections above: "And from his fulness have we all received, grace upon grace" (John 1:16), as well as St. Paul's exclamation with which this chapter opened: "My little children, with whom I am again in travail *until Christ be formed in you*" (Galatians 4:19, emphasis added). Every moral theology which is worth its salt will need to measure up to this high calling!

CHAPTER FOUR

Sin: "A Man Went Down to Jericho"

Sin, damnation, hell, vice: these are harsh words to our ears. Nobody likes to focus on such negative things! I am reminded of a story I heard regarding how some relatives reacted to a Byzantine-rite funeral. After the liturgy, several people commented that there was a discomforting number of mentions of sin throughout the prayers offered for the departed person. The Eastern churches are known for their liturgical repetitions, something that is less frequent in the Roman rite. In this particular case, the repetitions managed to draw attention to a troubling fact which we all too often do not trouble ourselves about: sin is everywhere in our lives, calling for ceaseless prayer for forgiveness and healing.

The biblical notion of sin is tied to the Greek term ἁμαρτία, *hamartia*, "missing the mark." The mark, the bull's-eye: the acts of the virtues, whether theological (faith, hope, and charity) or moral (prudence, justice, courage, and temperance, along with all of their various related subvirtues). By sin, we place ourselves outside of the circle of virtue. We gradually (or, if we sin with great vigor, quickly) sever the ties that connect us to the grace and love of God.

Note carefully one of the words in the previous sentence: "we." The great mystery of sin is the fact that *we* are the primary causes of it. It's very easy to say, "God is the cause of everything except for sin," and yet overlook the mystery involved in the correlative question: "Well then, who is the cause of it?" How can *we* cause something without God being active as cause? Many atheists jump on the logic and tell us that we believers are fooling ourselves. Their argument runs: according to you, God is the cause of all things, persons, and ultimately, of all actions; we are the cause of sin (but God is the cause of us and, ultimately, of our actions); therefore, God is the cause of sin. This argument is deceptive, but evil remains a paradox, one of the great problems discussed in philosophy and theology.

The key to unlocking this riddle is to see that sin is a *lack*, a kind of nonbeing, a kind of hole in what should be there, a kind of *privation*. All the good that we do, we do by participating in God's own activity. However, when we sin, *we* turn our hearts away from God, we *do not* participate in his activating presence in the depths of our souls. We are agents of *nonbeing*, the nonbeing that is *not observing the measure of the virtues*. The only thing that lies *purely in our own power* is to *not* be virtuous. Everything else, when we are truly acting virtuously, is a collaboration between us and God, with him as the first cause and us as the secondary cause.

These are immense mysteries. At once, sin places before us the great questions involved in the ways that human freedom interacts with the divine freedom. These topics open up discussions which are far too immense for this little volume. They have been discussed at length by faithful Catholic philosophers and theologians, whom I will cite in a note.[25] For our present purposes, we merely need to hold on to the basic truth: God is the cause of all that is good; *we* are the nihilists who weave sin into the story of history. Through sin, *we* cut off our relationship with God's grace. Obviously, we remain living, conversion remains a possibility, and God retains his love for us. But *from our side*, the bond is broken, leaving the initiative for renewal in his hands.

This bond can be cut in two different ways: one complete and the other partial. To explain this difference, the Catholic tradition draws an essential distinction between sins which are mortal and those which are venial. The Church affirms this distinction as being of central importance, for the entire question of the divine life is at stake here. The *Catechism of the Catholic Church* is rather direct in defining this distinction, so we should follow its clarity: "*Mortal sin* destroys charity in the heart of man by a grave violation of God's law; it turns man away from God, who is his ultimate end and his beatitude, by preferring an inferior good to him. *Venial sin* allows charity to subsist, even though it offends and wounds it" (CCC 1855). In short, mortal sins are *mortal—fatal*—to the life of grace; venial sins are not, but they are like the person who cuts threads off from the cords of love that connect us to God's grace.

It is tempting to say that mortal sins are only possible if we *directly* reject God. Some people have even proposed the idea that so long as we maintain a fundamental love for God, we will not fall into damnation, even if we commit a grievous sin. The God of mercy, they say, would not allow that. So long as we maintain a fundamental choice to love God, it would not necessarily be the case that particular actions must necessarily cut off a foundational love of God from our hearts.

This proposal is deceptive, however, and, in fact, has been condemned by the Church.[26] To understand why, think of a very concrete scenario. We must think of sin in *relational terms*. Therefore, imagine the case of two friends, one of whom murders his neighbors. No doubt, the other friend will pity him and perhaps even continue to feel great affection for him. However, we can say that by becoming a murderer, the guilty friend has now managed to cut off the relationship *from his side*. The other friend, all the while loving him, can nonetheless say, "I just can't be your friend until you show repentance." The continuous love expressed by the innocent friend is somewhat like (albeit still infinitely less than) the love that God retains for the most hardened of sinners. However, the guilty party must repent before the bonds of *mutual* friendship are fully restored.

Now, notice, in this example the murderer didn't set out thinking, "I'll break off my friendship with Bill." He merely committed murder. However, this murder *implied* that so long as he remained hardened in it, refusing to repent, he could not have the same relationships with those who were his friends before this act. So too, mortal sins do not always involve us *immediately* thinking, "To hell with God and his law!" Tragically, this can be merely implied in our mortal sins, inflexibly connected to them without being fully articulated in our own minds. In short: there are certain actions which are *intrinsically incompatible* with the love of God above all things. A list of such actions could be drawn from the Ten Commandments and related violations of divine morality: blasphemy, heresy, idolatry, not attending Mass on Sundays and holy days of obligation, despair of the divine assistance, neglect of parents, paying one's workers unjustly, greed, stealing, envy, sedition against legitimate authority, murder, abortion, euthanasia, adultery, contraception, homosexual sexual acts, and a number of others which can be found in resources for preparing well for confession.[27]

Now the Church does recognize that there are certain conditions for falling into mortal sin. While there are actions that are *objectively* mortal sins, it is necessary that these sins be committed in full knowledge and be fully and freely willed. In other words, certain circumstances can cause what is *objectively* mortally sinful to be *subjectively* not so. This does not mean that they transmute into non-sins! So long as there is some freedom involved, they are reduced to the status of being *venial* sins.

Now, venial sin does not cause us to fall out of a state of grace, but it does introduce into our soul kinds of "cross currents," waves of brackish spiritual water that no longer travel in grace's God-bound direction. In this way, venial sin predisposes us toward mortal sin, toward the loss of the life of grace. We are like self-sabotaging sailors, drilling holes into the hull of our ship. For a while, the holes remain above the water level, so we suspect nothing about the endangered condition of our hull, but all of a sudden the conditions change, the waters rise, and we find that the ship sinks, having been ill-prepared for this moment. This is the constant state of the human soul. Even though we *technically* are not bound to confess venial sins, the Church highly encourages this practice, directing us to the sacrament for healing and grace (see CCC 1458). How many such sins we commit! Each one is little, like a small drill bit adding yet another hole to the ship's hull, gradually placing its integrity in danger. We should end each confession by saying, "And in sorrow I confess many other sins which I no longer can recall." It calls to mind the words prayed by all present at the Byzantine Liturgy just prior to the reception of Communion:

> O God, be merciful to me, a sinner.
> O God, cleanse me of my sins and have mercy on me.
> O Lord, forgive me for I have sinned *without number*.

We must not think that these are merely the words of fire-and-brimstone preaching. Although many believe that the Church is obsessed with sin and that Catholics have a kind of masochistic feeling of guilt, the Church's teaching on sin is quite sane. It is, in fact, a recognition of our human frailty. Yes, sin is more than mere frailty. It is *much* more than a mere "character flaw" or "quirk." It is a kind of illness, sometimes mortal, which infects the most profound point of our soul: its relationship with God. Nonetheless, the ability to sin is a very pitiable human reality as well. God cannot sin. He does not need to achieve goodness. He *is* goodness itself, pure goodness, eternal goodness. We, however, are beings who are "on the way," works in progress. And how often do we slip along the path! How long do we miss the virtuous goal!

Our life is a kind of "race to heaven," but as any runner can tell you, a race is a grueling affair, requiring great exertion and subject to many potential pitfalls along the way: obstacles in the path, low blood sugar, hill training, etc. To be in shape requires constant exercise, and in our moral life as reborn children of God, the "divine marathon" requires us to pummel and subdue everything that might prevent us from running the race well and reaching our goal (1 Corinthians 9:24-27). We are forever ready to be lazy, and how often do we find ourselves falling short of our higher hopes for ourselves. St. Paul was not unique when he reflected on the drama of his own life and said, "For I know that nothing good dwells within me, that is, in my flesh. I can will what is right, but I cannot do it. For I do not do the good I want, but the evil I do not want is what I do" (Romans 7:18-19). St. Paul was a great saint, a man devoted to God and to his fellow Christians. What then can we say for ourselves? The words of the prophet are our own: "The heart is deceitful above all things, and desperately corrupt; who can understand it?" (Jeremiah 17:9).

The human readiness to sin calls to mind the words of the poet Rudyard Kipling, drawn in part from 2 Peter 2:22. Looking back over the devastation of World War I, Kipling, like many of his contemporaries, was crushed as he considered how all the hopes of modern progress had ended in such tremendous bloodshed. Reflecting on this calamity, he could not help but think of the human tendency to fail. As he closes his poem "The Gods of the Copybook Headings," he writes:

> As it will be in the future, it was at the birth of Man –
> There are only four things certain since Social Progress began: –
> That the Dog returns to his Vomit and the Sow returns to her Mire,
> And the burnt Fool's bandaged finger goes wabbling back to the Fire.[28]

All of us who are baptized are like the burnt fool who still reaches out for the fire, even though we know that it will burn us. Baptism remakes us into children of God. However, we remain in a kind of "moral field hospital" for the whole of our lives. We still have within ourselves the effects of sin, including an inclination toward further sin. Most often, this is referred to using the traditional theological term "concupiscence," but I have a fondness for another ancient expression used by the Church, *fomes peccati*, which could be translated "tinder for sin." Through grace, our soul is like a new and lush forest, putting down its roots into the river of grace which flows from eternity into each of our souls (Ezekiel 47:7-12; John 4:10-11, 7:38; Revelation 22:1-2). However, for the rest of our lives, there will be dry underbrush in this forest, tinder waiting for the spark of a fire which will then reignite the blaze and burn down this marvelous new and verdant landscape re-created and watered by God's grace.

This constant threat seems quite overwhelming, tempting us to look at all of our striving and say, "Vanity!" Is everything to be deficient or defective in human life? What are we to do? Is this message actually life-giving? Does the Church really want to "put down" humanity this much?

The response is simple. We do not need to search far to discover who is the chosen object of our Lord's love and compassion. He made this abundantly clear in the Gospels. His love rests upon the sinner (Mark 2:17; Luke 5:32). He is like the shepherd whose attention is turned to the one lost sheep (Matthew 18:12-14; Luke 15:4-7), like a father who receives his prodigal son (Luke 15:11-32), like the good Samaritan who cares for the man who has fallen by the wayside (Luke 10:25-37), a merciful God who looks upon the repentant publican with the greatest of affection (Luke 18:9-14).

Of course, we must never presume upon the mercy of God, for it is his free gift. Never should we say, "Let's sin. God will show us his mercy!" All of the "old man," the "old Adam," has been crucified with Christ, and our new life has come from our resurrected Lord. Freedom from sin does not mean that we can act like lawbreakers who willy-nilly act however we wish. Instead, we are free *from slavery to sin* so that we can be "slaves" of God, indeed his *friends* and companions, who receive something wonderful: "sanctification and its end, eternal life" (Romans 6:22; see John 15:15). This is the great goal and full fruit of our faith, the salvation of our souls (1 Peter 1:9). It is a gift which God is readier to give to us than a mother is ready to shower her child with love (Isaiah 49:15).

Every time we leave the sacrament of Reconciliation, even if we only have confessed venial sins, our ears should ring with the words of the Lord, proclaimed through the prophet Isaiah: "Behold, I am doing a new thing; now it springs forth, do you not perceive it? I will make a way in the wilderness and rivers in the desert" (Isaiah 43:19). These words apply above all to Christ, whose incarnation is the great "new thing" done by God, something at once expected by the prophets and, yet, how surprising, even to his closest disciples! But God also looks to do new things in our souls, to refashion us with the waters of eternal life.

Like ancient Israel, we are at fault, yet we blame God. We wander in a self-imposed desert of sin. We, who have received the great "bread from heaven," the Eucharist, look back at the easy life of self-gratification and echo the ancient words of God's people: "We remember the fish we ate in Egypt for nothing, the cucumbers, the melons, the leeks, the onions, and the garlic; but now our strength is dried up, and there is nothing at all but this manna to look at" (Numbers 11:5-6). And while we act as though we have no water, we, in fact, have a God who makes water gush forth in the valleys (Psalm 104:10), a God who is greater than the rock struck by Moses to give the Israelite people refreshment (Exodus 17:1-7), a God who gives us living water, flowing from Christ, in the sacraments (John 4:1-14, 19:34; 1 Corinthians 10:1-4; 1 John 5:6). How greatly we should desire that water, the gift of grace! How God stands ready to irrigate the dry and hard soil of our souls: "For I will pour water on the thirsty land, and streams on the dry ground; I will pour my Spirit upon your descendants, and my blessing on your offspring. They shall spring up like grass amid waters, like willows by flowing streams" (Isaiah 44:3-4).

The Fathers of the Church saw a profound example of God's mercy in the parable of the Good Samaritan (Luke 10:25-37). The man who goes down from Jerusalem to Jericho would be each and every one of us, falling from the state of grace into the state of sin. We lie upon the side of the road, bloodied and feeble. Yet Christ, the God-man rejected by the world, comes to us, taking us into his care, pouring the oil of grace and divine love into our wounds, and providentially placing us in the care of the innkeeper, paying the way—no matter the cost.

The story calls to mind a beautiful tale told in the prophecy of Ezekiel. There, the prophet lays forth the whole story of unfaithful Israel, a tale which applies to each of us as well:

> When I [the Lord] passed by you, and saw you weltering in your blood, I said to you in your blood, "Live, and grow up like a plant of the field." And you grew up and became tall and arrived at full maidenhood; your breasts were formed, and your hair had grown; yet you were naked and bare.
>
> When I passed by you again and looked upon you, behold, you were at the age for love; and I spread my skirt over you, and covered your nakedness: yes, I pledged myself to you and entered into a covenant with you, says the Lord God, and you became mine. Then I bathed you with water and washed off your blood from you, and anointed you with oil. I clothed you also with embroidered cloth and shod you with leather, I wrapped you in fine linen and covered you with silk. And I decked you with ornaments, and put bracelets on your arms, and a chain on your neck. And I put a ring on your nose, and earrings in your ears, and a beautiful crown upon your head. Thus you were decked with gold and silver; and your clothing was of fine linen, and silk, and embroidered cloth; you ate fine flour and honey and oil. You grew exceedingly beautiful, and came to regal estate. (Ezekiel 16:6-13)

And yet, the prophet goes on to tell of how Israel trusted in this new beauty, as though it was her own, not the gift of God. She used these gifts to evil and blasphemous ends. After a long litany of these faults and errant ways, God returns, nonetheless, to his great mercy: "Yet I will remember my covenant with you in the days of your youth, and I will establish with you an everlasting covenant" (Ezekiel 16:60).

And what is the implication for us? Christ makes it clear in the parable of the Good Samaritan: "Go and do likewise" (Luke 10:37). These words are merely a reiteration of those which bring the Sermon on the Mount to its close: "Love your enemies and pray for those who persecute you, so that you may be sons of your Father who is in heaven ... You, therefore, must be perfect, as your heavenly Father is perfect" (Matthew 5:44-45, 48). We are all sinful servants whose debt has been forgiven. Let us not fail to show this forgiveness to others (see Matthew 18:21-35). Through the gift of grace, we receive the reflection of Christ's love in our souls. Thus, just as he is the Good Samaritan, so too should we be good Samaritans in turn. This is the true Christian response to the problem of sin. In the words of a great twentieth-century theologian, "In other words, I become the neighbor of *the person upon whom I make my love fall*, and he becomes my neighbor. Others are 'other.' I am the one who must draw them close by making a ray of the love of God which has fallen upon me descend upon them."[29]

The Church does not speak of sin so that she can frighten and manipulate believers. The Church speaks of sin because it represents the greatest loss we could ever experience, the loss of the new divine life we have received through grace: "For what will it profit a man, if he gains the whole world and forfeits his life?" (Matthew 16:26). Allow me to finish with the words of the Dominican theologian Fr. Ambroise Gardeil, himself quoting a famous passage from St. Leo the Great:

> What woe will there be if we come to be deprived of this life by sinning! The Christian sinner is more than an errant being. Quite literally, he is a degenerate, a being who has corrupted the [new] nature begotten him by God, a being who has lost his divine vigor and his eternal value: "O Christian," exclaimed St. Leo the Great, "Be aware, therefore, of your dignity, and given your kinship with the divine nature, never consent to return by degenerate morals to the base vulgarity of your former existence!"[30]

CHAPTER FIVE

Forward, Always Forward: Continuous Conversion and the Moral Life

We have a life to live, a life that is shared with God. With the rising of the sun each morning, we should let loose the grace that is in our hearts: "What is it that you wish me to do today, Lord?" To go even further, we really must ask, "How do you want me to live *your life*, Lord—your life, which you have given to me?" And at the end of the day, we must examine once more whether we have in fact lived this life or, instead, have been somewhat like zombies, the walking dead, who were not animated by this new vitality, the vitality of Christ. The sun will set, the night will pass, and then we will find, yet again, the same need to press onward, as though we were just starting anew: "*Nunc coepi*. Now, I have begun upon the ways of the Lord." There is no end to the upward ascent to God. St. Gregory of Nyssa's description of Moses applies just as readily to each of us: "Once having set foot on the ladder which God set up (as Jacob says), he continually climbed to the step above and never ceased to rise higher, because he always found a step higher than the one he had attained."[31]

Here I would like to share words spoken by a holy old Hungarian Benedictine monk whom I had the honor of knowing, Fr. Sebastian Samay, OSB. You will see the point of the story in but a moment. Fr. Sebastian was a philosopher by training, and I was blessed to have him for an independent study in "epistemology," the theory of knowledge. One day, while sitting in his office for our weekly meeting, I remember—as clearly as though it were yesterday—how he looked off during his lecture and said something that I knew at that moment *needed to be copied down word for word*. I had been in the habit of taking abbreviated notes, but something deep within me shouted out, "Take this down!" I've kept these lines to this day, and I think they summarize so very well what I have been trying to communicate in the whole first section of this book:[32]

> What is the greatest mystery is shared life. Whenever we think of life, we think of it as *my* life, *her* life, *their* life. I cannot have your toothache or your life ... Or so we think. What we call salvation is precisely that; it is God's life extended to us by his generosity. Salvation means that he is going to extend his shared life, for his life is not individual either but, rather, is communal among Father, Son, and Holy Spirit. That shared life—there is *one* God—is the very life that God extends to us because of the merit of Christ through his death and resurrection.
>
> When people get married, they have this desire to share their life with the other person. In a certain sense, they do. They share their plans and their sympathies, but their life is not shared. That is why, as St. Augustine said, in sexual union "every animal is sad," for it seemed so close to being melted into the other person but, of course, when sexual intercourse is over, *he* turns away and starts smoking and *she* eats an apple, etc. That is why sex is repeated, for the illusion is created that since you were so close the last time it is going to happen ... but it doesn't.
>
> Therefore, shared life is one of the deepest cravings of human nature, and it is not satisfied except in the beatific union with God. He simply extends his life, so that it might flow through us. We have to give up our individual lives; we have to die. St. Basil did not mince words to call the Christian life *theopoesis* (=*theosis*, *divinization*), for our own self-focused life is, so to speak, replaced by his life.

This is not mere poetic fancy from a well-educated Hungarian tongue. The little expression "the life of grace" is pregnant with meaning. Grace is not merely a nice token given to us, a beautiful golden coin which, if we manage to keep it until our last breath, will pay our way into heaven. It is something that we must make grow, for if life does not progress, it falls backward into death. Indeed, one of the great marks of the spiritual nature of the human soul is the fact that, while our physical body falls apart as we "shuffle off this mortal coil," we can transform our dying into an act of great trust in God and even love for others, who will no longer have our physical presence after many years of shared existence together. Even in death, we are called to be more than passive spectators. As the character of the Dowager Countess of Grantham, Violet Crawley, once said in the TV show *Downton Abbey*: "Lord Grantham wasn't 'taken.' He died." Even in our last moments, to the degree that this is possible, we must live out our very death. Such vitality is so exceedingly powerful in our lives as Christians that, with Christ, we even overcome the very power of death!

We forever risk forgetting or ignoring one of the most important facts of moral theology: the language of "new birth" in relation to grace is not a fanciful, though ultimately empty, metaphor. Grace reaches down to the deepest fibers of our being in order to re-create us and divinize us, in order to give us a new life. It does not pass through us like light through glass, coming from God and going on its way. Instead, through the theological virtues of faith, hope, and charity, grace enables *us* to perform truly divine acts. And even in the case of the gifts of the Holy Spirit, where we are like ships catching breezes from heaven, *we* remain the ones who have these sails within our souls. Through these gifts, which we will discuss more fully in a later chapter, God makes *us* capable of receiving such inspirations from on high, and we have much work of prayer and expectation ahead of us if we are to prepare ourselves for receiving something so great.

In short, all the acts of our existence as Christians should be the expressions of a new and eternal life, one which in fact begins even now, here below. Just as the plant manifests its life throughout its life cycle, and the giraffe through its, so too does the grace-filled child of God manifest his or her life in and through the very actions that he or she is now capable of performing—an eternal "life cycle" which passes along its way, for the time being, within the flowing stream of time. What a great gift! What a responsibility! What a lofty calling!

In the end, however, the calling goes so high that we can never actually sit back and say, "I am finished. Now I can smugly rest on my laurels, self-satisfied in my achievement. How lovely a retirement package this is! Let us sip our mimosas and lounge by the poolside." Our sole satisfaction waits for the last day, the day which is no longer a day but, rather, is the eternal now of God himself, spread out before our gaze and inflaming our love, without any shadow of the passing world. In fact, that blessed vision of God contains a lesson for us in our "wayfaring" pilgrim state. In heaven, we will see God directly, "face-to-face." We will all share in one single, communal act of divine knowledge and love. (In the next section, in the chapter on the theological virtue of charity, we will see that the notion of *friendship* is the best means we have for understanding the mystery of charity and the deepest meaning of grace.) And yet, God will forever remain infinitely more than all that we share, joyously together, in that great throng which will feast upon the divine splendor. As is said by great theologians of both the East and the West, by St. Gregory Palamas and by St. Thomas Aquinas: even in that most intimate of moments, we will not know God as comprehensively as he knows himself. Or, as St. Gregory of Nyssa expresses it so perfectly:

> This truly is the vision of God: Never to be satisfied in the desire to see Him. But one must always, by looking at what he can see, rekindle his desire to see more. Thus, no limit would interrupt growth in the ascent to God, since no limit to the Good can be found nor is the increasing of desire for the Good brought to an end because it is satisfied.[33]

God alone has full knowledge of all the supernatural riches of his Godhead. Nonetheless, we will have an utterly true and certain knowledge of him, as we ourselves are transformed by the eternal light of this blessed and glorious vision: "We know that when he appears we shall be like him, for we shall see him as he is" (1 John 3:2). Such is the mystery of our redemption.

Here below, we only anticipate this glory; we hold it in seed, not yet in full bloom. We are in what theologians call the *status merendi*, the state of meriting (though even our merits are God's gift). So long as we do not grasp the beatific vision of God—or, better yet, so long as we are not ourselves grasped by God in this vision—we can forever merit more grace. We receive the gift of new life, something we *never* could merit *on our own*. However, we must perform acts befitting this life which we have received, thereby growing in this life—though only if and when God gives the growth. Hence, we do not speak merely of "the growth of the virtues," not even in the case of the theological virtues. Rather, we speak of merit, a notion which so beautifully combines our striving along with God's abundant gift: "For *he will render* to every man *according to his works*" (Romans 2:6, emphasis added). Or, as St. Paul wrote in the context of his apostolic labors: "So neither he who plants nor he who waters is anything, but only God who gives the growth. He who plants and he who waters are equal, and each shall receive his wages according to his labor" (1 Corinthians 3:7-8).

Hence, the apostles were rather strident about how much work the moral life of Christians must be. We only receive the crown of victory if we endure the trials of this life without losing our faith, hope, and love in God (James 1:12), above all if we endure despite unjust treatment (1 Peter 2:19-25). St. John was told, as he gazed upon the tribulations set forth in the book of Revelation, "Be faithful unto death, and I will give you the crown of life" (Revelation 2:10). And most famously, according to St. Paul, life is like a race, something calling for the greatest exertion and training: "Do you not know that in a race all the runners compete, but only one receives the prize? *So run that you may obtain it*" (1 Corinthians 9:24, emphasis added).

All of this is merely a kind of reflection on Christ's own strong words:

> If any one comes to me and does not hate his own father and mother and wife and children and brothers and sisters, yes, and even his own life, he cannot be my disciple. Whoever does not bear his own cross and come after me, cannot be my disciple ... *So therefore, whoever of you does not renounce all that he has cannot be my disciple* ... If any man would come after me, let him deny himself and take up his cross *daily* and follow me. (Luke 14:26-27, 33, 9:23, emphasis added)

Should we expect anything other than this, given the high calling which sounds forth in the words of the Sermon on the Mount? Where else could perfection lead but to God, who must replace everything in us that is not divine? He does not do this in order to pulverize and annihilate us but, rather, does so in order that each and every action of *ours* might be divine. Such seeming paradoxes are often the mark of great mysteries. Here we have a case of the "both / and" nature of the Catholic Faith: through grace, we are made divine; we are at once ourselves and yet also infinitely more! Theologians can explain all of these details in many treatises and through the course of many disputes. However, the practical importance remains: the whole of our life is to be poured out like an offering to God's glory: "And whatever you do, in word or deed, do everything in the name of the Lord Jesus, giving thanks to God the Father through him" (Colossians 3:17; see 2 Timothy 4:6; Philippians 2:17; 1 Corinthians 10:31).

Our virtue must forever increase. We are given a calling to, and the ability for, a perfection beyond all measure: "Unless your righteousness exceeds that of the scribes and Pharisees, you will never enter the kingdom of heaven" (Matthew 5:20). Each act must lead us to push forward on the pathway of unending progress, a kind of ongoing transformation from one glory to the next: "And we all, with unveiled face, beholding the glory of the Lord, are being changed into his likeness from one degree of glory to another" (2 Corinthians 3:18), until the dawning of the day whose glory will know no end.

We have the life of Christ, which is our calling. We walk with him in the truest of friendships, a life that is shared in the most profound sense. Our morality's aim is not merely "Do no harm" or even "Avoid evil and sin." We must go much further. We must live our life! Our moral task is to make the divine love radiate throughout all of our being, a task that is as infinite and endless as God himself. Traveling along the dust-covered paths of life, we are well aware that by ourselves we are not powerful enough for this task. However, our generous God has promised to be close to us, if we but ask. Let us pray and live every day as though we wanted to walk closer to him, moving forever onward toward that divine sunrise on the eternal shores:

> Just a closer walk with Thee,
> Grant it, Jesus, is my plea,
> Daily walking close to Thee,
> Let it be, dear Lord, let it be.
>
> I am weak but Thou art strong;
> Jesus, keep me from all wrong;
> I'll be satisfied as long
> As I walk, let me walk close to Thee ...
>
> When my feeble life is o'er,
> Time for me will be no more;
> Guide me gently, safely o'er
> To Thy kingdom shore, to Thy shore.[34]

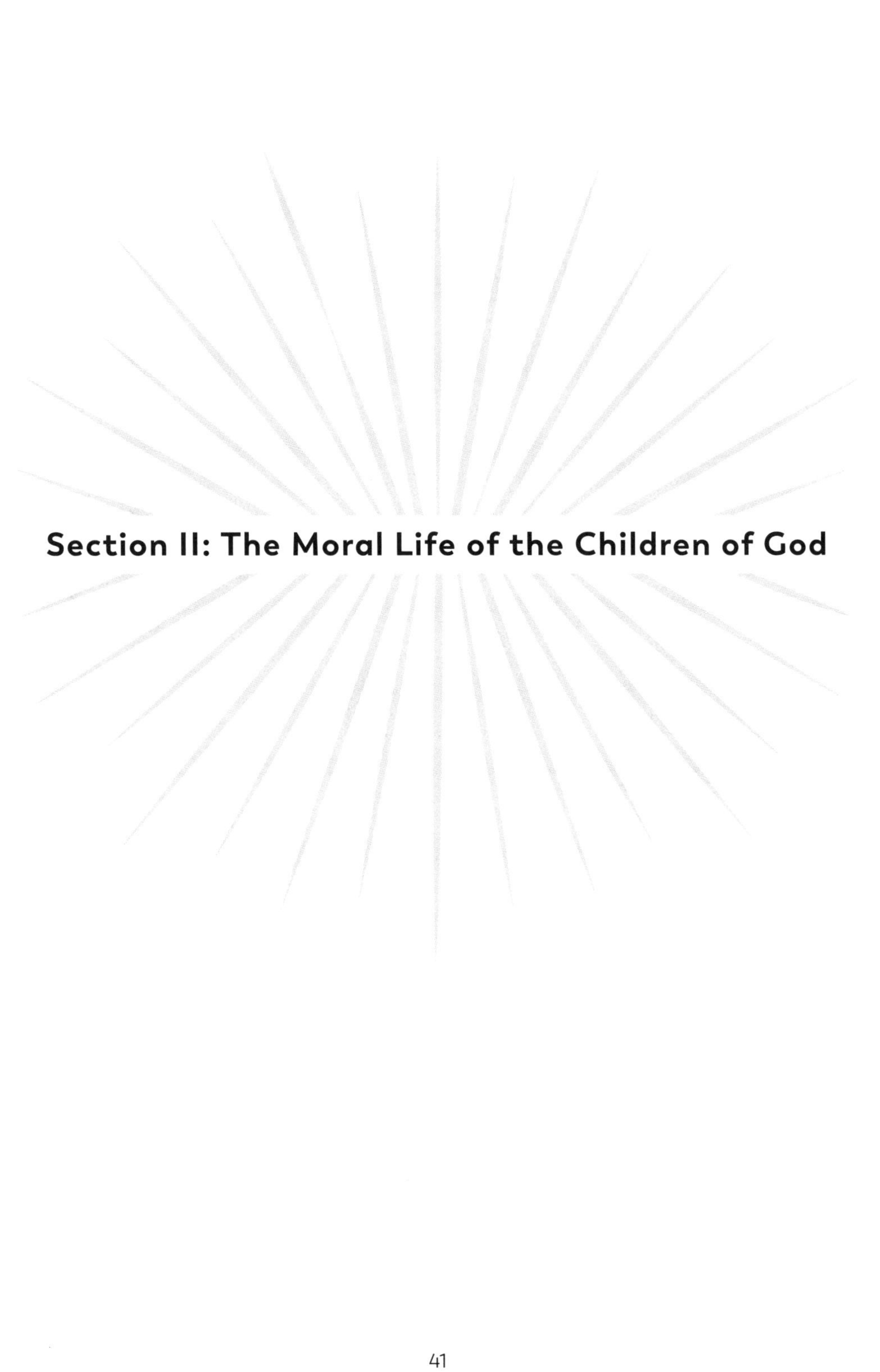

Section II: The Moral Life of the Children of God

THE THEOLOGICAL VIRTUES

Among all of the virtues that flower in our souls under the activity of God's grace, the most beautiful and central blossoms are the theological virtues of faith, hope, and charity. They place us in direct communion with God, as with our dearest friend, the bridegroom of our souls. The theological virtues are the greatest of all of God's gifts poured out upon us, and they are the most important aspect of our moral activity as Christians. The following chapters are dedicated to clarifying and illuminating their true character, so that we might understand the lofty heights to which we are called.

CHAPTER SIX

The Gift of Divine Eyes and Heart: Faith, Hope, and Charity

In the first section of this book, we discussed at length the way that the gift of grace truly re-creates us. As we saw in chapter three, salvation and redemption aren't just a kind of "get out of jail thanks to Christ" card. Salvation and redemption are, in fact, first and foremost about putting on "the new man, created after the likeness of God in true righteousness and holiness" (Ephesians 4:24; see Colossians 3:8-10). We are renewed by something greater than what Adam could have imagined: the gift of Christ incarnate, the second Person of the Holy Trinity and the source of all grace. The "grace of union," the grace by which human nature is united to the Word in Christ, is infinitely greater than the already-supernatural "grace of Adam," and from the fullness that was Christ's own grace we then have received, as from an ever-flowing fountain (see John 4:13-14).

Now, we have spoken already about this great theme, expressed in the West using the term *divinization* and in the East using the Greek term *theosis*, both meaning "being made divine." Through grace, we are truly remade in God's image. In the words of St. Peter cited in an earlier chapter, through grace we "become partakers of the divine nature" (2 Peter 1:4). However, we must be careful about this wording, "partakers." What does it mean?

I have heard friends and family jokingly using somewhat old-fashioned language to speak about having an alcoholic beverage: "Let us partake in libations!" Here, "to partake" means "to drink, to place something physically within me." We take a portion of wine and place it in our stomachs. This is, of course, quite natural and expected. The contents of a bottle of wine can be divided many different ways.

Can God be divided like this? No indeed! There is not a little bit of God here in me and a little bit of God there in you. God is not a large piece of cloth that we can divide up into pieces. Christianity is not a form of New Age religion. God is not the "divine spark within us." He is much more than that! And nonetheless, God is everywhere, as is said in the well-known opening of many Byzantine liturgies: "Heavenly King, Comforter, Spirit of Truth, *everywhere present and filling all things*." Merely skim Psalm 139, and you will indeed have a sense of this awesome mystery of his presence: he knows when we sit and stand; he is behind us and yet also in front of us; there is nowhere to flee and hide from his Spirit; he is present to the dead; he is at the furthest ends of the sea; and so forth ... Nothing would exist without his creative and conserving activity. And as Christ himself said, "Are not two sparrows sold for a penny? And not one of them will fall to the ground without your Father's will. But even the hairs of your head are all numbered" (Matthew 10:29-30). There is not a crevice of creation, not a little hidden speck in the corner of some solar system far, far away, which escapes its dependence upon God. "If he should take back his spirit to himself, and gather to himself his breath, all flesh would perish together, and man would return to dust" (Job 34:14-15). He is everywhere yet not contained; he calls all things *into* being while himself *eternally existing*. Thus, classical theological vocabulary spoke of his "presence of immensity," his presence to all the things he causes. They depend on him, completely, but he most definitely does not depend upon them.[35]

You see, therefore, even God's presence as the cause of all things is very mysterious. He is present yet not split up. All things depend upon him, but he does not depend upon them. Time and eternity coexist, but time depends upon God's never-changing eternity. This is one of the great mysteries reflected on by truly profound philosophers and theologians. In all of this, God isn't split up among all of his beings. He is not like a kind of water that soaks the sponge of creation. He is transcendent, even while we so immanently depend upon him for all that we are and do: "God is at work in you, both to will and to work for his good pleasure" (Philippians 2:13). How great a mystery! What beggars we are, flying from nonbeing into being! Yet here we are! All is gift.

As we already said many times, though it forever bears repeating, God pushes on further, giving us far more than our human natures. He gives us his nature. How? Not by merging with us like the Force from *Star Wars* but, instead, by making us capable of truly divine acts. Nature is made to act. Something or someone "acts naturally" when it fulfills what it is supposed to be. Nature isn't a "thing" inside of us. No microscope will find it. However, as sound philosophy teaches us, nature is the principle of our being enabling us to act. Merely as humans, we have unique "resources," ready to spring forth from our human nature. We are knowing and loving beings, capable of social relationships and of great conquests of the spirit. Our human nature makes us expand; it enables us *to act*.

Precisely as humans, our greatest actions are to know and to love. Yes, animals have their own kinds of knowledge and affection. They can know us and have a kind of love for us and for other things. But beyond this kind of animal knowledge, we humans can know the *natures of other things*, and we can love them *precisely for their own sakes*. This is what we mean when we say that the human person has an *intellect* and a *will*. By our intellects, we are open to *being*, and by our wills, we are tuned to *the good*. We have a spiritual mind and spiritual desire and joy. Our horizons span the whole of the cosmos. From all of this comes the great mystery of the human person, the greatest marvel of nature.[36] We can think of the intellect and the will as being the means at our disposal for spiritual-human activity. They are qualities we have—lasting qualities, in need of development and exercise—and by means of them, we are united to other things, striving after them and ultimately taking joy in them.

If we have a new nature, the divine nature, we should expect that we will have *new activities*, new ways of functioning in the world. "If any one is in Christ, he is a new creation; the old has passed away, behold, the new has come" (2 Corinthians 5:17). And God does just that. He gives us new capacities. Grace flows forth from the deepest part of our souls and gives us new minds and hearts. God divinizes our intellects and wills, enabling them to perform *truly divine* activities.

The gifts that make all of this possible are called the "theological virtues." But beware! Don't let the word "virtue" trick you! These are not skills which we could ever gain through practice and exertion. And even when we have them, they will forever be God's gift. We may *merit* greater faith or hope or charity, but only God enables its growth. There are other virtues, "acquired moral virtues," that we can cultivate solely through practice, deploying our merely human "resources." In a true sense, we have the tools in hand to grow in such virtues, like courage, temperance, or sobriety. By *our* nature, given to us by God, we cooperate with God to grow in the natural virtues. For this reason, they are called "acquired" virtues. But the theological virtues are different. Here, in the divine domain of grace, the words of St. Paul find an important application: "So neither he who plants nor he who waters is anything, but only God who gives the growth" (1 Corinthians 3:7). By the divine virtues given in grace, that is, by *God's* nature, given to us by God, we cooperate with God, who grows ever more present within us. This is why classical theology used a perhaps awkward but still helpful metaphor to try to capture this dependence. According to its terminology, these virtues are called "infused"; they are "poured into our souls from God." It is a metaphor which should be maintained, for it is, after all, scriptural in origin: "God's love has been poured into our hearts through the Holy Spirit who has been given to us" (Romans 5:5).

From an ancient tradition going back to Scripture itself, Christians speak of three theological virtues: faith, hope, and charity (see 1 Corinthians 13:13; Colossians 1:3-5; 1 Thessalonians 1:3). In the next three chapters, we will be discussing each of these virtues in detail. Here, let us only stress one very important point that they all share: they are *maximally* divine. Do not fall into a common error when using these terms, "faith," "hope," and "charity." Many believe that they are the equivalent of "trust," "optimism," and "generosity" or "kindness." No! They are something infinitely more. They are all uniquely divine, the most divine virtues in our souls as Christians. By each of them, we uniquely are "tuned up" to God's level. That is why they are called "*theo*-logical." By them, we truly think and love with God's own mind and heart, even though he remains still infinitely beyond us.

By faith, we truly put on the "mind of Christ" (1 Corinthians 2:16). We are enabled to know "the depths of God" (1 Corinthians 2:10). As we will see in the next chapter, faith is not merely trust. It is a kind of knowledge. By faith, we know the mysteries of the Triune God and his will to save all things. "For he has made known to us in all wisdom and insight the mystery of his will, according to his purpose which he set forth in Christ as a plan for the fulness of time, to unite all things in him, things in heaven and things on earth" (Ephesians 1:9-10). Through faith, we know *with God's own knowledge.* For now it is obscure, but in heaven it will give way to sight. Here below it is shrouded in mystery, but then the eternal morning will dawn. It is one and the same knowledge: here obscure and "on the way," but there "at home" and eternally spilling over into love-filled joy.

By hope, *we have a true and supernatural trust* that enables us to act with divine certitude that the gift of salvation and divinization is truly possible for us. As we have said, God gives all the growth in this divine life. This requires a radical trust, far more than we could ever "gin up" on our own. We must not trust in our own power to pull ourselves up by our bootstraps but, instead, must lean with all of our will on the God who saves. He alone is our help and our shield (Psalm 33:20). In rejection, affliction, and storm, he alone motivates the great hope we have—not only for ourselves, but for the whole world, whom we are called to comfort "with the comfort with which we ourselves are comforted by God" (2 Corinthians 1:4). We do not pridefully trust in our own righteousness but, rather, accuse ourselves and, like the tax collector, trust in God's abundant goodness and mercy (Luke 18:9-17). The motive of our hope is not sunny optimism. It is Christ crucified, "the power of God and the wisdom of God" (1 Corinthians 1:24). In the words of the powerful Latin hymn traditionally sung at the Good Friday Liturgy in the Roman rite: "*O Crux ave, spes unica!* Hail, O Cross, our only hope!" It is the supernatural God who gives us his very life through the gift of grace. We can say that God enables us to trust him, not by our own estimation of things but, rather, by God's own gift of his infinite trustworthiness.

By charity-love we don't merely give our money to others. This word *charity* is the Latin-derived term for the Greek term *agapē*. It is a unique kind of love, not merely "self-giving love," but far more than that. It is *God's own love*. In a beautiful image, taken from a slightly exuberant mystic, a great spiritual theologian has written that this is a kind of heart transplant with God.[37] Yet God retains his heart, so perhaps the wonderful theme from St. Thomas Aquinas deserves to be placed in relief: charity is divine friendship, God with us and us with God. In fact, this is the principle that guides the whole of Aquinas' theology of charity.[38] Indeed, this theme long predates St. Thomas, for Christ himself said, "No longer do I call you servants, for the servant does not know what his master is doing; but I have called you friends, for all that I have heard from my Father I have made known to you" (John 15:15). Through charity, we do not love and trust God merely because he will save us. No, that is hope. The love that unites us in friendship with God in charity loves God wholly because he is lovable. In the beautiful words of the traditional Roman Catholic act of contrition, "I detest all of my sins ... most of all because they offend you, my God, who are all-good and deserving of all my love." Moreover, friends share all things. Yes, we share God's love, above all God's own love for his own infinite goodness. However, we also share in his love for all things. As St. John reminded his flock, "Beloved, if God so loved us, we also ought to love one another. No man has ever seen God; if we love one another, God abides in us and his love is perfected in us" (1 John 4:11-12). "Fraternal charity" is truly divine.

And charity has a unique characteristic. It alone will last beyond the breaking of the world. Faith and hope are the theological virtues of wayfarers, of pilgrims. While we are not united with God through the beatific vision, we need a kind of "supernatural supplement," faith. And while we have not achieved this full union with God, our wills must be strengthened. We need courage beyond courage. In short, we need theological hope. Charity, however, will remain forever. Faith and hope will pass over into the great love of heaven, no longer needing faith and hope. And how great will that love be! How great will be the joy that we will share in that communion with God and with all the redeemed in Christ, partaking in one knowledge and one love, a reflection of the Triune God, in whose image we are being re-created even now.

CHAPTER SEVEN

Faith: The Substance of Things Hoped For

"Any one who goes ahead and does not abide in the doctrine of Christ does not have God; he who abides in the doctrine [of Christ] has both the Father and the Son" (2 John 1:9). Church "doctrine" is not merely an abstract intellectual teaching like some form of geometry or paleontology. The truths of faith are, ultimately, the self-revelation of the tri-personal God who wishes to give us a share in the divine life. Some thinkers in the early twentieth century went so far as to say that the truths of faith are, ultimately, a kind of moral advice. They held that faith teaches us how we should act in relation to God. According to these thinkers, "the modernists," who were ultimately condemned by St. Pius X, the truths of faith were *truths of action*, not *truths about how things really are*. Such truths supposedly would communicate instructions for human action, not the mystery of God and his saving works. This claim may seem very pious and utterly respectful of God's mysterious nature. How could our words or thoughts ever contain the great and transcendent God? Did God himself not say through the prophet Isaiah, "For as the heavens are higher than the earth, so are my ways higher than your ways and my thoughts than your thoughts" (Isaiah 55:9)? Nonetheless, despite how humble the modernist claim might seem, it ultimately is a poison against the very notion of faith.

We cannot repeat this enough: *faith is a form of knowledge*, even though it is obscure and is experienced, as it were, "in a mirror dimly" (1 Corinthians 13:12). When we have human faith in a teacher's words, we aren't completely unaware of what he or she is telling us about. We have some vague idea of what his or her words mean. We *believe* them on the basis of his or her authority. I have never been to the Alps, but based upon what I have been told about them by others, and based on the many images of them that I have seen, I have *some* idea of them. And my life is all the richer for having these beautiful images. In short, even merely human faith is a replacement for direct knowledge, and although direct vision is preferable, we nonetheless are enriched by such a substitute for the time being.[39]

Now, there is a temptation to relativism in our modern idea of knowledge: you have your truth; I have mine. However, does this kind of armchair philosophy really measure up to our own personal experience of knowledge? Does knowledge really separate us from other people and from the very things that we know? Just because we never perfectly know things, is our knowledge false? Am I more "distant" from the Alps through this knowledge I have of those beautiful mountains, even if I have never been there? Am I more distant from things because I know them? If I am a doctor, am I better or worse off if I know about a new procedure that might help my patients?

Let us stand up against the relativist claim that you have your truth, and I have mine, and say with confidence that even though we can fall into mistakes, when we know things, we are "in touch" with them. Indeed, for many of the Church's philosophers and theologians, knowledge actually is a way of being united to other things. When we know a truth, that truth becomes "ours," without itself changing. In fact, one and the same truth can be had by many people at once. We speak of "a profound union of minds." Many people can lovingly know about the Alps (or the Appalachian Mountains, more local and well-worn for those of us, like me, whose roots are there). The fact of this union is experienced in the excitement we feel when we can discuss a topic of shared interest. We say with gusto, You've seen that too? You have been there too? You *know* about that too? Through knowledge, the external world comes to dwell *within us and between us* in a new and unique way.

Most profoundly, when we truly know someone whom we love, we share in that person's life in the deepest possible way. Here, the biblical euphemism "to know," used to speak of sexual relations, conceals a profound truth (see Genesis 4:25). In loving marital-sexual relations, spouses know each other and are emotionally vulnerable to each other in ways that cannot be put into words. The most profound kind of knowledge is the sharing of a single viewpoint and a single life, at least to the degree that this is possible. This scriptural metaphor for "knowing" should always be in the back of our minds when we talk about knowledge. Knowledge is a way of dwelling with other things and persons. An ancient image expresses this perfectly: the human soul is like a reflection of the wide universe within itself.

Granted, there is such a thing as personal moral knowledge or practical knowledge. We will have an opportunity to reflect on this when we come to discuss conscience and the virtue of prudence. Such personal moral knowledge teaches us how to set *our lives* in order. In that chapter, we'll see that the Catholic Faith has a decisive answer to all proponents of ethical relativism. Catholic moral theology is well aware of the fact that *my* choices will not necessarily be the same as *yours*. The prophets themselves were well aware of the hidden depths of the human heart: "The heart is deceitful above all things, and desperately corrupt; who can understand it?" (Jeremiah 17:9). And the great St. Paul cautions, "I do not even judge myself. I am not aware of anything against myself, but I am not thereby acquitted. It is the Lord who judges me" (1 Corinthians 4:3-4). Above all, do we not have Christ himself cautioning us greatly against judging others? Moral knowledge is very mysterious and very personal. We will be able to affirm all of this. In fact, we will affirm this even better than does worldly wisdom, which makes false claims to be ever so merciful.

However, the Church is also clear: such personal-moral knowledge must have a solid foundation in reality. The skyscrapers of New York City rest upon a solid rock foundation, called Manhattan schist, without which their heights would have been impossible. If we can't build on shifting sand in physical architecture, how much more is this the case for the moral architecture of the soul, whose depths are hidden even from our own eyes? As we will discuss in a future chapter, there are two solid foundations for our morality: the natural law and revealed truth. Faith puts us in touch with the latter: the truth of who God is, the truth of who Christ our Savior is, the truth of who we are as fallen and redeemed creatures, truths taught by the Church and lived by the saints. In short, theological faith is knowledge, putting us in touch with our supernatural destiny. It is more than mere "trust" in God; it is theological and divine. In the words of St. Paul: "Now we have received not the spirit of the world, but the Spirit which is from God, that we might *understand* the gifts bestowed on us by God. *And we impart this in words not taught by human wisdom but taught by the Spirit*, interpreting spiritual truths to those who possess the Spirit" (1 Corinthians 2:12-13, emphasis added).

In the life of grace, faith provides us with the rock-solid foundation which builds up the Church, who through the sacraments, the Liturgy, and her teaching is the dwelling place of supernatural faith.[40] Through faith, we have knowledge of realities beyond our loftiest philosophical or scientific reflection. The philosophy of Plato, Aristotle, or even the great Plotinus could not even imagine the marvels of God which are known by the simple working man or woman who has faith. These great philosophers knew God *as the Cause of reality*, and the Church herself teaches *with full certainty* that the human mind by its own powers can know God in this way. However, God is infinitely more than the First Cause. God is the Trinity, Father, Son, and Holy Spirit, united in an eternal communion of knowledge and love beyond what the words of philosophy could ever stammer. And yet this is what faith puts us in touch with. It enables us to hear the voice of the heavenly Father. Through faith, the simple old grandma—as we Slovaks say, the old "baba"—knows truths that Plato and Plotinus would envy. What a great gift is given to the humble of heart! Christ himself did not merely speak but, rather, "rejoiced in the Holy Spirit" when he thought upon this great fact: "I thank you, Father, Lord of heaven and earth, that you have hidden these things from the wise and understanding and revealed them to infants" (Luke 10:21; Matthew 11:25). And was this not proclaimed, years earlier, by Our Lady, the Mother of God: "He has put down the mighty from their thrones, and exalted those of low degree" (Luke 1:52)?

With the new eyes of faith, we see a whole new world open up before us. No longer are we merely creatures. Yes, we are this. How could we not be? However, beyond being mere men and women, we see our true vocation: to be sons and daughters who can say with St. Paul, "It is no longer I who live, but Christ who lives in me" (Galatians 2:20). Through faith, we see that we are to be remade in Christ, through the Spirit, so that we might be true worshippers of the Father in spirit and truth (John 4:23-24), offering in loving homage to God the whole of our lives (Romans 12:1). No longer is God merely the Cause and Creator of all things. Indeed, through faith, we come to know a far more intimate title for God than "Lord": he is the unbegotten heavenly Father, the eternally begotten Son, and the all-holy and eternally life-giving Spirit. Here we have the profound meaning hidden in those words spoken to Moses so long ago: "I AM WHO I AM" (Exodus 3:14). Through the new eyes of faith, we see our true and primary identity: we are sons and daughters of God. This will have repercussions throughout all the details of our lives.

Likewise, with the eyes of faith, we no longer look at the Church as do nonbelievers, thinking that she is merely a kind of massive society, though ultimately one more moral community among others, a kind of international nongovernmental organization. No, she is the mystical body of Christ (see Ephesians 5:22-33, Colossians 1:24), an extension of Christ's incarnation, his means for acting here and now, indeed in *every here and now*, until the end of time, as he himself promised: "If you forgive the sins of any, they are forgiven; if you retain the sins of any, they are retained" (John 20:23); "I am with you always, to the close of the age" (Matthew 28:20). And finally, to give one more example, with the eyes of faith, we see that the moral life of Christians is not merely a kind of "souped up" morality, a kind of turbocharging of our moral engines. Rather, it is "a new creation" (Galatians 6:15), a "new life of the Spirit" (Romans 7:6), being buried with Christ to rise to a new life (Romans 6:4; Colossians 2:12).

It is easy to be exhilarated by this great and marvelous reality that is the gift of faith. When we hear that "now" is the day of salvation (2 Corinthians 6:2), let this word "now" ring in our ears! In an earlier chapter, we already saw how it is that grace establishes the kingdom of God in our hearts *even now*. Through grace, the deepest part of the soul, what the theologians call "the substance of the soul" is changed. We receive a kind of new nature; we "put on the new man" (Ephesians 4:24); we become "conformed to the image of his Son" (Romans 8:29). And this new life pours forth, communicating eternity to our faith. In the words of St. Thomas Aquinas: "By faith, eternal life begins in us."[41]

This is why, in the book of Hebrews, faith is said to be the "substance of things hoped for, the proof of things not seen" (Hebrews 11:1).[42] Through faith, we are put in touch with the most vital truths we will ever know:

God's life in the Trinity, given to us through grace, above all by the Church in the sacraments. Here below, what we know by faith is still obscurely known, for faith is not the same as full knowledge. Faith is a knowledge that we believe on the authority of another person, in this case on the authority of God who has revealed himself to us as Father, Son, and Holy Spirit. However, *what* we believe is *exactly the same* as what we will *know* in full light in heaven. "For now we see in a mirror dimly, but then face to face. Now I know in part; then I shall understand fully" (1 Corinthians 13:12).

Each Sunday, we pray the Creed: "I believe in one God, the Father ... the Son ... and the Holy Spirit." *We believe*. Nonetheless, if we are asked, "Do you know that God is a Trinity, Father, Son, and Spirit," we can answer, "Yes, I know through the gift of faith." Indeed, we can say this with full certitude, for our faith rests on a rock-solid foundation: God who reveals this, giving us the very gift of faith, this "infused, theological virtue." Again: "Faith is the substance of things hoped for, the *proof* of things not seen." Yes, our words never can completely match up with these realities. As Christ himself said, "[No one] has seen the Father except him who is from God" (John 6:46). However, the same Gospel opens up saying, "The only-begotten Son, who is in the bosom of the Father, *he has made him known*" (John 1:18). The truths known through faith are a gift given to us by the Son, and even though they remain shrouded in mystery, we will know them fully in heaven. Faith puts us in touch with one and the same life as that which will animate our eternal bliss: "By faith, eternal life begins in us."

To take an image from St. John of the Cross, we are like people who are not ready for the radiant gold of eternity.[43] God, in his largesse, his astonishing generosity, reveals the divine truth of himself to us by placing a kind of silver upon the gold. When we reach heaven, the silver will not be needed, for we will *see*. However, the deepest substance of what we now believe will indeed remain. The truths of faith are an eternal gold wrapped in the divine gift of a beautiful silver veil, like the most beautiful of brides. When the Church hands on to us the teachings of Christ, she plays her role in helping God give us a great gift, like a loving bridegroom giving his gift to his bride: "We will make you ornaments of gold, studded with silver" (Song of Solomon 1:11). Have you ever thought of this when you have recited the Creed on Sunday? Have you ever thought of this when you opened the *Catechism*? Do you have the profound desire, like a passionate lover, to know what the Church teaches and what her greatest saints have written? You should! It is a wedding gift, one that is shared by each of those who gather at the wedding feast of the Lamb, not only at every Mass and Divine Liturgy but, above all, in eternity (Revelation 19:6-9).

For now, though, we are not in our heavenly homeland. We are wayfarers, in classical theological language, *viatores*. We are "on the way," and in a sense, we look at heavenly realities "from afar," even though we also really and truly know them through faith. And like everyone who travels on the road, we can take wrong paths; we can go astray, like the Prodigal Son, who sleeps in each of our breasts. If faith is a light, the loss of faith plunges us into a kind of darkness, indeed of the worst sort: "If your eye is sound, your whole body will be full of light; but if your eye is not sound, your whole body will be full of darkness. If then the light in you is darkness, how great is the darkness!" (Matthew 6:22-23). If we are truly called to be children of God—which we certainly are, by a God who never tires of giving us his love and grace!—then, we must know this God who has given us a new birth: "Any one who goes ahead and does not abide in the doctrine of Christ does not have God" (2 John 1:9). Otherwise, we will be like the Gentiles spoken of by St. Paul: "They are darkened in their understanding, alienated from the life of God because of the ignorance that is in them, due to their hardness of heart ... greedy to practice every kind of uncleanness" (Ephesians 4:18-19).

In short, the loss of faith is a shipwreck for one's life. Do we reflect enough on sins of unbelief? People tend to think, "Heresy is too strong of a word! How old-fashioned!" Still, sins *against faith* are akin to constructing a rocky outcropping upon which the ship of our life bottoms out and sinks into the sea. Switching our metaphors: if we snuff out the light of faith, all will be darkness: "If then the light in you is darkness, how great is the darkness" (Matthew 6:23). Do we cultivate the light of faith every day? If not, this is a true moral failure! Do we confess this? How often are we guilty of it, if only venially! The well-known words of the book of Revelation often ring true for all of us: "Because you are lukewarm, and neither cold nor hot, I will spew you out of my mouth" (Revelation 3:16). To not care about the gift of faith is like saying to one's spouse, "I don't want to know you." Let us pray that this never ends in the dread divorce: mortal sin against the theological virtue of faith.

Of course, keeping faith is no easy affair! It is something which, ultimately, must come from God. "Every good endowment and every perfect gift is from above, coming down from the Father of lights" (James 1:17). But our God does not wish to save us without our own involvement. As St. Augustine put it so beautifully, he who created us without us did not will to save us without us (see CCC 1847). Thus, we have a moral obligation to practice our faith, to strengthen it, to embrace it fully. This is not merely a kind of duty, a matter of justice. It is a matter of supernatural life and death! If the plant does not draw water from the ground, it will not fulfill the aspiration of its nature: to grow to its fullness. So too, if we do not cultivate the gift of faith, we will not fulfill the great aspiration of the "new nature" that we have been given through the gift of grace. We will fail to be like trees planted by the waters of God, bearing good fruit in due season with ever-youthful leaves (Psalm 1:3), drawing from the living water "welling up to eternal life" (John 4:14).

Yes, even after a life lived in devotion and love of God, we may find ourselves like St. Teresa of Calcutta (Mother Teresa) still overshadowed by a kind of darkness. But let us not confuse this kind of "doubt" with real and true doubt. With every fiber of our being, we can believe and yet still call out, like the father spoken of in the Gospel, "I believe; help my unbelief!" (Mark 9:24). This is a fundamental quality of a truly Christian character. Paradoxically, we are at once beggars and wealthy; we open our hands to God who alone can fill them. We are often like the apostles on the Sea of Galilee, tossed about in the midst of the storms of life, relying solely on the Lord for surety of faith (see Matthew 8:23-27). In the next chapter, we will reflect on how our good God comes to our aid with another theological virtue to give us even more strength of will: hope. But let us also practice our faith, let us cultivate it like good gardeners who wish to help the great eternal Host in the eternal banquet!

We opened this chapter by mentioning certain errors from the past, the errors of the modernists who held that faith was not really so much about *knowledge of reality* as it was *knowledge about how to act*. Very often, errors are correct in what they affirm but wrong (sometimes *very* wrong) in what they deny. We can affirm the modernist claim while profoundly correcting it: faith is knowledge about how to act *because it tells us who we are, children of God, reborn in Baptism and called to be perfect like our heavenly Father whom we know through what Christ and his Church teach*. Yes, we must not treat faith just as a question of "mere knowledge." The truths of faith are eminently "practical" and moral, without being *merely* practical and moral. Through faith, we learn about realities that should influence all of our lives. In fact, since we can only love what we know, our love of God, our charity, presupposes faith. As a great theologian once expressed the point poignantly, we can say, at least to a degree, that "faith is the intellectual mouth by which charity is nourished on the Divine Good."[44] The knowledge of faith must become the rule of our action, the light which inflames the fire of divine love, charity!

All of this can seem very abstract. Therefore, let's consider just two examples of how it is that faith *in divine realities* informs our very living. Remember, however, there are many such "flowers of faith" among the dogmas taught by the Church. There is much sweetness to be drawn from these blossoms, and the best preachers know how to elevate their hearers' minds, revealing to them just how far the sweet smell of these flowers spreads throughout the whole of our lives. For our part, let's smell a pair of blooms drawn from the great garden of the Church's dogmas, the first from Christology and the second from sacramental theology.

We will take up first a mystery which we discussed in an earlier chapter: the mystery of the Incarnation. The early Church was shaken by great battles, lasting for centuries in fact, as she strove to articulate her faith in the mystery of Christ. It all seems very abstract: Christ is one person with two natures, two minds, and two wills. Can't we just say, "Let's just treat Christ as though he were God," and stop there? No, for the question remains: just how is it that he is God? To say that Christ has two natures, one divine and one human, is not merely an idle speculation. Christ's *humanity* was able to be made *supremely holy* by the Incarnation. Through what later theologians would call the "grace of union," his human nature was united to the eternal Word, and as a first illumination of this primordial grace, his humanity was carried also to the heights of holiness.[45] Christ's humanity is the holiest humanity which ever will exist, "full of grace and truth" (John 1:14). Moreover, we know that this grace was not "bottled up" within Jesus. He who was truth incarnate stood before Pontius Pilate and said, "For this I was born, and for this I have come into the world, to bear witness to the truth" (John 18:37). He has come so that we might receive life and light from him, so that he may radiate his grace to us: "And from his fulness have we all received, grace upon grace" (John 1:16). In the language of theology, this is Christ's "capital grace," a kind of "overflow" of the grace which filled his human nature. In English, the expression is opaque, but its meaning is luminous if we know how it fits into older theological language, as we mentioned in an earlier chapter: Christ's grace radiates forth to us inasmuch as he is the head (*caput*) of the Church, which is his mystical body.

What, today, is the choice means for this radiation? Here, we have our second example of dogma: the sacraments in the Church, above all the Holy Eucharist. Yes, God dwells deep within our souls. He works in the silence, and we are called to pray in secret so that our "Father who sees in secret will reward you" (Matthew 6:6). However, let us take care not to misunderstand our Lord. We cannot read the Acts of the Apostles without realizing that the early Church did not interpret Christ's words as meaning "Never pray out loud with other people." The first disciples saw the simple meaning of his words: external actions are done for the sake of internal ones. As embodied creatures, we most often perform our most internal actions *in external ones*. When we pray the Our Father, this is not merely "vocal prayer," as though it weren't also "mental" or "spiritual" prayer. When we recite the Creed, we're not merely mouthing words; we're actually proclaiming the most profound mysteries of the Faith! When we pray the Rosary, we find ourselves alongside Mary, the Mother of God, pondering the mysteries of redemption in our hearts (see Luke 2:19). The Church does not practice abstract spiritualism. Instead, she practices the sacraments and prays the Liturgy, doing so as the body of Christ. Indeed, in the Great Commission Christ tied the sacrament of Baptism to his promise to remain present to the Church forever: "Go therefore and make disciples of all nations, baptizing them in the name of the Father and of the Son and of the Holy Spirit, teaching them to observe all that I have commanded you; and behold, I am with you always, to the close of the age" (Matthew 28:19-20). These are the various *means* for grace to arrive at us, so that it may animate the whole of our lives. In short, the sacraments are the continued application, today, of the fruits of the incarnate Christ's saving action.

Thus, we have two very abstract truths of the faith: the *hypostatic union* and the *causal presence of Christ's activity in the sacraments*. Bound together by the "law of the Incarnation," they are centrally important for our very lives. In the dogma of the hypostatic union, we affirm that the divine and human natures can exist in the one Person who is the Word of God, without those natures getting mixed together into some kind of divine-human substance. Christ retains all that belongs to his divinity, while drawing to himself everything that makes for humanity. The *eternal Word* saves us *by taking on humanity*. And how appropriate is it that, for the rest of history, he doesn't limit his activity to private inspirations but, instead, draws us together through the sacraments of the Church, who herself is "the universal sacrament of salvation."[46] So we have a kind of divine ebb and flow which should be stamped on the whole of our lives: The eternal Word, begotten of the Father before all ages, in Christ, draws human nature to himself and then radiates over all of creation his light and life. And through all the ages following his ascension and Pentecost, he acts through his body, the Church, calling all peoples to her sacramental life, so that they all may be made members of Christ's body and be drawn back to the Father, through Christ, in the Holy Spirit, who has been poured forth into their hearts. Is this merely abstract knowledge? Could we think of anything more *vital* and necessary? I dare say not!

We believe—and rightly so!—that the Church teaches us with certainty in "matters of faith and morals" (see CCC 890–892). But let us never build a high wall between these two domains. We must never say, "Dogmas on this side of the wall; morals on the other." Christian morals are grounded in supernatural faith. This is why it is important to understand that moral theology is really not some separate discipline cut off from dogmatic theology. Thus, faith and morals are not isolated from each other, for dogma, in a real sense, lives within us. If we put the dogmas about Christ on a nice little island, we will never understand the nature of the Church and the sacraments, through which he continues to be active today. Nor would we ever understand our own moral life as Christians, for if we didn't understand something about *who Christ is*, how could we say, in full truth, "we have the mind of Christ" (1 Corinthians 2:16)?

Obviously, we must bear in mind St. John's challenging words, "He who says 'I know him' but disobeys his commandments is a liar" (1 John 2:4), along with the well-known words of St. James, "Faith apart from works is dead" (James 2:26). The truth of these declarations will be affirmed repeatedly in the chapters that follow. In this chapter, however, I have merely wished to stress this very important fact: the truths of faith are the very truths of our lives. We have been called to be supernatural sons and daughters, to live a divine life. Through faith, we *know*—yes, obscurely, at a distance, like wayfarers and pilgrims, but nonetheless *really* and *truly*—the truths that enable us to begin to grasp eternal life, even now. Doctrine and life, faith and morals, belief and action: these are not separate domains. It is our *moral* duty to strengthen our *faith*! Without it, our entire life as a Christian is a sham. Indeed, without this faith, we do not live the true Christian life. Thus, the practice of reading and reflecting on the Scriptures and on the Church's teaching is *vitally* important. It is a matter of (supernatural) life and death! One great gift of Benedictine spirituality is the practice of *lectio divina*, divine reading, slow and penetrating meditation on the Word of God. Likewise, the Church has promoted devotions like the Rosary because they encourage believers to meditate on the very mysteries of Christ's life, thereby feeding their own lives. These mysteries are the soul of this devotion, and they are the most vitally important truths we shall ever know!

Morals and faith, faith and morals—they intertwine around each other like the vines of a heavily laden grape arbor. They cannot be separated without both of them being killed. Through the gift of grace, which ultimately comes from the greatest grace—namely, the mystery of Christ's incarnation—we live the divine life. We feed upon this life through faith, which we receive above all through the sacraments, a faith which we *live* in hope, in charity, and indeed throughout all of our moral actions. Without God, we can do nothing (John 15:5), and we must draw sap from him through faith. With the life that we receive from this divine source, we can echo the words of St. Paul: "I can do all things in him who strengthens me" (Philippians 4:13). Thus, doctrine and life are not two separate domains. This is the profound meaning of St. James' words: "Be doers of the word" (James 1:22). In and through faith, we can be said to live God's own life. He is in us, and we are in him. He is our source and our ultimate end. He is the home in which we dwell, and we are the true temples of his Spirit (1 Corinthians 6:19).

Take the theological virtue of faith seriously! Meditate on the Church's teachings. Read the Scriptures lovingly. Each article of the Creed should be like a banquet to nourish your whole life until your last breath—and then the great banquet will come, like a long-expected continuation and fulfillment of the feast we began here below in faith. Each of these truths of faith is the truth of the new life that we have received in grace. Each of these truths is a light, radiating from God through Christ, in his Church, to us so that we may radiate the light of Christ to all: "Let your light so shine before men, that they may see your good works and give glory to your Father who is in heaven" (Matthew 5:16). And all of this starts with the light of faith, which the Church Fathers often referred to as a true form of "illumination." Will you be illuminated? Will you illuminate others? Well, then, take doctrine seriously, for without it neither you, nor the world, will know Christ. In short, in the words placed at the head of this chapter, "Any one who goes ahead and does not abide in the doctrine of Christ does not have God; he who abides in the doctrine has both the Father and the Son" (2 John 1:9).

CHAPTER EIGHT

"In Hope We Are Saved"

As we have been emphasizing in each of these chapters dedicated to the theological virtues, each of these magnificent gifts of God "tunes us" to him in a different way. We have seen how faith gives us divine vision even here below, a kind of supernatural eye so that we can know the revealed truths of God. This viewpoint will affect everything that we will consider and "see" in our moral life. It gives us a God's-eye view in the loftiest possible sense, even if our "faith-knowledge" is slim and dark here below, as though looking into a dim, old mirror (1 Corinthians 13:12). In a similar manner, hope is a supernaturally God-oriented virtue, building up a trust that is founded precisely on the fact that our Trinitarian God is our refuge and our strength, a help close at hand in times of trouble and distress, giving us surety throughout all the tumult of the world and upheaval among the nations (Psalm 46). Theological hope is a trust that rests upon the supernatural omnipotence of God!

In this chapter, I think it necessary to engage in a bit of rhetoric in order to stir up hope as well as to explain what it is. Such will be our approach to this mystery, this "infused" virtue which is often treated merely as a kind of pious optimism. We must raise our minds much higher than this. We must raise them to the divine heights where God wishes to lead us!

And what greater elevation could there be than to meditate on salvation history? If the motive for our hope is *God himself, our Savior,* then we should turn to the great tale of his salvation offered to mankind. The whole story of Israel is a kind of reminder of the fact that God is the sole strength of his people. Their many falls were due to their refusal to trust in him. The people grumbled against God after leaving Egypt, remembering the many riches they had while living there, and God responded to their lack of trust by leading them through the desert for forty years, in a sense, left to their own designs. As the psalms later recounted this, "But my people did not listen to my voice; Israel would have none of me. So I gave them over to their stubborn hearts, to follow their own counsels" (Psalm 81:11-12); "For forty years I was wearied of that generation and said, 'They are a people who err in heart, and they do not regard my ways.' Therefore I swore in my anger that they should not enter my rest" (Psalm 95:10-11). But, note, they were only *in a sense* left to their own designs, for God did not hold back his generosity, giving his recalcitrant people manna in the wilderness (Exodus 16), providing for them a gift so great that it was, in fact, a foreshadowing of the true bread from heaven, Christ Eucharistically present among us (see John 6). And the people of Israel saw how wonderful this was:

> Therefore, when the LORD heard, he was full of wrath;
> a fire was kindled against Jacob,
> his anger mounted against Israel;
> because they had no faith in God,
> and *did not trust his saving power*.
> Yet he commanded the skies above,
> and opened the doors of heaven;
> and he rained down upon them manna to eat,
> and gave them the bread of heaven.
> Man ate of the bread of the angels;
> he sent them food in abundance. (Psalm 78:21-25, emphasis added)

Pray the Psalms and you will find this theme of trust and hope repeated over and over again. (For example, see Psalms 4, 37, 73, 84, 115, 130–132, and especially the beautiful Psalm 107.)

We could tell the story over and over again. God gives us infinite reason to trust in his saving power, from the days of Noah to the years of exile, from the victories of Judith and Daniel to the greatest victory: the triumph of Christ, the Redeemer, he who we could say is redemption incarnate.[47] There are many instances of this theme, which is fulfilled in Christ. This great source of hope is reflected in the Hebrew word used by Scripture for God's love: *hesed*, which one will find in some scriptural translations as "loving kindness" or "steadfast love," what we might call his "covenant fidelity."[48] God's love is expressed in the form of a constant faithfulness.

Isaiah proclaims God's wrath, only to follow the proclamation with God's loving "turnaround," for he is forever ready to save his people:

> But now thus says the LORD, he who created you, O Jacob,
> he who formed you, O Israel:
> "Fear not, for I have redeemed you;
> I have called you by name, you are mine.
> When you pass through the waters I will be with you;
> and through the rivers, they shall not overwhelm you;
> when you walk through fire you shall not be burned,
> and the flame shall not consume you.
> For I am the LORD your God,
> the Holy One of Israel, your Savior. (Isaiah 43:1-3)

What could inspire hope more than such a history with all of its repeated refrains, all the way up to this refrain's greatest recapitulation: the death and resurrection of Christ? "Through him you have confidence in God, who raised him from the dead and gave him glory, so that your faith and hope are in God" (1 Peter 1:21).

Such hope is not something purely lighthearted, an optimistic grin looking at the pain of the world. The theological virtue of hope has a realistic view of things. In fact, according to St. Thomas' way of classifying things, the Holy Spirit's gift of knowledge, which strengthens our faith, does so by showing us the fleeting nature of the world and the way that sin has marred all things. Did not St. Paul see this in a quick but penetrating glance: "We know that the whole creation has been groaning with labor pains together until now" (Romans 8:22)? A true faith cannot help but look upon the world and see how fleeting and fickle it is. And hope will be marked by this sober awareness of how things stand.

It brings to mind a song performed by the famed country singer Roy Acuff, "This World Can't Stand Long."[49] It is perhaps no surprise that Acuff, the son of a Baptist preacher, took up such a harsh religious sentiment, unhesitatingly speaking of the "fire and brimstone" to be rained down by God. But if you read the homespun words with a sympathetic eye, you can see the expression of a simplc faith which is trying to express something of the hope which we must have in God.

However, Protestant Americana is not the only place where we can find this kind of insight. We can draw from the hymnody of our own traditions in order to see this same hope expressed, even in the face of the harshest of realities and experiences. In the older form of the Roman rite, the extraordinary form, funerals use a medieval hymn, *Dies Irae*, "The Day of Wrath," chanting about the judgment day in poetic and breathtaking imagery:

> That day of wrath, that dreadful day,
> shall heaven and earth in ashes lay,
> as David and the Sybil say.
>
> What horror must invade the mind
> when the approaching Judge shall find
> and sift the deeds of all mankind!

And yet, after many ominous stanzas, this liturgical poem does not close in despair. It too is marked with an expression of hope in God's mercy:

> Before You, humbled, Lord, I lie,
> my heart like ashes, crushed and dry,
> *assist me when I die*.
>
> Full of tears and full of dread
> is that day that wakes the dead,
> calling all, with solemn blast
> to be judged for all their past.
>
> *Lord, have mercy, Jesus blest,*
> *grant them all Your Light and Rest.* Amen.[50]

Or, drawing from the Byzantine tradition, in the poetic words of St. John of Damascus in the funeral liturgy, we have the same intermingling of the awareness of the world's passing nature, alongside the commendation of the departed soul to God, trusting in Christ:

> What earthly delight endures unmingled with grief? What earthly glory remains immutable? All things are less than a shadow, more deluding than a dream. In a single moment all these are effaced by death; *but in the light of your countenance, O Christ, and in the enjoyment of your beauty, grant rest to the one whom you have chosen; for you love mankind.*[51]

I cannot help but think of our hope as being somewhat marked with this sort of sublime melancholy. Yes, it is more certain than anything we could imagine, for it is founded on God's omnipotence and love, an unbreakable hope which inspired the early Church to undergo great sufferings and to maintain her faith in the midst of the tumult of her birth:

> But recall the former days when, after you were enlightened, you endured a hard struggle with sufferings, sometimes being publicly exposed to abuse and affliction, and sometimes being partners with those so treated. For you had compassion on the prisoners, and you *joyfully accepted the plundering of your property, since you knew that you yourselves had a better possession and an abiding one*. Therefore, do not throw away your confidence, which has a great reward. For you have need of endurance, so that you may do the will of God and receive what is promised. (Hebrews 10:32-36, emphasis added)

"Joyfully accepted," indeed, but like everything in this changing world, it is intermingled with the sorrow and endurance of wayfaring pilgrims. We are all somewhat like the people of Israel in exile: "By the waters of Babylon, there we sat down and wept, when we remembered Zion" (Psalm 137:1).

The story of the patriarch Joseph (Genesis 37–50) is rich with imagery that is instructive regarding the meaning of supernatural hope. The favored son of Jacob, the young Joseph was hated by his brothers. Experiencing one injustice after another, he found himself nonetheless settled firmly upon the strongest of foundations, God's *hesed*: "But the LORD was with Joseph and showed him mercy [*steadfast love*], and gave him favor in the sight of the keeper of the prison" (Genesis 39:21). From slavery and imprisonment, Joseph ended up in charge of the whole of Egypt. And yet, when he was blessed with children, Joseph gave his little ones names which reflected his simultaneous trust in God's providence and his sorrow at being separated from his family: Manas'seh, for "God *has made me forget all my hardship and all my father's house*," and E'phraim, "for God has made me fruitful *in the land of my affliction*" (Genesis 41:51-52).

There is a paradox here, for Joseph at once is in a land of his affliction and yet claims to have forgotten his father's house. It is as though God's great omnipotence has given him supernatural trust in his lot, while he nonetheless bears this affliction upon his heart. And we see this same paradox when his brothers come before him, begging for food. Standing before them in full strength, without them knowing who he is, Joseph nonetheless must leave the room to weep: "They did not know that Joseph understood them, for there was an interpreter between them. Then he turned away from them and wept" (Genesis 42:23-24). Then, later, when they bring his brother Benjamin forward, Joseph once more rushes from their presence in order to let loose his tears: "Then Joseph made haste, for his heart yearned for his brother, and he sought a place to weep. And he entered his chamber and wept there" (Genesis 43:30). And when Joseph at last revealed himself to his brothers, "he wept aloud, so that the Egyptians heard it, and the household of Pharaoh heard it" (Genesis 45:2). What tears, which could be heard throughout the whole of the great kingdom! And, indeed, the tears continued flowing, a kind of beautiful intermingling of sorrow and joy, as Joseph's trust in God was fulfilled before his very eyes: "Then he fell upon his brother Benjamin's neck and wept; and Benjamin wept upon his neck. And he kissed all his brothers and wept upon them" (Genesis 45:14-15). Indeed, yet again, upon seeing his father, "he presented himself to him, and fell on his neck, and wept on his neck a good while" (Genesis 46:29).

Finally, as the "Joseph cycle" draws to its close, with words which are among the most sublime words of human drama, with his brothers falling before his feet after the death of their father, imploring that he not harm them, Joseph sees at last, in full, the meaning of the dreams he had experienced as a young man. He was not to be like a kind of childish princeling. His life's meaning was not to hope in goods *for himself.* No, he was to be an instrument of God for the sake of salvation. This was the meaning of his whole vocation, of all the suffering that he endured, as well as the meaning of all the great things that happened to him over the course of his life. And yet, once again weeping, he said to his brothers, "Fear not, for am I in the place of God? As for you, you meant evil against me; but God meant it for good, to bring it about that many people should be kept alive, as they are today. So do not fear; I will provide for you and your little ones" (Genesis 50:19-21).

There are few things more mystical than such hope. It attaches us to heaven prior to the full dawning of that eternal day. Our faith sees from afar, and so our hope too is a condition of being a "wayfaring" pilgrim. It is not fulfilled but, instead, looks forward with great eagerness, as we "groan inwardly as we wait for adoption as sons, the redemption of our bodies" (Romans 8:23), "forgetting what lies behind and straining forward to what lies ahead ... [pressing] on toward the goal for the prize of the upward call of God in Christ Jesus" (Philippians 3:13-14). We are indeed saved through grace, yet we still do not yet see the full dawning of our salvation: "For in this hope we were saved. Now hope that is seen is not hope. For who hopes for what he sees" (Romans 8:24).[52] Thus, we must hope in God's strength to save us. Our salvation depends *upon him.*

Take care to understand the apostle's words aright! This hope-filled patience isn't merely a good-mannered attitude, a refusal to get "all worked up." That can also be a virtue, one associated with the virtue of courage. The truly moral person must indeed keep an "even keel" when faced with evils and pains, not giving in to them out of abrupt frustration. This may seem like a minor affair, but it is something quite important in our lives. How many sins have we run headlong into out of a lack of patience? Nonetheless, the "patience" involved with the theological virtue of hope is something far more sublime.

When we see someone buoyed up by such hope, it is like watching our saving God on the march through the world: "Since we have such a hope, we are very bold" (2 Corinthians 3:12). Nothing can stop this virtue, which presents a masterful countenance, a kind of detachment from all things of the world, in order to climb the highest mountains. Because of faith, we can say, "Yes, *you* light my lamp; *the Lord my God* lightens my darkness" (Psalm 18:28). And then, spilling over from this light of faith into our conduct, we reflect the fact that we place an utterly great trust in our God's power in our lives, for he is omnipotent in bringing about all goods, above all and primarily the good of salvation for us and for those whom his providence has placed in our lives: "Yes, by you I can crush a troop; and by my God I can leap over a wall" (Psalm 18:29). And in the words from the wondrous canticle with which the prophecy of Habakkuk draws to a close:

> Though the fig tree does not blossom,
> nor fruit be on the vines,
> the produce of the olive fail
> and the fields yield no food,
> the flock be cut off from the fold
> and there be no herd in the stalls,
> *yet I will rejoice in the Lord,*
> *I will joy in the God of my salvation.*

God, the Lord, is my strength;
he makes my feet like deer's feet,
he makes me tread upon my high places
(Habakkuk 3:17-19, emphasis added)

This is a truly supernatural form of hope! By it, we grasp eternity, not at all by our own strength but, rather, by the strength of God who gives our grip an ironclad assurance. And this is not for human victory but, rather, for the divine victory being worked out *in and through us*. We must indeed pray and turn to our God to ask for an increase in this great virtue! When we examine our consciences, do we truly ask ourselves whether we have fallen short in cultivating and living this hope? How many other sins are, in fact, rooted in a fundamental deficiency in this theological virtue? How many cases of self-indulgence are, in the end, nothing more than a fault by which we trust in ourselves and not in God's omnipotent power actively working in and through our lives?

We must strive every day to live and to communicate this hope. In whom do we hope? Do we hope in our own strength, in our own abilities, in our current good health, in our wealth and the balance in our retirement accounts? Should we not look upon all of this as something fleeting, something subject to all the chance happenings of life, the danger that besets everything that is passing? We all know how precarious health is, how relationships can change so quickly, how even the hard reserves of precious metals can be stolen or devalued, and how, as we age, our relatives and friends pass from our sight here below.

Our Lord does not ask us to be hopeless in the face of this! Rather, he wishes us to allow all of these loves and attachments to be remade into tools to be used or set aside, depending upon what *he* calls us to. Through virtuous living, and above all through charity (which we will be discussing shortly, in the next chapter), we are to transform these earthly treasures into heavenly ones. Thus, we have the most profound fulfillment of his words: "Do not lay up for yourselves treasures on earth, where moth and rust consume and where thieves break in and steal, but lay up for yourselves treasures in heaven, where neither moth nor rust consumes and where thieves do not break in and steal" (Matthew 6:19-20). Every increase in our love of God, gushing up from the depths of our souls and splashed out over all of our relationships, will last into eternity if we are faithful to the end—when hope will give way to vision, with expectation blossoming forth with what it already contained: God himself, our eternal shield and strength.

All of this inspired St. Paul to write the stirring words with which he draws the eighth chapter of the letter to the Romans to a close, spelling out the infinite, unbending assurance we should have in God's providential love, in which we find the sure foundation for our hope:

> What then shall we say to this? *If God is for us, who is against us? He who did not spare his own Son but gave him up for us all, will he not also give us all things with him?* Who shall bring any charge against God's elect? It is God who justifies; who is to condemn? Is it Christ Jesus, who died, yes, who was raised from the dead, who is at the right hand of God, who indeed intercedes for us? Who shall separate us from the love of Christ? Shall tribulation, or distress, or persecution, or famine, or nakedness, or peril, or sword? As it is written,
>
> > "For your sake we are being killed all the day long;
> > we are regarded as sheep to be slaughtered."
>
> No, in all these things we are more than conquerors through him who loved us. For I am *sure* that neither death, nor life, nor angels, nor principalities, nor things present, nor things to come, nor powers, nor height, nor depth, nor anything else in all creation, will be able to separate us from the love of God in Christ Jesus our Lord. (Romans 8:31-39, emphasis added)

This is the nature of the theological virtue of hope. In it, we find the whole attitude of *a true Christian sense of triumph*, an attitude of soul which is founded not upon our triumphs but, rather, upon our God's triumph, brought about in dolor upon the Cross and shining forth in radiant and joyous splendor in the Resurrection. Our whole moral life should be infused with this divine hope: *O Crux ave, spes unica!* Hail, O Cross, our only hope! All our other virtues should be affirmed by this God-founded assurance in salvation, an assurance which rests not on us (for we can indeed fall into mortal sin) but, rather, on God if we cultivate a life of grace and virtue like little children who ask only to receive holiness from our God (Luke 18:17).

How the world would change if we took the words of the New Testament seriously! Instead of fashioning our family lives around careers and the rat race, we would seek first what God, not the market and contemporary opinion, is calling us to do. No longer slaves of the future, we would live by Christ's words, which are well-known but perhaps so readily and easily doubted: "But seek first his kingdom and his righteousness, and all these things shall be yours as well. Therefore do not be anxious about tomorrow, for tomorrow will be anxious for itself" (Matthew 6:33-34). Instead of fearing what the world might say when we speak our faith in the midst of an increasingly godless, militantly secular world, we would trust in the truth which frees us, in a Father who loves us and cares for us:

> And do not fear those who kill the body but cannot kill the soul; rather fear him who can destroy both soul and body in hell. Are not two sparrows sold for a penny? And not one of them will fall to the ground without your Father's will. But even the hairs of your head are all numbered. Fear not, therefore; you are of more value than many sparrows. (Matthew 10:28-31)

Hymns and poems, including (perhaps especially) those written by the little ones of God, often say far more than fancy words of theology. With my Appalachian upbringing, I am reminded of the verses of the gospel song "Hold to God's Unchanging Hand" as I think of the theological virtue of hope:

> Time is filled with swift transition.
> Naught of earth unmoved can stand.
> *Build your hopes on things eternal.*
> *Hold to God's unchanging hand.*
>
> Trust in Him who will not leave you.
> Whatsoever years may bring.
> If by earthly friends forsaken,
> Still more closely to Him cling.
>
> Covet not this world's vain riches
> That so rapidly decay.
> Seek to gain the heav'nly treasures.
> They will never pass away.
>
> When your journey is completed,
> If to God you have been true,
> Fair and bright the home in Glory
> Your enraptured soul will view.[53]

Our lives are divinized lives, and through hope, God places within our hand the hand of him who was crucified for our salvation. Those pierced wounds should give us all the strength needed in order to say, with Thomas who himself had doubted, "My Lord and my God!" (John 20:28). All our courage should radiate with this great assurance, the surety that enables us to say with Job, "I know that my redeemer lives and at last he will stand upon the earth" (Job 19:25). Too often Christian hope is presented as mere optimistic confidence when, in fact, it is the sure fixing of our will in eternal life, which we strive to incarnate in all our deeds. Faced with our frailties, our sins, the sometimes-crushing difficulties of life, along with all the injustices committed against us by others, it is only through theological hope that we will be able to stand erect and exude the holiness to which we are called by Christ. May we be worthy of the words of St. Paul, written to the Church in Colossae: "We always thank God, the Father of our Lord Jesus Christ, when we pray for you, because we have heard of your faith in Christ Jesus and of the love which you have for all the saints, *because of the hope laid up for you in heaven*" (Colossians 1:3-5, emphasis added).

CHAPTER NINE

Charity: Merely Giving Money or the Fire of Divine Love?

On occasion, we will encounter a troublesome linguistic dynamic. Words change meaning, sometimes so much so that their new meanings completely overshadow their more ancient ones. This is true for the word "charity," a word which should be the most beautiful and most profound of all words in the English language, though it has become commonplace. We normally use this word to indicate financial generosity ("give money to charity") or kindness ("be charitable"), but these meanings are quite distant from the original sense of the word, ultimately coming from the Latin *carus*, meaning "dear, beloved, costly, or precious." In the Western Church, historically dependent as it is upon the Latin language, this word became the translation of the Greek term *agapē*, used for God's outpouring love in Christ, a love which becomes the Christian's own love thanks to the gift of grace. Therefore, the word "charity," when used with strict theological rigor, means God's own supernatural love, graciously given to us. Charity is something utterly supernatural, in fact the most divine thing which exists in this world, a kind of dawning of eternity right here in the midst of time. It is God's very own love, given to us so that we might love with God's own heart! Charity is much more than a social virtue of good grace and unselfishness. It is the most divine of all virtues!

Now, when we know things through faith and through theological reflection, we need to have a "toe-hold" on our day-to-day language, at least if we plan to make any sense and not just be making things up. For example, the word *supernatural* is a relative term, indicating something which is *above our nature*. The loftiest form of supernaturality is *God himself*, he who is above all created natures. However, God is not supernatural in relationship to himself. He is God, one and three. The word "supernatural" itself already bears witness to our status as finite beings. *Above us* there is something, someone, indeed three Someones who are one God. Our Triune God is *super*-natural in relation to us. Already, this basic threshold word in theology, "supernatural," is relational, from the created order to the Uncreated One-in-Three. It is also negative, in the sense that it is really saying that *he* is not finite like us in *any* way. And yet, it is also supremely positive, asserting that *he is infinitely more and above us created beings*. We must have some notion of the natural in order to form a notion of the supernatural, but then we find that we leave the former behind as we springboard upward into the blinding light of God!

This dynamic occurs in all of the words which we apply to God. They all have one foot in our experience and one in the heavens. Some of them are mere metaphors: God grieves over his fallen world (Genesis 6:6); he is a rock and a fortress (Psalm 18:2); and in Christ he is the Lamb of God (John 1:29; Revelation 5). These metaphors are infinitely meaningful: in the words of a great Catholic thinker, they are like simple and poor livery with which God clothes himself in order to humbly reveal himself.[54] But other notions really do apply to God in the truest of ways: he is the highest good; he is the most beautiful one; he is omniscient; he is all-loving. And yet, in all these cases (and a number of others), these attributes take on an infinitely loftier meaning when applied to him: "For as the heavens are higher than the earth, so are my ways higher than your ways and my thoughts than your thoughts" (Isaiah 55:9). This is true for all of these "divine names" which we apply to God.

Now, it seems strange to bring up these points of methodology in this chapter. Perhaps they would have been better placed in our discussions of faith, or perhaps in a kind of prologue to the book. However, I place them here with full awareness, for it is here that we must take care to understand how our words are functioning. We must not mistake their meanings, for in the domain of charity, our words, notions, and judgments will all lead us into the depths of the Divinity, if we are docile to the movement of faith. The words we apply to this reality will present us with the one thing necessary in our lives (Luke 10:41-42).

The divine love, charity, "God's love ... poured into our hearts through the Holy Spirit" (Romans 5:5)—what is the best way to understand it?

What is the best word to apply to it? Here, as on many other occasions, I find myself following St. Thomas Aquinas because he gives us a truly illuminating ordering of principles. The central notion which should guide our reflection on the theological virtue of charity is *friendship*.

To understand this assertion, let us begin in the domain of our experience. We need to appreciate the fact that the word "love" is said in many ways. Many know of C.S. Lewis' book *The Four Loves*. It is neither my place nor my desire to challenge the words of the famed Anglican apologist. However, I will follow a slightly different path, one laid out with great clarity by the Swiss cardinal Charles Journet, himself following a long line of Aquinas' own followers.[55]

The first great division of loves is between a love which ultimately rests *in us* and a love which rests *in another person*. Theologians once upon a time called the first kind of love *amor concupiscentiae*, the love of "concupiscence," using the latter word in a neutral sense meaning "desire." Such love can be either good or bad. We can desire inferior things for ourselves so that we can live, such as food, housing, etc. We can desire superior things for our own sake as well; for instance, we can wish to be virtuous because it is a human perfection. But we can also have such loves for wicked purposes. We can love alcohol to the point of intoxication and impoverishment, and we can "love" virtue so much that we turn it into vice, becoming so attached to the mere *idea* of "being good" that we, in fact, become puffed up with pride.

The second sort of love, resting *in another person*, can take on two primary forms. In both cases, we find ourselves in a kind of ecstasy, standing outside of ourselves. When we love other persons, we are in some way *within them*—and the true question will be this: Can they also be *within us*? We will find that they can indeed, and in the case of God, this will be primary, for he must first come to dwell in us so that we might therefore dwell with and in him. Before pushing on to this ultimate case, however, let us continue our upward ascent.

We can have for another person a love which takes on a unilateral form: *benevolence*, "well-wishing," in the strongest sense. I can have such benevolence-love for people who do not wish to have any relationship with me. In fact, we are called to do this regarding our enemies: "Love your enemies and pray for those who persecute you" (Matthew 5:44); "If your enemy is hungry, feed him; if he is thirsty, give him drink" (Romans 12:20). Indeed, virtuous parents should have a benevolence-love for their children, something which will never depart from their hearts no matter how much their child may wander afar and abroad, like the character singing in the bluegrass song "When It's Lamplighting Time in the Valley," who knows that his mother is praying for him as she keeps a lamp burning for him.[56]

Hearing the words of the song, one cannot help but think of the wandering children of God. Such maternal love is reflected in God's own love for his errant people: "Can a woman forget her sucking child, that she should have no compassion on the son of her womb? Even these may forget, yet I will not forget you" (Isaiah 49:15). And so poignantly in the prophet Hosea:

> When Israel was a child, I loved him,
> and out of Egypt I called my son.
> The more I called them,
> the more they went from me ...
> Yet it was I who taught Ephraim to walk,
> I took them up in my arms;
> *but they did not know that I healed them.*
> I led them with cords of compassion,
> with the bands of love,
> and I became to them as one
> who raises an infant to his cheeks,
> and I bent down to them and fed them ...
> How can I give you up, O Ephraim!
> How can I hand you over, O Israel! (Hosea 11:1-4, 8, emphasis added)

"But they did not know that I healed them." This is often how people interpret the ancient adage that friendship is *willing the good of the other person*, as though there were no further perfection to be had. And this is what people may be tempted to think of God's love. Charity would be "self-gift," and Christ would be the *Redeemer*, buying us back from the debt of sin, giving us eternal life like a kind of external gift, *solely* something given to us.

This misunderstanding comes across in the way that popular consciousness thinks of the Scriptural Greek term *agapē* used for the love of God and the love which Christians should have for him and for others. All too often, *agapē* is rapidly defined as "self-giving love," as though the most divine of loves were unidirectional, *benevolence-love*. But it is more, for there is a loftier form of love still: *friendship-love*. Yes, we will our friend's good with a kind of benevolence. We can even do so when he or she goes astray, perhaps injuring us in some way. And yet, this is not the *essence* of friendship. Friendship is most truly itself when it is *mutual*, when we share a single life, a single love. Friendship is most truly itself when our friend is somehow "within us" through love and we ourselves are within him or her, when love creates a kind of single soul out of two persons. This is the most profound union possible in all the world, a union which is so profound in God that it manifests itself in three Persons who all share one and the same knowledge and one and the same love. According to theological terminology, the persons of the Trinity "circumincess": they *dwell within each other*. Our Lord says, "I and the Father are one" (John 10:30).

Take care! We are now making an infinite somersault! We must push the analogy of friendship beyond all human friendships, using a kind of superanalogy. Faith is needed here, for it must be revealed to us that this life of friendship-love with God is truly possible. (And it has indeed been revealed!) All of this is summarized in the words of the apostle of love, St. John the Evangelist: "Beloved, let us love one another; for love is of God, and he who loves is born of God and knows God. He who does not love does not know God; for God is love. In this the love of God was made manifest among us, that God sent his only-begotten Son into the world, so that we might live through him ... If we love one another, God abides in us and his love is perfected in us" (1 John 4:7-9, 12). And let us recall Christ's words in St. John's Gospel, words which we have already reflected upon: "No longer do I call you servants, for the servant does not know what his master is doing; but *I have called you friends*" (John 15:15, emphasis added). And in the Gospel of Luke he reassures his disciples, "I tell you, *my friends* ..." (Luke 12:4, emphasis added). Let us never downplay the fact that God has called us his friends!

Christ and his apostle are not saying, "Love God so that you can become divine." He is no Pelagian who thinks that we can merit salvation and bring about supernatural love through our own human action. God's love is made manifest through the Incarnation, and this "manifestation" is not merely a kind of good example given to us in Christ. Rather, in that great Johannine theme, we are told that we are given a new life in Christ, like vines grafted onto the branch filled with divine sap "so that we might live through him." This new life enables us to love *with God's love*. He gives us the power, so to speak, to turn back around in response to his gift and love with his own love. Cardinal Journet sums all of this up so well:

> What could I give to God in response to His immense love, if He, in coming to meet me, did not Himself begin by filling me to the brim with His own love for Himself, if He did not give me a source from which I can draw, so that I might give back to Him in return? He comes in order to give Himself to me in His love, thus becoming my own, and if I possess Him, He is at my disposal, enabling me to return Him to God: *to give God to God* ...
>
> Charity is like a net that I throw over the Trinity so as to hold It captive in me. The Trinity is God by nature and by essence, and for my part, I am God by participation. Quite unthinkable! Yes, of course, it goes without saying that God belongs to God: He dwells within Himself. But ... what an idea: He comes into me so as to dwell within me; I can be not only myself but, indeed, *myself along with God who is given to me*; I give myself to Him with Him who is in me![57]

And all of this is summed up in the words of St. Athanasius in his work *On the Incarnation*: "The Son of God became man so that we might become God" (see CCC 460).[58] Once again, we see how *everything* in moral theology cannot help but return to its source: God's self-gift, given in grace, lived in our current wayfaring state, and then brought to its consummation in heaven. Here, we are directing our gaze toward this great truth of the meaning of charity: it is God's own love, given to us, so that God dwells within us, and we within God! We walk around in the halls of heaven even now, and we love with the very love of God because he has made us his friends. And this is why charity will not perish; this divine friendship is one and the same now and in eternity, with no change except the fact that then we will see our God face-to-face, meaning that this love will be fed eternally by the sight of our God. We will no longer be as wayfarers as we are now but, rather, as those who rejoice in their homeland, there forever with our greatest friend, the Bridegroom of our souls, whom we now receive in the Eucharist:

> And humbly I'll receive thee,
> The Bridegroom of my soul,
> No more by sin to grieve thee,
> Or fly thy sweet control.[59]

Grasping onto the word "friend," we feel ourselves launched into the heavens. And we are! This divine friendship spoken of by Christ and by the apostles is something which transports us into the celestial heights! We were already there, of course, through grace, faith, and hope. But in charity, we are most truly in our eternal homeland. Without any change to himself, God stoops downward *precisely in order to draw us upward.*

This is most true in the incarnate Christ himself, where human nature is *drawn to the Word of God.* But it is true for us as well. Through the gift of grace, God changes us so that we then may be truly capable of being united to him in supernatural knowledge and love, friendship-love.

In their most profound moments, even the pagans grasped this fact: by themselves, no human can truly be a friend of God, for he is too transcendent. We do not ascend to heaven in order to bring God down to us. The loftiest "natural religion," the loftiest "natural love" for God, is still infinitely distant from true friendship, from a true sharing in life. However, we need not ascend to heaven to find him, for he has first descended to us—from the start and throughout all of salvation history (see Deuteronomy 30:12-14; Romans 10:5-13). He comes to dwell in us through grace if we merely "get out of the way" and allow him to do so, thereby becoming sharers in his life. Just as he calls us out of nothingness, so too does he draw us to the heights so that we might be his friends.

Here, allow us to pause for a moment yet again in order to meditate on this by considering the poetic words of St. John Henry Newman:

> O wisest love! that flesh and blood,
> which did in Adam fail,
> should strive afresh against the foe,
> should strive and should prevail;
>
> And that a higher gift than grace
> should flesh and blood refine,
> God's presence and his very self,
> and essence all-divine.[60]

And what will this charity, this love, do to us? It will enable us to do all things. In the Roman rite, many couples choose a famous passage from St. Paul for their wedding day. It sounds very nice, yes:

> Love is patient and kind; love is not jealous or boastful; it is not arrogant or rude. Love does not insist on its own way; it is not irritable or resentful; it does not rejoice at wrong, but rejoices in the right. Love bears all things, believes all things, hopes all things, endures all things. (1 Corinthians 13:4-7)

It all seems so charming and domestic. But have we heeded its full context, that which gives it its most profound meaning, the meaning which then can be applied to the couple's own love? St. Paul continues:

> Love never ends; as for prophecies, they will pass away; as for tongues, they will cease; as for knowledge, it will pass away. For our knowledge is imperfect and our prophecy is imperfect; but when the perfect comes, the imperfect will pass away ... For now we see in a mirror dimly, but then face to face. Now I know in part; then I shall understand fully, even as I have been fully understood. So faith, hope, love abide, these three; but the greatest of these is love. (1 Corinthians 13:8-10, 12-13)

The love he is speaking of is *charity*, the divine love, something greater than supernatural faith and greater than supernatural hope, something greater than all other things in the whole universe, something which lasts beyond death. It is an eternal seal upon our hearts in fulfillment of the words of the Song of Solomon: "Set me as a seal upon your heart, as a seal upon your arm; for love is strong as death, jealousy is cruel as the grave" (Song of Solomon 8:6).

Now, if we are God's friends, we are all closer to each other in Christ than we even are to our blood relatives, sharing this one seal of love. We have been received into the great family of Christ: "And stretching out his hand toward his disciples, he said, 'Here are my mother and my brethren! For whoever does the will of my Father in heaven is my brother, and sister, and mother'" (Matthew 12:49-50; Luke 8:20-21). Our mother Mary, the Mother of God, was *most profoundly Christ's mother in her faith and grace*, for all of creation awaited that holy response from which the future of redemption flowed: "Let it be to me according to your word" (Luke 1:38). Grace gathers us all together into the one family of God as the "fellow citizens with the saints and members of the household of God" (Ephesians 2:19), the mystical body of Christ (see Ephesians 5:22-33, Colossians 1:24).

Think of the long list of people whom St. Paul names at the end of the letter to the Romans. He readily presents nearly thirty names in a land distant from his own, all of whom he holds dear to his heart (see Romans 16:1 and following). These are the bonds knit together by charity, gathering together the many new brothers, sisters, and mothers whom Christ promised he would give us if we give up all things and follow him (Mark 10:29-30). And St. Paul is clear, throughout his writing, that there are moral requirements to this brotherhood:

> Bear one another's burdens, and so fulfil the law of Christ. (Galatians 6:2)
>
> Walk in a manner worthy of the calling to which you have been called, with all lowliness and meekness, with patience, forbearing one another in love, eager to maintain the unity of the Spirit in the bond of peace. (Ephesians 4:1-3)
>
> Let all bitterness and wrath and anger and clamor and slander be put away from you, with all malice, and be kind to one another, tenderhearted, forgiving one another, as God in Christ forgave you. (Ephesians 4:31-32)

All of this is a reflection of the charity, the divine love, that we share with our brothers and sisters. It is called, in traditional theological language, "fraternal charity." But again, *sursum corda*, "lift up your hearts"! This is not mere kindness, mere geniality, mere generosity. It is the divine love! The gift of charity has made all of us brothers and sisters, for God "desires all men to be saved and to come to the knowledge of the truth" (1 Timothy 2:4). Even those who are only *potentially* in a state of grace are still to be loved just as Christ loved sinners: so much that he died for them! Thus, fraternal charity is a true extension of the divine love. God loves us with his infinite love, enabling us to love with his love.

And let us not forget Christ's own words, affirming his divine presence in such acts of "fraternal charity":

> Then the King will say to those at his right hand, "Come, O blessed of my Father, inherit the kingdom prepared for you from the foundation of the world; for I was hungry and you gave me food, I was thirsty and you gave me drink, I was a stranger and you welcomed me, I was naked and you clothed me, I was sick and you visited me, I was in prison and you came to me." Then the righteous will answer him, "Lord, when did we see you hungry and feed you, or thirsty and give you drink? And when did

> we see you a stranger and welcome you, or naked and clothe you? And when did we see you sick or in prison and visit you?" And the King will answer them, *"Truly, I say to you, as you did it to one of the least of these my brethren, you did it to me."* (Matthew 25:34-40, emphasis added)

This passage is explained with supreme balance by one of the greatest Dominican spiritual theologians of the twentieth century, Fr. Ambroise Gardeil, who compares fraternal charity directly to the Eucharist and to the mystery of the Church, both of which are mysteries concerning God's continued presence among us:

> *You did it to me!* God says it, and He says it by pledging His truth. Just as the omnipotent Christ consecrated bread as His body, He consecrated the poor as another self. And here the full extent and depth of God's design is uncovered before us. The object of our love for God remains unknown for us, and this fact presents the great difficulty that frustrates this love and disconcerts us. Doubtlessly, Jesus Christ filled the gulf. Nobody has seen God. The Son who is in the Father's bosom has described Him to us. He has done even more than this. In Him, we have touched the Word of Life with our hands! However, this humanized vision of our God itself only existed for a few moments, after which Jesus Christ departed, becoming in His own turn an invisible object of faith for us. Nonetheless, He did not completely depart, and we here come into contact with these visible survivals of the God Man, namely the Eucharist and the Church, next to which our neighbor finds his place. "This is my body"— "He who hears you, hears me"—"You do them to me": the three creative utterances which consecrate those things that substitute for our Savior-God's physical presence, each corresponding to a particular need felt by our soul, which wishes to love God.[61]

Charity looks to soak all of creation in the divine love, to make all things, all actions, all persons, everything be stamped with the seal of God and to become a kind of great banquet of divine grace, a true communion even among enemies! This is a great mystery, but it is something much more than mere kindness or mere generosity. It is a desire to share, *together,* in the divine friendship of grace which God pours out into our hearts. It is a desire, with a true joy, to love *Christ as truly present* in our brothers and sisters, sharing together in the mystery of God's grace forever active in the depths of our souls.

A touching example of such fraternal charity (or we might say "sororal" charity) can be found in the life of St. Benedict. The great monastic saint's sister, St. Scholastica, would visit him yearly. On the last such visit, he went down to his monastery's guest house. There the siblings, along with several of Benedict's monks, "spent the whole day singing God's praises and conversing about the spiritual life." Then, when the somewhat strict Benedict declared that he must return to his monastery, Scholastica wept and prayed that he might be prevented from leaving her. The heavens let loose a great storm, preventing the monk from returning to his monastery. Thus unable to return, he spent the night with his sister, "and both of them derived great profit from the holy thoughts they exchanged about the interior life." And St. Gregory the Great, who wrote the tale of this encounter, makes clear what inspired and enabled this graced moment as St. Scholastica's life drew onward to its close. It was her love: "Do we not read in St. John that God is love? Surely it is no more than right that her influence was greater than his, since hers was the greater love."[62] *This* is fraternal charity in its highest manifestation: not merely doing well for others, not merely self-sacrifice, but, in the heights, *a communal joy in the divine friendship shared by those who have one and the same love, the love of charity, the very life of God lived even now*.

This gives the true meaning to the famous maxim of St. Augustine: "Love God and do what you will!"[63] This does not mean that sinning is an option sometimes. It means, instead, that the ruling impulse of your life should be the love of charity. And this charity, animating the whole of your life, will bear fruit in eternity. Faith will pass away, giving way to vision. Hope will be done away with too, passing over into this eternal and sure enjoyment of God's presence. But love will remain, blossoming forth in heaven with all the intensity that our merits deserve—merits which are nothing more than the crowning of God's own gifts to us. As the Roman rite prays in the first preface to the saints: "For you are praised in the company of your Saints and, in crowning their merits, you crown your own gifts."[64] Let us pray that our hearts may be ablaze with the love which will find itself again, one and the same love, crowned with the eternal vision of our friend, our Bridegroom, our love, our God.

CHAPTER TEN

The Universal Call to Mysticism: The Gifts of the Holy Spirit

Having now discussed all of the theological virtues, I hope that you see a very important fact: to be a Christian is a bold and lofty vocation. There is nothing pedestrian about our calling, nothing ho-hum. By Baptism, we are given a life which is truly superhuman. Sanctity should be shocking! Holiness is something more than the merely human. Missionaries have traveled the world to spread the Gospel. St. Benedict threw himself into a thorn bush in order to overcome sexual temptation. St. Simeon Stylites lived an ascetical life on top of pillars. What could they have told their more (supposedly) sober relatives who perhaps thought all of this was crazy? St. Thomas Aquinas' family wanted him to be a powerful abbot of the great monastery Monte Cassino, but he followed another path, joining a group of poor beggars, the Dominican friars. In response, his relations kidnapped him, locked him up, and attempted to have him break his vow of chastity. Even in a family who wanted their son to be a monk, the choice to be a "mere friar" seemed like throwing one's life away. When the Holy Spirit moves us, things get quite shaken up indeed, at least to the eyes of the world!

But what if I said to you that *your* life should be like this? What if I told you that there is no such thing as what Bishop Robert Barron has called "beige" Christianity?[65] No doubt, this might seem like zealotry on my part. Obviously, we're called to be holy and good citizens. But, really, throwing ourselves into bushes and living on pillar tops? We have children to raise and the rat race of work to attend to!

Nonetheless, my words are nothing more than a reiteration of the truths stated in the New Testament, lived by the first Christians, and reiterated by the teachings of the Church through the ages. Should we limit our God's power? He is well enough equipped to fashion saints in suburbs and holy men and women in the homeliest of existences. Christ does not call together a coterie of elitists, a little clique of the great and glamorous. His circle is much more down-to-earth, men and women who are well aware of their weakness. The religious leaders of his day looked upon Jesus' dining partners and indignantly asked, "Why does he eat with tax collectors and sinners?" And he had a ready answer: "Those who are well have no need of a physician, but those who are sick; I came not to call the righteous, but sinners" (Mark 2:16-17). God has quite enough power to make the divine life shine out in our day-to-day lives. And John the Baptist proclaimed a truth which holds firm even to our own day: God can take the driest and hardest material and make it a fitting instrument of his praise, for he "is able from these stones to raise up children to Abraham" (Luke 3:8).

How is this possible? In short, it is possible through the Holy Spirit, who is given to all believers as the great gift bestowed on our souls. This great gift flowers in a variety of individual *gifts*, a number of perfections that stay with us so that we might await the breeze of the Spirit blowing from God through our depths. In the history of theology, these gifts have been described in different ways by various theologians and spiritual writers. In this chapter, we will continue drawing inspiration from St. Thomas Aquinas, who I believe helps to provide some useful distinctions regarding these matters. In what he says about this topic, he develops what he found in the earlier Western tradition, especially in St. Augustine. While his teaching is not a universal doctrine, it does help to lay out some very important distinctions about one of the most vital truths concerning our perfection as Christians.

Let us begin by dispelling a potential confusion. When we speak of the "gifts" of the Holy Spirit, this expression is being used in a very specific sense. Here, we do not mean to refer to the various charisms which have been experienced throughout the history of Christianity even to the present day. St. Paul spoke of such special "charismatic gifts," by which believers are enabled to build up the Church, manifestations of the Spirit for the sake of the common good of the body of Christ. These include words of wisdom, understanding, and of faith and gifts of healing, miracles, and prophecy, along with others (1 Corinthians 12:4-14; Ephesians 4:11-14). The contemporary charismatic movement has helped to reinvigorate an awareness of the importance of such gifts in the life of the Church.

However, the Holy Spirit comes to us for something more than merely these external gifts, important as they may be. His primary "mission" is a sanctifying one. Here we see the most profound meaning of the opposition between the "flesh" and the "spirit." Even though many Christians have been tempted, through the centuries, to oppose Christian "spirituality" to the "dirty physical world," this temptation has forever been condemned by the Church, who ceaselessly proclaims that flesh itself can become the mediation of salvation: "And the Word became flesh and dwelt among us" (John 1:14). Instead, "flesh" represents the world inasmuch as it is opposed to God and his ways. God sends forth his Spirit in order to fashion Christ in us, making flesh the servant no longer of itself and of the ways of the world but, instead, of God: "If the Spirit of him who raised Jesus from the dead dwells in you, he who raised Christ Jesus from the dead will give life to your mortal bodies also through his Spirit who dwells in you" (Romans 8:11). We find ourselves in a situation analogous to Mary the Mother of God. The Holy Spirit overshadowed her, so that the power of the Most High might fashion Christ in her womb, something infinitely beyond anything she ever could do on her own (Luke 1:35). In a similar, though different, manner the Spirit must dwell within us to bring the true life of grace:

> O Holy Spirit, mighty defender,
> To all who love you, comfort you give.
> Everywhere present, *fountain of virtues,*
> *Without your kindness, no one could live.*
>
> O Holy Spirit, treas'ry of blessings,
> Come, as was promised, *life-giving* Flame.
> Come, dwell within us, *quicken our cool hearts,*
> *Strengthen our purpose to praise your name.*[66]

All of this means that there is a sense in which the world should look upon Christians as though we don't quite fit in. St. John never tired of contrasting the world with the children of God. Our vocation calls us to a way of life that is quite different from the world's ways: "And I will ask the Father, and he will give you another Counselor, to be with you forever, even the Spirit of truth, whom the world cannot receive, because it neither sees him nor knows him; you know him, for he dwells with you, and will be in you" (John 14:16-17). The most perfect choices of the Christian life should have a kind of strangeness to secular eyes. They should radiate with so much divine love that they reflect Christ's own striking and unexpected holiness: a "sign of contradiction," revealing the hearts of many (see Luke 2:34-35) and drawing great hatred down upon his head. Of course, we must not go about trying to anger the world though our actions and choices. No, merely by living our lives as Christians, living the Christ-conformed life to which we are all called, we will find ourselves set in opposition to the world, which will look upon this life of "enthusiasm" (a word that literally means "inspired") and will find it quite strange and, perhaps, quite foolish: "The unspiritual man does not receive the gifts of the Spirit of God, for *they are folly to him, and he is not able to understand them* because they are spiritually discerned" (1 Corinthians 2:14, emphasis added).

In fact, our salvation requires the activity of the gifts of the Holy Spirit, a fact which we do not appreciate well enough. One of the things that I have stressed in this volume is that Catholic moral theology is not merely a kind of "high-voltage" moral philosophy or a pious gold plating on the words of Aristotle and the Stoics. Christian morality is far more than this. It is a calling to the perfection of our heavenly Father, a calling to the perfection of charity. All of us share one and the same vocation, inscribed in our Baptism: die to self, live in Christ. Our circumstances may differ and our particular paths may twist this way and that, but the end remains the same: the perfection of divine love. This is what the Second Vatican Council meant in speaking of the "universal call of holiness" discussed in the fifth chapter of the conciliar constitution *Lumen Gentium*. It can be pithily summarized: "The classes and duties of life are many, but holiness is one."[67]

We have emphasized this point many times, and yet it is quite necessary to keep it in the forefront of our minds: holiness is not the province of experts. Christ does not call merely vowed religious and priests to holiness. He calls *all* of his disciples to his life. Yes, St. Paul, in his letters to Timothy and Titus, writes immortal instructions to those who are ordained, words which should ring in the hearts of every bishop, priest, and deacon until the end of time. Nonetheless, this same Paul wrote *to all believers*: "For our sake he made him to be sin who knew no sin, *so that in him we might become the righteousness of God*" (2 Corinthians 5:21, emphasis added); "He chose us in him before the foundation of the world, that *we should be holy and blameless* before him" (Ephesians 1:4, emphasis added); "Hold fast what is good, abstain from every form of evil. May the God of peace himself *sanctify you wholly*" (1 Thessalonians 5:21-23, emphasis added). The citations could be piled up to the heavens. It is all a reiteration of Christ's own unqualified call to holiness, proclaimed with vigor in the Sermon on the Mount and forever applying to the faithful, even if we—alas!—forget it.

With his characteristic eagerness to enumerate and distinguish things, St. Thomas turned to Scripture to find a list of the Spirit's gifts, which are aids in this quest for holiness: "There shall come forth a shoot from the stump of Jesse, and a branch shall grow out of his roots. And the Spirit of the Lord shall rest upon him, the spirit of wisdom and understanding, the spirit of counsel and might, the spirit of knowledge and the fear of the Lord" (Isaiah 11:1-2). In the Latin Scripture used in St. Thomas' days, there was a seventh gift listed after knowledge: piety. Trying to harmonize this Scripture with the tradition that came before him, St. Thomas related each gift to a particular virtue, as well as to the Beatitudes found in the Sermon on the Mount. We do not need to follow him in all of his technical details, for that would take up a whole book![68] However, we will merely note this high-level distinction: some gifts (knowledge, understanding, and wisdom) are more "contemplative," while others (counsel, might, piety, and fear of the Lord) are more "active." Let's briefly consider each of these groups in overview fashion.

Our faith is supernatural. By it, we know mysteries which far exceed anything human reason could reach on its own. We come to know that God is the Father, the Son, and the Holy Spirit. What could this mean to someone who does not have faith? Indeed, what does it mean to those of us who have faith? We will never fully understand the profound meaning of these revealed words. We will always have a kind of "infinite margin" remaining, for the only one who fully comprehends this mystery is God himself, for only he fully knows what his own life is: "No one comprehends the thoughts of God except the Spirit of God" (1 Corinthians 2:11). And this fact applies to so many other things in which we believe, all things with great practical importance: the Church is *the body of Christ*; the sacraments are the *channels of God's grace*; the Mass is *Christ's own sacrifice today present*; grace and the theological virtues are *God's life poured out into our souls*. In all of these mysteries, the Triune God is present like their "inner core." If he alone understands himself, then we need a great aid indeed! We need the Holy Spirit's gifts of knowledge, understanding, and wisdom so that our faith may be purified. We need to be mystics!

Let us, however, repeat an important point once again: this requirement applies to *all Christians*, not merely to contemplatives, to monks and nuns. Nor are priests and bishops the only ones added to such a list, as though they cornered this market on the Holy Spirit's illuminating inspirations. No, indeed! The theological virtues are given to all, and we are all baptized into Christ. All Christians are "supernaturalized"! Again, to repeat the instructive words from the Second Vatican Council cited earlier, "the classes and duties of life are many, *but holiness is one*." If there is a universal call to holiness, there is also a universal call to mysticism. That is, everyone should look to set up a small hermitage of contemplation in his or her soul. All believers are entitled to draw abundantly from the spiritual riches of the great authors who have written concerning spiritual matters: the desert fathers, St. Gregory of Nyssa, St. Gregory the Great, Blessed Henry Suso, the monks whose writings are gathered in the *Philokalia*, St. Francis de Sales, and so many others. And with their texts in hand and the Word of God in our hearts, we will await, with the gifts of the Holy Spirit in our souls, the inspirations of God so that we may indeed "taste" and, to the degree possible, "see" the Lord's goodness (Psalm 34:8).

We all are given supernatural faith, supernatural hope, and supernatural charity-love. We all must strive after great holiness, which requires close communion with God, who dwells in our souls as our closest friend. These words of St. Paul apply to all Christians: "We have the mind of Christ" (1 Corinthians 2:16). And by this new mind that we are given, we know these great mysteries, "the depths of God": "'What no eye has seen, nor ear heard, nor the heart of man conceived, what God has prepared for those who love him,' God has revealed to us through the Spirit. For the Spirit searches everything, even the depths of God" (1 Corinthians 2:9-10).

Moreover, in our day-to-day moral life, the Spirit is present to guide us as well. Hence, St. Thomas lists out the other gifts: counsel, might, piety, and fear of the Lord. At times, we hear it said that we should pray in order to see "what God wants us to do." But do we really know what we are saying? Too often, this advice seems like a nice and pious idea but not really all that important. However, it is a duty of the Christian life! We must be ready to await the Spirit's arrival! We open our hearts and minds so that he may then direct us in his own way: "And when they bring you before the synagogues and the rulers and the authorities, do not be anxious about how or what you are to answer or what you are to say; for the Holy Spirit will teach you in that very hour what you ought to say" (Luke 12:11-12). Such readiness to await the divine inspiration is the work of the gift of counsel.

And we need a might (or, courage) beyond what any virtue could give, and we need a holy fear, by which we never would desire to depart from God. Placing all of our surety in him and in the victory of the Cross, we press forward, though with hearts that are all too ready to be fickle. The Lord made dire promises to his followers: "The hour is coming, indeed it has come, when you will be scattered, every man to his home, and will leave me alone." However, he also gave us a firm foundation for keeping ourselves erect in hope and true Christian courage: "Yet I am not alone, for the Father is with me. I have said this to you, that in me you may have peace. In the world you have tribulation; but be of good cheer, I have overcome the world" (John 16:32-33). By the gifts of might and fear, we can truly fulfill the words which St. Paul enjoined upon the community in Rome: "Never flag in zeal, be aglow with the Spirit, serve the Lord. Rejoice in your hope, be patient in tribulation, be constant in prayer" (Romans 12:11-12).

And how can we truly pray as we should? Before the inscrutable mystery of God, along with his transcendence and holiness, how could we truly raise up our voices? We need a tongue that is trained by God (Isaiah 50:4), ready to speak his praises in a fitting way. We need a truly pious soul, ready to give voice to the worship which we owe to God in justice. How appropriate, here in the domain of prayer, where we open our hands before God, is it for us to learn to open our hearts to receive the gift of piety, the gift of true reverence in relation to God, who alone is fully aware of just how glorious he is. He alone can teach us how to pray in a truly befitting manner: "Likewise the Spirit helps us in our weakness; for we do not know how to pray as we ought, but the Spirit himself intercedes for us with sighs too deep for words" (Romans 8:26).

These seven gifts are the patrimony given to all the baptized, something we need in order to live our lives, merely as Christians, to their full perfection. How merciful our God is! In order to fulfill the vocation he gives us, he does not merely command us to climb up mountains on our own. No! He tells us to learn how to open our hands so that he can give us great gifts, better than any earthly parent. He does not set up a narrow gate so that he can fashion a kind of divine obstacle course that would render our lives impossible to live. We merely need to ask, and he is ready to give us what we need in order to enter through this gate, blown along by the wind of his Spirit (Matthew 7:7-14).

Thus, let us pray in the words of the sequence *Veni Sancte Spiritus* sung in the Roman rite on Pentecost:

> Grant to Thy faithful, dearest Lord,
> whose only hope is Thy sure word,
> the sevenfold gifts of grace.[69]

How great a Father indeed! He fills us with himself so that we can soar to the heights to which we are all called. Buoyed aloft by the Spirit, may we be able to say with the great apostle,

> For this reason I bow my knees before the Father, from whom every family in heaven and on earth is named, that according to the riches of his glory he may grant you to be strengthened with might through his Spirit in the inner man, and that Christ may dwell in your hearts through faith; that you, being rooted and grounded in love, may have power to comprehend with all the saints what is the breadth and length and height and depth, and to know the love of Christ which surpasses knowledge, that you may be filled with all the fulness of God. (Ephesians 3:14-19)

CHAPTER ELEVEN

The Church and the Sacraments: The Wellsprings of Eternal Life

As we bring this section to a close, let us once more draw some connections between moral theology and the rest of theology. Here again, we will see that the mysteries of the Faith are all intertwined with each other. Each mystery has something to tell us about the others, and moreover their hierarchy helps to reveal to us, with greater clarity, the meaning of each mystery.[70]

The greatest of all the mysteries of the faith is the mystery of the Most Holy Trinity, the eternal life of the three Persons in the one God, the Father, the Son, and the Holy Spirit. This is the mystery that is reflected within every other revealed mystery—their central reference point. In order to understand all the others, this mystery is the first thing that is necessary. Alongside the mystery of the Holy Trinity, there is the mystery of the incarnate Christ, he who has revealed the Trinity to us, precisely because he is the second Person thereof, the Word, eternally related to both the Father and the Holy Spirit.

These are the two great *credibilia*, the two great "things to be believed": God-in-himself and God-in-the-world. In the ancient Church, these two domains were called "theology" and "the economy (of salvation)," in order to designate the difference between the two greatest mysteries. All the anticipations of these mysteries—whether in ancient Israel or in whatever truth is found in other religions, though mixed with error—ultimately find their fulfillment in these two great mysteries, and all the truths of the Christian Faith are, in the end, connected to them. There is *the economy of salvation*: "For he has made known to us in all wisdom and insight the mystery of his will, according to his purpose which he set forth in Christ as a plan for the fulness of time, to unite all things in him, things in heaven and things on earth" (Ephesians 1:9-10). And there is *the economy leading to "theology" (i.e., to the eternal life of the Trinity in heaven)*: "When all things are subjected to him, then the Son himself will also be subjected to him who put all things under him, that God may be everything to everyone" (1 Corinthians 15:28). "For all things are yours, whether Paul or Apollos or Cephas or the world or life or death or the present or the future, all are yours; and you are Christ's; and Christ is God's" (1 Corinthians 3:21-23).

Now, we have already reflected on this at great length in the chapters up to this point. We have spoken about the supernatural, divinizing character of grace and of the theological virtues. In fact, in our chapter concerning "putting on Christ," we reflected on some quite technical points of theology in order to show how the mystery of the Incarnation reveals to us the nature of grace. However, before we move on to our other particular discussions concerning the moral life, it is important to make one final connection. We must connect the mystery of the incarnate Word to the mystery of the Church, his "mystical" body (see Ephesians 5:22-33, Colossians 1:24), into which we have been incorporated through grace. Up to this point, our connection of the mysteries risks looking like this, at least in overview:

The Most Holy Trinity → The Incarnate Word →
The Sending of the Spirit → Grace →
Theological Virtues → Moral Virtues

However, we need to add another mystery:

The Most Holy Trinity → The Incarnate Word →
The Sending of the Spirit →
The Building up of the Church, the Place of Grace →
Grace → Theological Virtues → Moral Virtues

The Church is the "place of grace," the rich and fertile soil wherein the divine life is meant to grow. Now, this does not mean that God does not act outside of his Church. In the words of a famous medieval maxim, "God does not deny grace to him who does what is in his power." However, we must understand these words aright. All grace is Christ's grace. Here, we must repeat a text which expresses this so completely: "And from his fulness have we all received, grace upon grace" (John 1:16). Wherever there is grace, it comes from Christ and *it, by rights, leads to him*. All who live outside the Church are in what we could call an "abnormal" situation, for the deepest longing placed in their souls actually wishes to be fulfilled in the Church, the true garden where they will blossom forth in all that is good. This is why the Church remains *missionary* and never must tire in her task of spreading and cultivating the gospel. Her message and activity bring true fulfillment, for all grace aims to be incorporated into the Church: "These elements, as gifts belonging to the Church of Christ, are forces impelling toward catholic unity."[71]

In this book, my intention is to speak to those who already believe and who are looking to grow in the moral life *as God has ordained it to be lived*. Thus, we must consider the mystery of the Church and the sacraments, by which the incarnate Word continues to act, even today.[72]

The mystery of the Church is subordinate to the mystery of the incarnate Word. Through his incarnation, death, and resurrection, Christ is the fount of all grace. The culmination of the whole Incarnation, that which gives it its *raison d'être*, is the Crucifixion, by which glory is given to God through this redemptive action: "Now is my soul troubled. And what shall I say? 'Father, save me from this hour'? No, for this purpose I have come to this hour. ... For this I have come into the world, to bear witness to the truth" (John 12:27 and 18:37).[73] All the graces ever given after the Fall anticipated this moment, and all graces thereafter will merely be applications of this great act through the rest of time: "I, when I am lifted up from the earth, will draw all men to myself" (John 12:32).

The sacraments are not just external rituals. They are the acts of Christ, alive and acting through his body today. The ministers of the various sacraments are *free* ministers, and this is something taken into account in how the Church understands the sacraments. However, they remain true instruments of Christ's activity, for the sacraments function as the means for the continued expansion of his saving mission through the world and for all time. After his resurrection, Christ tells Mary Magdalene not to hold on to him, for he must return to his Father (John 20:17). Soon thereafter, he breathes his Spirit upon the apostles, giving them the power to forgive sins (John 20:22-23). Here begins the fulfillment of what he said to them before his death: "It is to your advantage that I go away, for if I do not go away, the Counselor will not come to you; but if I go, I will send him to you" (John 16:7). Yes, the Spirit of grace *interiorly* renews the Christian community. However, he also is present in establishing the Church, extending the power of the Incarnation and of Christ's grace and merits through all of time.

As Catholics, we have a kind of "incarnational consciousness." Christ's ascension is not the end of his incarnate presence. I am a great lover of traditional Protestant hymnody, which has much beauty and grandeur. However, it is difficult not to be a little troubled as a Catholic when one sings the words of the third stanza of Charles Wesley's "Hail the Day That Sees Him Rise":

> Highest heaven its Lord receives; Alleluia!
> yet he loves *the earth he leaves*. Alleluia!
> Though returning to his throne, Alleluia!
> still he calls us all his own. Alleluia![74]

"The earth he leaves ..." In a sense, yes, of course, for his physical bodily presence is gone. However, we must not overemphasize this departure. Rather, to use the somewhat odd-sounding but still informative language of classical theology, just as Christ's humanity was the *conjoined* instrument of his divinity, so too, the sacraments are his *separated* instruments. St. Thomas summarizes this idea as follows, showing how the sacraments are part of the logic of the Incarnation: "The saving power of the sacraments must be derived from Christ's Godhead *through His humanity*."[75]

In point of fact, the Ascension inaugurates a new kind of incarnate presence, an ecclesial presence, a presence through the Church, which is his *body*. Was this not the great theme of St. Paul?

> We, though many, are one body in Christ, and individually members one of another. (Romans 12:5)

> For just as the body is one and has many members, and all the members of the body, though many, are one body, so it is with Christ. For by one

> Spirit we were all baptized into one body—Jews or Greeks, slaves or free—and all were made to drink of one Spirit. For the body does not consist of one member but of many. (1 Corinthians 12:12-14)

> So then you are no longer strangers and sojourners, but you are fellow citizens with the saints and members of the household of God, built upon the foundation of the apostles and prophets, Christ Jesus himself being the cornerstone, in whom the whole structure is joined together and *grows* into a holy temple in the Lord; in whom you also are built into it for a dwelling place of God in the Spirit. (Ephesians 2:19-22, emphasis added)

> Speaking the truth in love, we are to grow up in every way into him who is the head, into Christ, from whom the whole body, joined and knit together by every joint with which it is supplied, when each part is working properly, makes bodily growth and upbuilds itself in love. (Ephesians 4:15-16)

Yes, this body is quite different from the one that is joined to the Word through the hypostatic union. This is why the Church is called his "mystical" body. The word "mystical" does not mean "ghost-like," something invisible hovering in between all of us. The union of this body is not a physical union; however, it is more than a mere moral union, like what we experience in a club or even in a national political community made up of many people. The Church really and truly knits us together, marked as we are with the seal of Baptism, as members of one body connected by one life, the life of Christ given through the Spirit.

The connection of the sacraments to Christ is so tight and close that, in fact, we must first and foremost say that Christ is the one who acts through the sacraments. Obviously, these sacraments lead to the outpouring of the Spirit and ultimately lead us back to the Father. Moreover, God can certainly work grace outside of the order of the sacraments (though, as we have already said, that grace *draws such a person who receives it to the Church and to her sacramental life*). However, the sacraments themselves pass through all the intermediaries which stretch from the incarnate Christ to the external action of the ministers of the sacraments, which confer grace through these bodily actions. Through this long chain of sacramental action—from Christ's divinity, through his risen and glorified body, through his body the Church, into which we are incorporated through Baptism and in which he continues to act in a special way through his priests and bishops—we can truly say that in and through the Church's activity, exercised by her sacramental ministers, "Christ baptizes in every baptism; Christ absolves whenever absolution is given; Christ offers, and offers himself in, every Eucharist sacrifice."[76] This is merely a theological reformulation of the truths which were revealed directly after the Resurrection, when Christ made it clear that he would remain present in and through the sacraments: "All authority in heaven and on earth has been given to me. Go therefore and make disciples of all nations, *baptizing them in the name of the Father and of the Son and of the Holy Spirit,* teaching them to observe all that I have commanded you; and behold, I am with you always, to the close of the age" (Matthew 28:18-20, emphasis added); "When he was at table with them, he took the bread and blessed and broke it, and gave it to them. And their eyes were opened and they recognized him ... Then they told what had happened on the road, and *how he was known to them in the breaking of the bread*" (Luke 24:30-31, 35, emphasis added).

The sacraments call for a complete book of their own. What is important here is for us to understand that the theological life of grace is not merely something "internal," something completely private. Our moral life is tied to the public life of the Church. Her Liturgy is a kind of garland wrapped around her sacraments, which themselves contain and cause the great gift that enlivens our entire moral lives: the gift of grace. Our holiness is Christian holiness, and as Catholics we know that this means that it is *ecclesial holiness.*

Through the ministers of the sacraments, Christ acts today. These outward actions are not merely signs of what God happens to be doing in our soul at the same time. This was true of the "sacraments" of the old law, in Israel. The sacraments of the new law go further. *They themselves* are causes of grace, for Christ is the one who acts here and now in the sacraments.

And all of the sacraments have an abiding effect, though this effect differs from sacrament to sacrament. Three of them confer a seal which will last the entire life of its recipient: Baptism, Confirmation, and Holy Orders. Traditionally speaking, these three sacraments have what is called an "indelible character," something which remains in the soul forever. This indelible character marks the soul and forever functions as the source of future activity as Christians, precisely as reborn children of God (for Baptism and Confirmation) and as men exercising some degree of Christ's hierarchical priesthood (for Holy Orders). For this reason, these sacraments cannot be repeated.

The case is somewhat different for the other four sacraments (Matrimony, Anointing of the Sick, Reconciliation, and the Holy Eucharist). In their cases, there are more or less abiding states which are the source of that particular sacrament's grace. (And we must be careful to understand that this grace is nothing more than a kind of particularized reflection of the gift of divinizing-sanctifying grace, *received and reflected here and now in a unique, sacramental activity*.) In Matrimony, the sacramental bond of union is not as lasting as the character of Baptism, Confirmation, and Holy Orders. However, it does last the whole of the marriage until one's spouse dies. Anointing of the Sick is not merely a single action like a point in time but, rather, gives its recipient the spiritual strength to face illness as a child of God who has been touched by Christ. Even the sacrament of Reconciliation, or confession, marks us with the grace of forgiveness, to which we respond through our penance, which flows forth as a kind of effect from the graced encounter we have had in and through the sacrament. Finally, the most unique case is the Eucharist, which *abides in itself as the Body and Blood of Christ*, thus giving rise to the great practice of Eucharistic Adoration and veneration, a devotion that is dear to the Western Church and which is a gift to the universal Church, arising from a wondrous appreciation of the *abiding* nature of the Eucharistic conversion through transubstantiation, leading to the abiding sacramental presence of Christ in the Church's tabernacles.

As Christians, all of our grace flows from our baptismal "character," which is the "living spring" (see John 4:14) by which we are incorporated into the great life of Christ lived in the Church. Thereby we are made fit to receive the Eucharist, for through Baptism we truly are made participants in his own self-offering and resurrection (Romans 6:3-4), the reality of which is reactualized in every Eucharist. As we fulfill our duties as spouses and parents, we are not merely being upright citizens and good human beings. We are allowing the abiding grace of Matrimony to reveal something of the very mystery of Christ and his Church (Ephesians 5:21-33). Our own sufferings can be conformed to Christ through the Anointing of the Sick.

And the virtues of humility and of penance are uniquely supported by the sacrament of Reconciliation.

Above all, all of these sacraments lead to the Eucharist, and all things flow from this most holy sacrament of the altar. How appropriate this is, too, for the Eucharist is the very sacrifice of Christ offered today through the hands of the priest who through Holy Orders is made Christ's *instrument* for bringing about this great and awesome mystery. If the Cross (along with the Resurrection, whereby victory is announced) is the culmination of the redemptive Incarnation, and if the Incarnation is the source of all graces and, moreover, if the Eucharist is the abiding offering of that sacrifice until the end of time, then we can only draw the necessary conclusion: the Eucharist is, in the oft-quoted words of the Second Vatican Council, "the source and summit of the Christian life."[77] Given that our very life of grace makes us members of Christ's body, the Eucharist—by which the Incarnation's fulfillment is actualized for us day after day, building up the body of Christ here below—also builds up the very life of grace in our souls. It is the source of all "moral" perfection which we will ever have, for our moral perfection is a divine perfection, the very perfection of the heavenly Father (Matthew 5:48). "The Eucharist is the efficacious sign and sublime cause of that communion in the divine life and that unity of the People of God by which the Church is kept in being. It is the culmination both of God's action sanctifying the world in Christ and of the worship men offer to Christ and through him to the Father in the Holy Spirit"[78] (see CCC 1324–1327).

You see now, I hope, that the sacraments are not just a kind of "add-on" to the moral life, something to be handled by dogmatic theology or a mere question of "spirituality." They are the conduits of the life which Christ has brought to us. When you think of the various themes that we have discussed up to this point, as well as the various virtue-related topics which will be taken up in the chapters that follow upon this one, never forget to ask yourself how it is that these various "moral virtues" are connected, in the Christian life, to the conduits of grace which are the sacraments. Through them, Christ acts in us, so that our action might be enlivened by this life of grace, given to us in and through Christ's action. In this world, our action becomes, at least to some small degree, a kind of coming of Christ to all whom we meet: "Truly, truly, I say to you, he who receives any one whom I send receives me; and he who receives me receives him who sent me" (John 13:20). And all of this is like a golden chain made up of the mysteries of faith, connecting us today to the Trinity through the mystery of the redemptive Incarnation made present through the Church and her Christic activity in the sacraments. This is no metaphor. Everything is connected by a sure and strong chain, one which comes down from heaven and draws all things to God:

> It shall come to pass in the latter days
> that the mountain of the house of the Lord
> shall be established as the highest of the mountains,
> and shall be raised up above the hills;
> and peoples shall flow to it,
> and many nations shall come, and say:
> "Come, let us go up to the mountain of the Lord,
> to the house of the God of Jacob;
> that he may teach us his ways
> and we may walk in his paths." (Micah 4:1-2)

THE CHRISTIAN MORAL VIRTUES—GENERAL REMARKS

Before we discuss particular moral virtues, we will dedicate two chapters to some basic, overarching reflections. In the first of the chapters in this brief section, we will reflect on the way that many of the Christian virtues can be discussed even with nonbelievers. Historically, this has been called the "natural law." Although Christian morality is infinitely more than this natural morality, it includes everything that is in it. In the second chapter in this section, we will consider a virtue which is essential for all holiness (humility) and a very pernicious vice which is devastating for the whole of the moral life (acedia, also known as sloth).

CHAPTER TWELVE

A Few Remarks on the Natural Law

This book is mainly concerned with moral theology—that is, with the way that the life of grace transforms our human activity into a truly divine activity, a true participation in Christ's own life in our own deeds and relations. In order to stress this *theological* character of moral theology, I have felt it necessary to depend principally upon Scripture as an open and rich source for moral reflection. Moreover, all of my discussions have been guided by the theological reflection of the Church through the centuries, even when I do not cite any works explicitly. In short, our perspective has been "within the household of faith."

My insistence on this point is important. It is very tempting to turn Christian ethics into a kind of "gilded moral philosophy." We could look at the Christian life as though it were the most sublime morality, the loftiest fulfillment of what human nature is capable of, a kind of gold plating upon our humanity. In a sense, this is true, though only inasmuch as grace *fulfills nature precisely by surpassing nature*. Our perfection is not merely human. Through grace, our perfection is truly divine—a theme which I have repeated very often, yes, but one which nonetheless is pivotally important and often overlooked in preaching and teaching. Christianity brings something greater than the most sublime morality: it brings the very life of God, measured out into our souls. Christ is not merely the moral model whom we must imitate. He is the source of our life, of our supernaturalized vitality: "In him was life, and the life was the light of men ... 'I am the way, and the truth, and the life'" (John 1:4 and 14:6).

Now, there is another kind of temptation, one which is perhaps equally perilous: to treat moral theology as though it did not involve any nonreligious moral truths. There are some very technical dangers involved in making this mistake. (For example, one such danger is what certain theologians call a form of "pseudo-supernaturalism," denying nature so much that we actually end up denying what is truly supernatural, for we can only define the *super*-natural in terms of the *natural*.) However, there is a much more practical (and quite pernicious) error which arises when it is said that morality is really just a matter of religion, without making any further distinctions. This assertion risks turning all moral arguments into religious arguments, potentially leading morality itself to be relegated to the private sphere, indeed, to the sphere of individuals' private moral preferences.

Do we not know of this state of affairs? It is reflected in an often-cited quote from a legal opinion written by former justice Anthony Kennedy in the United States Supreme Court case *Planned Parenthood of Southeastern Pa. v. Casey* (1992): "*At the heart of liberty is the right to define one's own concept of existence, of meaning, of the universe, and of the mystery of human life*. Beliefs about these matters could not define the attributes of personhood were they formed under compulsion of the State."[79] In *Roe v. Wade* (1973), the Supreme Court, claiming to argue on the basis of the Fourteenth Amendment, defined a domain of privacy into which the government supposedly could not step, thereby making the act of abortion broadly legal, at least up to the point of viability.[80] At that time, the Court had some small measure of good sense, noting in its majority opinion that such "zones of privacy" are not absolute. With the 1992 case, however, the Court allowed its rhetoric, at least under the pen of Justice Kennedy, to become much more sweeping.

We will dedicate a future chapter to the moral evil of abortion, there also acknowledging the sad situations faced by those who have tragically faced this sorrowful experience. Here, however, we must take a moment to dwell upon Kennedy's text, for it reflects a kind of "atmospheric idea" unreflectively held by many concerning the nature of morality. The sentence that is emphasized in the quote above makes a striking claim: the core of human freedom directly involves our ability to *define* what the meaning of existence is. In a limited sense, of course, this is true. A profound reality about human nature is the fact that we must seek out our meaning and then must work also to express this meaning in our actions. All of this is indeed part of our glory as free, truly human beings.

We freely come to know the meaning of our existence. However, this sort of *defining* does not aim at having *us fabricate the truth of reality*, as though *we* were setting its boundaries, delimiting its scope, *defining it in the sense of giving reality itself its contours*. Rather, the sane sense of defining something involves delimiting and expressing just where the joints of reality cut. The primary characteristic of *defining* things is *stating the way things are*: Man is a rational animal; justice is the virtue enabling us to give each his or her due; courage means that we should not fear things so much that we would commit unjust acts; and so forth. We cannot pave a path forward through reality, thus "defining ourselves" in Justice Kennedy's sense, without first having some basic idea about what we are and what reality is. Consider how inventive the physical and biological sciences are, designing experiment after experiment with great ingenuity. However, why does the scientist do all of this? Because he or she is on a quest, a quest *for the truth of reality*. The same is true for humans in general, and even when we command our actions and define the path we will take, we do this first and foremost by being conformed to the truth of what it means to act as a virtuous human and as a son or daughter of God.

The aforementioned quote deals with questions surrounding American abortion jurisprudence, but it reflects a deeper bias—namely, that ultimate questions of meaning are, in fact, merely private opinions. This is reflected in contemporary language in expressions like "your truth" or "my truth." If someone were talking about the virtue of prudence (which we will discuss in a later chapter), there might be some sense to these expressions. It is quite correct to say that your decision in X circumstances will not be the same as mine in Y, even though we both might make a truly moral choice. However, personal moral prudence presupposes some basic bedrock foundation. In the language of classical moral theology, we ultimately need our knowledge to *conform to reality*—namely, to the *reality of the virtues*. This alone gives a firm and sturdy foundation on which we can build all the rest, all the essential ornamentation in the particular circumstances of our lives.

Now, not all moral truths depend *directly* on religious proclamation. There are many moral truths that can be known without the Church teaching them, though as the steward of Christ's grace, she also teaches these natural moral truths so that her children may not be turned aside by the wiles and temptations of the world. Nonetheless, these are not truths which are *intrinsically supernatural*. They are truths about virtues that perfect us *precisely as human beings*, precisely as men and women, not necessarily as children of God reborn through grace.

Later in this book, in the chapter on fasting, I will briefly discuss a thesis held by some theologians (among whom are numbered the disciples of St. Thomas Aquinas, including myself), stating that, in addition to the theological virtues, there are also Christian *moral* virtues given along with grace. In the theological literature, these are called the "infused moral virtues," with the word "infused" being used to indicate the special way that they are gifts coming from God. Technically, this theological thesis is not something that all believers must hold, though the Thomists believe it helps to illuminate certain problems regarding the way that we are fully remade in Christ's image through grace. Nonetheless, for the purposes of this book, we will consider the virtues in a very general sense, presupposing that we are talking about how the Christian life should reflect itself in these various actions. We will not directly discuss whether or not these actions presuppose a new set of infused moral virtues.

Now, returning to the natural law: what kinds of moral truths can we know as belonging to the natural law? The simplest—at once vague and yet rich with everything that will be needed for the rest of our natural moral life—is quite obvious: "That which is good must be done, and what is evil must be avoided." This principle, which is often called "the first principle of practical reason," is akin to what is called the "principle of noncontradiction": "something cannot both be and not be at the same time and in the same respect." These principles are like lights illuminating all of our thought. They are the first principles guiding (or implied in) all the rest of our knowledge, at least in the natural order (and they will be presupposed for everything that God reveals to us concerning his supernatural life and his providential plan for our salvation).

Now, everyone can agree on the simple claim that what is good must be done. But a quick retort will come, no doubt: "However, I have my good, and you have your good." A very easy way to flesh out the first principle of practical reason is to consider the various basic virtues that perfect us in our moral activity. Christian tradition, drawing on ancient

Greek sources, including Plato and Aristotle, though also later Greek and Roman thinkers, calls the most basic categories for these moral virtues the "cardinal virtues." The word "cardinal" comes from the Latin word *cardo*, meaning "hinge," like the hinge on a door. The rest of our moral life "swings" upon these four hinges: prudence, justice, courage, and temperance. There is nothing mysterious involved in this enumeration. Our minds must be ready to choose moral goods (prudence), our wills must be ready to enter into rightful relations with others (justice), our fear and anger must be of service to higher goods (courage), and our desires must not be so rapacious as to overthrow the whole of our lives in pleasure-seeking self-"fulfillment" (temperance).

Now, the nature of these virtues is so clearly true and sane that they are technically what classical philosophers call "self-evident truths." This does not mean that we drop into life knowing them. Nor can you just pull someone over on the street and ask, "What is justice?" No, indeed! If you read the tales of Socrates, you will see that in his quest for truth he needed to meander all around Athens asking so many questions about the virtues that he inevitably was put to death for showing just how many supposedly wise people had very little knowledge, indeed so little knowledge that they didn't even know their ignorance! However, the nature of these virtues is self-evident in the sense that all we need to do is define our terms clearly, and people will find that they can't deny them without falling into absurdities. The virtues are all first principles for "natural" morality, and all other natural moral notions will be illuminated in their light. Let's merely consider the four cardinal virtues themselves, though they have many relatives too.

The loftiest part of our soul is, in fact, something more than "mere soul." According to the philosophy of Aristotle, followed by many later Catholic theologians, plants and animals, because they are living beings, have souls. Unlike rocks or other nonliving things, they are alive, and as living beings, they are "animated," a word that comes from the Latin animus, "soul." No, this does not mean that "plants are people, too." Nor does it mean that plants or animals are spiritual beings. Instead, it means that they are *unique centers of self-directed activity*. By contrast, human beings have *spiritual* souls, and this makes humans unique. Now, the human soul does share with the animal kingdom the powers of sensation (including memory and active imagination, called the "estimative sense" by ancient and medieval psychology) as well as the sense-derived desires and joys, fears and vexations that we can see in "mere animals." Moreover, like plants, we must process food and grow, making something higher (namely, human-organic life) out of something lower (namely, physical food). Yet above all of this, our souls have a spiritual light and a spiritual power of desire and joy: the intellect and the will. This is what makes us unique in all bodily reality, a kind of being with our feet upon the ground and our heads in the heavens. We exist on the border between beings which are purely material (minerals, plants, and animals) and those which are purely spiritual (the angels and God).[81]

Now, our lowest powers don't define us as humans. They need to be fully "integrated" into the story of human life, this spiritual-bodily life which should forever amaze us, the greatest marvel in all of nature.[82] We never would look upon someone who drinks his family into poverty as though he were a good person, and someone whose bad eating habits lead to poor health, while perhaps a tragic case, ultimately is not someone whom we would emulate. Nor would we like to emulate someone who is so needlessly picky over food that he or she is always a social pest.[83] The same could be said in the domains of fear and anger. The hotheaded person who always rushes too quickly into things is, in fact, not in right order. Indeed, he or she only looks courageous while, in fact, not being so. True courage knows how to stay put and even to suffer pain and fear while waiting for the appropriate circumstances in which to act. However, the person who pauses far too long out of fear—or even out of a lack of sensitivity—also falls short in matters of courage. The courageous person does not lack fear, but he or she will not let it have the driver's seat. Fear is a mere instrument to inform us of our surroundings at best. It is not what drives the actions of a truly rational being. Such are the stringent requirements of two of the so-called cardinal virtues: temperance and courage.

Our wills and intellects need perfecting as well! We must turn our wills toward all of the various relationships we have with others and with various institutions. We must be ready to give others what is owed to them, in whatever form this may be. Sometimes this will take place in relationships like those we have with our parents or with the nation into which we are born. Sometimes, this will merely be to other human beings, to whom we owe many spoken and unspoken debts—strict contractual debts or "debts" of truthfulness, of gratitude, of generosity, of kindness, and indeed even of a ready wit when necessary! In all of these various relationships, we can fall short or go too far. We need to be made just. Finally, we must be able to coordinate all of these various requirements of morality. We need to draw on our past experience and upon the experience of others, without being biased. We must know how to come to the right path *for ourselves, in our own particular circumstances*. We must be ready to bring head and heart, intellect and will, together in order to do the right deed here and now! In other words, we need the virtue of prudence.

These virtues—prudence, justice, courage, and temperance—are all moral goods which will shape our character, but they also are moral goods which we can describe in words, and while they are still very basic, they provide an eminently clear first example of truths which can be shared between believers and nonbelievers alike. They are like the largest, hardest bones of the natural moral edifice. Temperance: "Pleasures of food, drink, and sex are not the final word in life but, instead, must be integrated into higher goods, duties, and relationships." Courage: "Fear and anger are instruments to be wielded, and sometimes suffered, in defense of the other goods of life." Justice: "Where a debt is owed, whatever its form may be, it is good (that is, *necessary*) to repay it in an appropriate way." Prudence: "All these moral goods must be weighed out so that we do not fail to forge forward in making good decisions." All of these virtues concretize that very first principle: "That which is good must be done, and what is evil must be avoided." And ultimately, the person who spurns them will fall into self-contradiction, as well as tragic dissipation.

Traditionally, the Church has called this domain of "naturally" accessible moral truths *the natural law* (see CCC 1954–1960). The seeds for her teaching are reflected in Scripture, most famously in words with which St. Paul opens the letter to the Romans:

> For the wrath of God is revealed from heaven against all ungodliness and wickedness of men who by their wickedness suppress the truth. For what can be known about God is plain to them, because God has shown it to them. Ever since the creation of the world his invisible nature, namely, his eternal power and deity, has been clearly perceived in the things that

> have been made. So they are without excuse; for although they knew God they did not honor him as God or give thanks to him, but they became futile in their thinking and their senseless minds were darkened. (Romans 1:18-21)

However, fuller development of the idea of the natural law required a great deal of further philosophical refinement. Throughout antiquity, Greek and Roman philosophers, especially those who have received the name Stoics, worked out a moral vocabulary which spoke of the natural law or the natural moral law which all men can know. To the Christian ear, this admittedly pagan idea helped to flesh out insights like those found in Scripture. It also helped to articulate a basic datum of experience: men and women who are not believers still have moral knowledge. Thankfully, orthodox Christianity is almost always a religion of "both / and," not "either / or." Thus, the natural law was readily integrated into the moral outlook of Christianity, not only in the West but also in the East, even though the histories of these integrations were different.[84]

Now, we should step back and admire this fact, something not always publicly appreciated about Catholic Christianity, though it is true all throughout the Church's long history. The Church is the bearer of supernatural truths. She teaches us about the Trinity, the Incarnation, the sacraments, the life of grace, the theological virtues, and many other truths that *wholly* exceed what we could know through human reason. As we discussed in an earlier chapter, these are truths that require the theological virtue of faith in order for us to know them. They are truly *super*-natural, above the natural powers of reason. However, the Church is also the steward of the prerogatives of natural reason in addition to the prerogatives of faith. Grace is a *new nature*, but this does not mean that we must cast aside human nature in order to explain our rebirth. No, indeed! Grace in fact requires a soil in which it might be received, what theologians refer to as a "receptive subject," or even more opaquely, an "obediential potency," an openness to that which exceeds itself. This is the most profound part of our created nature, by which we turn to our God to receive anything that is not contradictory to our nature, including the gift of his own supernatural life.[85] Obviously, this gift must expand and elevate this nature, which itself could not possibly anticipate so great a gift. Nonetheless, no such expansion, nor any such elevation, would be possible without such a nature being first presupposed. This is what distinguishes creation from our graced re-creation. The former presupposes nothing; the latter presupposes (conceptually, not temporally) something—namely, nature.

Thus, in order to be the steward of the things of God, the Church (yes, her leaders, but indeed all her faithful) must defend human nature itself. Though she has had a tumultuous history with certain figures of culture and science, she has fostered many branches of human knowledge and has forever defended the possibility of having shared moral knowledge. The religious outlook of Christianity is fertile soil for scientific endeavors, for we proclaim a world that is created by a God who is wise and intelligent. In fact, we proclaim that a Word, a truly intelligible expression, is at the root of all things: "In the beginning was the Word, and the Word was with God, and the Word was God. He was in the beginning with God; all things were made through him, and without him was not anything made that was made" (John 1:1-3). And historically, the encounter between philosophy and the Catholic Faith helped to sow the seeds for the development of modern science, for even though Aristotle's thought was limited in many ways, one of his great accomplishments was the laying out of the outline of scientific methodology, above all in his logical works the *Topics* and the *Analytics*. The Church is the defender of human reason, not its foe.[86]

Such is the case when it comes to the idea of natural moral truths. The highest duty of the Church is to hand on the supernatural truths of the Faith, including the moral truths which point us toward our lofty calling as brothers and sisters of Christ. However, she also teaches many truths of morality which are, by rights, accessible to all. Merely to name a few of these truths: the evils of abortion and contraception, the need for employers to pay just wages, the rights of citizens and parents in relation to the state, and the basic kindness owed to all people no matter who they are. Against the tide of relativism which sweeps through the world like an all-consuming fire, claiming that everything is up to debate, the Church preaches many truths which even nonbelievers should be able to know!

Now, we should not misunderstand this notion of the natural law, thinking that it is necessarily irreligious. At its deepest roots, the natural law is religious in character. There is nothing more natural to man than the fact that he is finite and created. This means that *by our very nature* we are religious beings. If we use the title Homo sapiens to designate who we are, it is equally proper to refer to our species as *homo religiosus*. Because we are intelligent and wise (*sapiens*) we are also moral and religious (*religiosus*). The foundational duty of the natural law is, in fact, the fulfilling of our religious duties. A later chapter will be devoted to this topic.

Many have looked upon all of the varied and sundry ways that people live throughout the world and have doubted the existence of the natural law. Everything seems shifting, and every civilization seems to have its own moral code. However, at other times, often when faced with the horrors of war and the truly important questions of life, humanity has seen what binds us together in common: justice, the pursuit of truth, the joys of family life, and so forth. Back and forth, the popularity of the natural law has forever waxed and waned, all the way back into the first philosophical speculations concerning it. Such is the nature of what Heinrich Rommen referred to as the "eternal return of the natural law."[87] However, the fact that there are so many deformations does not undercut the fact that this natural moral law exists. There are many ways to fall down, but few in which to stand erect.[88] Nonetheless, in all of these various cultures, there are groping attempts to express these very basic moral goods. And throughout all of this history, with ebb and flow, with doubt and certitude, with relativism and sure moral proclamations, the Church will stand on this firm and sure footing, echoing words whose truth she herself humbly acknowledges to have drawn from the works of the great Roman orator Cicero:

> For there is a true law: right reason. It is in conformity with nature, is diffused among all men, and is immutable and eternal; its orders summon to duty; its prohibitions turn away from offense. ... To replace it with a contrary law is a sacrilege; failure to apply even one of its provisions is forbidden; no one can abrogate it entirely.[89]

CHAPTER THIRTEEN

Acedia and Humility: Two General "Atmospheric Conditions" in the Moral Life

As we transition into our discussion of the various moral virtues, it is useful to think about the general "moral atmosphere" of the Christian life. While the life of grace is, above all, the life of the theological virtues, it involves a great host of other virtues as well. Our whole person must be altered, and this will involve all the moral virtues to be discussed in our upcoming chapters (and, indeed, many others as well, though an introductory text can only give the broad outlines of this rich and verdant garden). By means of all the various forms of Christian prudence, justice, courage, and temperance, everything that is human is requisitioned for divine service: our minds, our wills, our fears and sorrows, our anger, our desires, and our enjoyments. All of these must be marked with the face of Christ, leaving nothing at all untouched.

Blessed be God that he gives us the ability to shoulder this divine task! Nonetheless, how strenuous an undertaking it is! Dashing forward at the beginning of the day, we risk finding that by midday our strength will flag. The noonday devil will strike!

This expression "the noonday devil" is an ancient Christian adage. It was immortalized scripturally in the text of the Latin Vulgate text prepared by St. Jerome and expressed in the first edition of the Douay-Rheims English translation of the Bible: "Thou shalt not be afraid of the terror of the night. Of the arrow that flieth in the day, of the business that walketh about in the dark: of invasion, or of the noonday devil (*daemonio meridiano*)" (Psalm 90 [91]:5-6). Although contemporary translations, based upon the Hebrew and Greek of the Old Testament, do not reflect St. Jerome's Latin, we can say that the expression has managed to stick.

We tend to think of the "noonday devil" as being the exhaustion we feel as the day moves onward: we need a coffee to help us overcome the temptation to lazily neglect the tasks at hand. However, for ancient spiritual authors, this "devil" was something quite nefarious. For the influential monastic author Evagrius Ponticus (346–399), this sinister figure was the very demon that would strike monks in the desert in the middle of the day, distressing them, making them lose their attention and discipline of prayer. It was numbered among the "eight tempting thoughts" besetting the monks living in the Egyptian desert. In the Christian West, these *eight* thoughts have come down to us in a slightly amended form as the *seven* deadly sins. For Evagrius, this noonday devil was called "acedia," which we today call "sloth."[90]

Now, we must take care. This word "sloth" has resonances that can confuse us regarding the nature of this particular vice. To our ears, it sounds like a kind of plump laziness. We imagine someone who sits lazily upon the couch, binge watching shows while avoiding work. However, in traditional spirituality and moral theology, this vice is something far more pernicious. Evagrius described it thus:

> The demon of *acedia*, which is also called the noonday demon (Ps 90[91].6), is the most burdensome of all the demons. It besets the monk at about the fourth hour (10 am) of the morning, encircling his soul until about the eighth hour (2 pm). First it makes the sun appear to slow down or stop, so the day seems to be fifty hours long. Then it forces the monk to keep looking out the window and rush from his cell to observe the sun in order to see how much longer it is to the ninth [hour, *i.e.* 3 pm], and to look about in every direction in case any of the brothers are there. Then it assails him with hatred of his place, his way of life and the work of his hands; [it tells him] that love has departed from the brethren and there is *no one to console* him ... If anyone has recently caused the monk grief the demon adds this as well to amplify his hatred [of these things]. It makes him desire other places where he can easily find all that he needs and practice an easier, more convenient craft. ["]After all, pleasing the Lord is not dependent on geography,["] the demon adds; ["]God is to be worshipped everywhere.["] It combines this with remembrance of his relatives and his former way of life, and depicts to him a long life, placing before his eyes a vision of the burdens of the ascetic life. So, it employs, as they say, every [possible] means to move the monk to leave his cell and flee the racecourse.[91]

This description of a monk looking around for "something else to do," something to distract him in the midst of the desert struggle, could be readily adapted to our own life experience. How often do we spend time avoiding our direct duties, convincing ourselves that we need to do something greater, something more influential than "merely" loving our family and neighbors? The world of social media is a great temptation for us to look out our digital window into the lives of others, just in case something "interesting" is happening somewhere ... anywhere! (How tragic! In fact, something great is happening right now within us: God is continually calling us to closer union with him through the exercise of love.) And how ready can we be to turn online to find something that will stir up our outrage, the great addiction of our age, making us feel as though we are virtuous merely because we stumble around angry at all things.

The vice of acedia is underneath all of this. What is its root source, the main poison that it allows to seep into our souls? Quite simply, we no longer take joy in the things of God. It is a profound sorrow, a truly spiritual sorrow which turns us away to look for joys elsewhere—away from our current duties, away from our current situation, away from the place where Divine Providence has placed us. Delight and joy are said to "crown" our activity, and our lives are all the better when we take delight in things that are *deserving of delight*. But woe unto the person who feels sorrow in such good and divine things—not a merely psychological sorrow but a true repulsion, as though one were saying, from the depths of the soul, "Lord, it is *not* good that you are here." Hence, for St. Thomas Aquinas, the vice of acedia (or sloth) is opposed to the greatest of the theological virtues: charity.[92] Often without realizing it, the slothful soul feels sorrow in the face of the divine love.

This pained state of soul sends us away looking elsewhere for delight. We turn away from the quiet, virtuous, and divine garden which God wishes to be ours, filled with flowers of his own making. Hoping to find greater meaning and enjoyment elsewhere, we plunge ourselves into a garden of personal, earthly delights. All of this seems so much more enjoyable than sticking to our basic duties and obligations. "How tedious all of that is! How humdrum," we tell ourselves. But, alas, are we well enough aware that we might be placing ourselves into a kind of Hieronymus Bosch painting, filled with grotesque forms that, ultimately, suggest the hell which inspires all of this supposed delight and fills it with its congenital rot?

No doubt, this rhetoric may seem overcharged. Nonetheless, the sane spirituality of ancient Christianity is correct in this regard. The vice of acedia is a dangerous affair, against which we must always be on the watch. If the theological virtue of charity should be a consuming fire, the vice of acedia is an asphyxiating, oxygen-free atmosphere which stifles the flames of the divine love. Or, to return to our garden metaphor, this asphyxiating, airless atmosphere chokes off all of the growth God wishes to make bloom forth in beauty through and in us. When we examine our consciences, do we heed the pernicious presence of acedia, even if it is only in the form of venial sins? Woe for the day when such sins burst forth as mortal wounds against the life of grace!

How can we counterbalance this suffocating air? Humility. No doubt, this virtue is readily misunderstood. When we speak about someone being "very humble," we think of a poor, bowed-over person who is always ready to say that he or she is the worst of all people, not worth anything. Aren't such "humble" people really just spineless worms, not men and women of great deeds? Do we not teach our children to have "self-esteem" and to be proud of themselves? Why would we counsel humility?

Here again, it is useful to draw from Evagrius. Consider how he describes the vice of pride:

> The demon of pride conducts the soul to the very worst fall. It urges ... [the soul]: [1] not to acknowledge God's help; [2] to think it is responsible for its own success; [3] and to be arrogant towards the brethren as unintelligent because they do not all share the same opinion concerning this.[93]

In pride, we can see the clearest example of the so-called "capital vices," those particularly pernicious faults which give rise to many others, like heads (*capita*) which lead the whole organism in the wrong direction. What could be more delusional for a creature than to ignore the fact that it is not the source of its own existence (and, ultimately, of its activity, which is also a gift from God)? And for a Christian, what could be more blindly stupid than to claim that *we* are the source of the divine life of grace? Through pride, we convince ourselves of such foolish things, relying on ourselves, not on God. In this way, we turn all of the virtues away from their true end, poisoning the whole of our life. Therefore, the fundamental atmosphere of the Christian life should be humility, a ready recognition of God as the source of all that is truly good in what we have, in who we are, and in all that we do.

This utter reliance upon God is likewise the reason why we should always be ready to emphasize the fact that we are sinners. There are two senses of the Lord's words "Apart from me you can do nothing" (John 15:5). Most often, we rightly read this expression as stating the fact that all things come from God. However, we can also emphasize the fact that *on our own*, all that we can do is *nothing*, the nothingness and darkness that is sin. In fact, as we discussed in the chapter on sin earlier in this book, God is not the cause of sin; *we alone* are its cause. Its cause is *our* deficiency, our *falling short*. The whole mystery of the problem of evil is involved in this fact: God is the primary cause of all things, *except for sin*, but nonetheless, while merely *permitting it*, he is forever active in drawing good out of such evil.[94] The mystery of Christ is the great witness to this superabundant mercy of God, drawing from this evil quite literally the gift of the greatest possible good, the "grace of union"—that is, the hypostatic union of his two natures in his one Person. In the words of the Exsultet, which is chanted at the Easter Vigil in the Roman rite: "O happy fault that earned so great, so glorious a Redeemer!"[95]

Though we must never despair of our God's love, we should also be quite struck by this fact: that all that is *solely us* (and not *us-and-God*) is sin. Thus, before we approach the sacrament of charity, the Eucharist, we should be ready to pray, "Lord, I am not worthy to received you ..." or, in the words used in Byzantine liturgies prior to the reception of Communion, "O God, be merciful to me a sinner. O God, cleanse me of my sins and have mercy on me. O Lord, forgive me for I have sinned without number." These words are not meant to "beat up" on ourselves but, instead, to frankly acknowledge how small we are and how great indeed God is.

But this outlook in no way involves burying the talents given to us, like the wicked servant who had the wrong sort of fear of his master: "Master, I knew you to be a hard man, reaping where you did not sow, and gathering where you did not winnow; so I was afraid, and I went and hid your talent in the ground" (Matthew 25:24-25). Rather, humility requires us to be quite ready to do great deeds—*the great deeds we are called to do, not those which we merely devise for ourselves*. An acceptance of providence, of our place in *God's tale*, is the mark of the truly humble person, and if we live our lives in this atmosphere, we will find that it is far from asphyxiating. Instead, it is the only natural environment for the growth of grace and virtue!

In the seventh chapter of his rule for monks, St. Benedict provides a kind of original Christian twelve-step program: the twelve steps of humility. Although his recommendations are written for those who are living in the monastic enclosure, under the rule of an abbot, these guideposts remain quite applicable to all Christians. After all, all Christians share the same *end*: the perfection of charity. Vowed religious differ only inasmuch as they take on something to help speed their steps along the shared path, vowing themselves to take up well-tested tools in the spiritual life: poverty, chastity, and obedience—or, as is the case for the ancient monastic tradition, still reflected in the vows taken by Benedictine monks, stability (to a particular monastery), obedience, and *conversatio morum* ("conversion through a monastic way of life"). These vows are merely instruments taken by the religious who, nonetheless, shares in the one vocation of Christ-centered perfection to which all Christians are called. A married layman or laywoman cannot live *the same* life as a vowed religious, but with a bit of "onsite adaptation," we can readily see how the ancient wisdom of monasticism can apply even in the midst of the bustle of an active family life.[96]

Let's briefly consider the wisdom contained in the twelve steps presented by St. Benedict. Whereas our main metaphor to this point has been that of a garden, the great father of Western monasticism chose a different image for humility: it is like a ladder rising up to heaven, akin to what Jacob saw in a dream, with angels ascending and descending to and from heaven (Genesis 28:12). How surprising a metaphor: through humility, we lower ourselves so as to be elevated to heaven! But is it really so surprising? Is it not, in the end, a mere case of the logic of the Cross: "For whoever would save his life will lose it, and whoever loses his life for my sake will find it ... Whoever humbles himself like this child, he is the greatest in the kingdom of heaven" (Matthew 16:25, 18:4)? Take care, however, not to be deceived by the metaphor. These steps are not merely rungs to be left behind as we travel upward. Rather, with each of St. Benedict's steps, we must maintain and deepen whatever we have already accomplished. The second step of humility will presuppose and improve upon the first, and the same is true throughout this ascent.

St. Benedict remarks that the sides of the ladder are made up of our body and soul, "into which our divine vocation has fitted the various steps of humility and discipline as we ascend."[97] Here, we should pause to see an important connection to the problem of acedia discussed at the opening of this chapter. The "spiritual life" is, in fact, a life which we live as embodied creatures. Christian holiness is not about out-of-body experiences. Rather, true holiness is a question of *transfiguration*. Indeed, in Byzantine Christianity, the event of the transfiguration of Jesus on Mount Tabor represents an important image for the mystery of our own divinization.[98] We are to be filled with the divine light of grace, so that every small nook and cranny of our humanity may, in fact, radiate with this luminosity. Thus, our exercise of humility must be something that we live out in practices and habits. Through such devoted, "embodied holiness," we learn how to overcome the temptation to give in to the "noonday devil" of acedia and the vaunted spirit of pride.

The upward ascent begins with a pivotal first step: keep the fear of God forever before your eyes. Yes, St. Benedict begins with the fear of hell, something that is not illicit! Certainly, we must go higher than this, but we begin with such fear so that we may pass onward to the truly mature fear to be felt by sons and daughters of God, "filial fear," that is no longer afraid of hell but, rather, of being separated from God through sin. These two fears have two completely different outlooks. The first is a fear *for our own sake*; the second is a fear *inspired by the very love of God, which we wish not to lose*. This is an awe-filled fear aware of the greatness of our Triune God, who is our dearest friend, he who *makes us to be such friends* through his grace. And when charity blossoms forth in perfect glory in heaven, then will the words of St. John be fulfilled in whole: "There is no fear in love, but perfect love casts out fear" (1 John 4:18). Hence, just as the fear of the Lord is the beginning of wisdom (see Psalm 111:10; Proverbs 1:7, 9:10; etc.), it also is the first step on the way of humility, for it acknowledges two great truths: God's infinite lovableness and our own weakness.

The next three steps, steps two through four, all deal with overcoming attachment to our own wills and desires. St. Benedict focuses on monastic obedience to the abbot of the community and how the monk must quietly embrace obedience even when it causes suffering or involves injustice. This can seem quite harsh and medieval. Nonetheless, it was Christ, not a harsh human taskmaster, who enjoined his disciples, "If any one strikes you on the right cheek, turn to him the other also; and if any one would sue you and take your coat, let him have your cloak as well; and if any one forces you to go one mile, go with him two miles" (Matthew 5:39-41).

Is such long-suffering all that rare? How many parents must endure the harsh trial of raising children who certainly will break their hearts on more than a few occasions? How many times are we misunderstood by friends and relatives who impute malice (or at least ill will) to our best intentions? How often do people perform tasks of great devotion and generosity, all without being noticed by those who think themselves to be "truly" important and great?

This is an important truth: holiness is easily overlooked. It does not parade around, making waves. It does not assert its rights. We find many things to which we must be obedient, all these little duties and relationships which make up the fabric of our lives. We see the quiet holiness of dutiful parents and of adult children who care for their aging parents, the dutiful holiness of good neighbors and of those who suffer loss without speaking a word of bitterness. There are many supposedly "great" people whom we might have the pleasure of meeting, but all of the prideful pomp of the world pales in comparison to the company of an aging mother who gracefully bears the true and great sorrow of the loss of an adult child to cancer. We will see more of Christ's visage in her peaceful yet sorrowful face than we will in all of the self-congratulatory gatherings of the great and the beautiful. We will see more of him in her face because we will see a kind of reflection of his own obedience: "Although he was a Son, he learned obedience through what he suffered; and being made perfect he became the source of eternal salvation to all who obey him" (Hebrews 5:8-9)—all who obey him even in the simple and humble details of day-to-day existence.

Here too, we have one of the reasons why stability is a vow taken by the Benedictines. The desert fathers—the true and great founders of Christian monasticism—knew very well that we must put down our roots in order to grow in holiness. The monk who suffers from acedia wanders about, looking for a guest to come, hoping that something will disrupt the boring details of his day-to-day life in his hermitage. And what did the wise desert fathers recommend to such a monk? Quite simply, they said that their disciples must strive to keep up their rule of life, in short, *their routine of prayer and work*. Even the most influential of all the desert hermits, St. Antony the Great (251–356) fell under the cooling spell of acedia, and for him too, the remedy was quite simple: be faithful in all the small details of day-to-day monastic life in the desert:

> Once, when Antony was living in the desert, his soul was troubled by boredom and irritation [*akèdia*]. He said to God, "Lord, I want to be made whole and my thoughts do not let me. What am I to do about this trouble? How shall I be cured?" After a while, he got up and went outside. *He saw someone like himself sitting down and working, then standing up to pray, then sitting down again to make a plait of palm leaves, and standing up again to pray*. It was an angel of the Lord sent to correct Antony and make him *vigilant*. He heard the voice of the angel saying, "Do this and you will be cured." When he heard it, he was very glad and recovered his confidence. He did what the angel had done, *and found the salvation* that he was seeking.[99]

We may not live in a desert hermitage, nor in a monastic enclosure, but all of us have our boring, daily duties. We have our often-tedious relatives, friends, and neighbors. Instead of looking to run away from them, so that we might go and "do great things," perhaps we should find a kind of "lay obedience," a kind of ungrumbling (indeed joyful) acceptance of the necessities of our day-to-day life, thereby truly fashioning virtue out of necessity![100] And consider the wondrous effect of this simple stability: "And [Antony] found the salvation he was seeking!" How true a fulfillment of the Lord's words: "He who is faithful in a very little is faithful also in much" (Luke 16:10).

The fifth step of humility is to confess one's sins, even secret ones, to the abbot of the monastery. We may not live under an abbot, but are we honest and vulnerable to our spouses? Do we conceal wounds and bitterness, like the monk mentioned by Evagrius, forever looking to be distracted by thoughts of what makes us bitter? We must learn to be open and honest with those people whom Providence has placed in our paths, not playing little games to cover over our sins and even our frustrations. Obviously, all of this takes a careful touch, but holiness calls for this kind of vulnerability, so that we might avoid the self-satisfied conclusion that we are purely "in the right." If we confess our frustrations and our faults to true friends, they may indeed correct us for being wrong or, at the very least, unbalanced. Is not this a good thing, an honest way of *living in the truth*?

St. Benedict's sixth and seventh steps of humility have to deal with being treated as lowly and learning to recognize our lowly status. In the monastery, someone might be given the most boring tasks: cleaning up prayer books, setting tables, weeding the fields. Such a monk might be temped to say: "I have great talents! I am so misunderstood!" Perhaps this is even true about this monk, but really, in point of fact, are any of us all that great and separated off from the rest of humanity? This book is being written in the wealthiest of first-world nations. Do we Americans not convince ourselves that there are many things we need not worry about, tasks that are "beneath us"? Life has a way of teaching us otherwise. A parent learns that cleaning up dirty diapers and cooking rather unrefined toddler meals is a necessity. Helping out at a small local fundraiser seems so much less important than trying to do some greater task, something far less parochial! A choice must be made: will we grumble at this task or, rather, will we accept it gladly? The same applies to so many of the tasks of life. What happiness there is in accepting them without a murmuring tone!

Moreover, when we feel exalted and full of self-assurance, we do well to remind ourselves that our task is to deal with the log that is in our own eye, not to rush off to dust off the specks in the eyes of others (Matthew 7:4). This is not a question of making up faults and weaknesses to attribute to ourselves. Rather, it is a recognition that we are the sole source of only one thing: sin. Everything good that we do, we do it together with God, indeed, with God being the one who gives this good deed to us!

In the eighth step of humility, St. Benedict gives a maxim which, in fact, informs much of my own reflection on this chapter of his rule: do only what is endorsed by the common rule of the monastery and the example set by the superiors of the community.[101] In other words, don't go seeking out oddities when trying to be holy. Instead, strive for holiness on the pathways that are placed right before you. In your prayer life, stick to those devotions which simply answer the needs of your soul. Don't go running after all sorts of new and strange devotions day after day. Dust off your Bible, a small book by one of the Church Fathers, or something by one of the Doctors of the Church or by the popes. Draw humbly from them, not looking to feel special because you have found a secret wisdom. Instead, experience pure gratitude at having such deep wells ready to give you spiritual refreshment.

Moreover, we don't need to go running out all over the world to find people to love. We aren't called to love an abstract "Humanity" but, instead, are called to love whoever it is that happens to be given to us. This will be enough! In fact, our neighbors (by which is meant "all those who happen to be placed in our *direct* path") are gifts from God for the exercise of virtue and the divine life of grace. As the English author G. K. Chesterton once wrote,

> We make our friends; we make our enemies; but *God makes our next-door neighbour*. Hence he comes to us clad in all the careless terrors of nature; he is as strange as the stars, as reckless and indifferent as the rain. He is Man, the most terrible of the beasts. That is why the old religions and the old scriptural language showed so sharp a wisdom when they spoke, *not of one's duty towards humanity, but one's duty towards one's neighbour* ... But we have to love our neighbour *because he is there*—a much more alarming reason for a much more serious operation. *He is the sample of humanity which is actually given us.* Precisely because he may be anybody he is everybody. He is a symbol because he is an accident [of our particular history].[102]

Steps nine to eleven in the Rule's advice on humility are rather grim sounding, admonishing us not to readily speak and laugh, to be serious in our talk. Obviously, there is such a thing as virtuous humor, which lifts the spirit and celebrates true causes of joy. However, how often do we use our words to waste time and to tear down others or, at the very least, to feel better about ourselves! And, a great deal of our complaining about the evils surrounding us in fact covers over a kind of veiled pride, implicitly asserting our own holiness in contrast with this supposedly horrible "world." Often—and I speak from my own self-examination!—we are like the Pharisee who thought only of his own righteousness: "God, I thank you that I am not like other men" (Luke 18:11). God's favor rested, however, on the tax collector who was praying next to this "righteous" follower of the Law and pleaded, "God, be merciful to me a sinner"

(Luke 18:13). And what was the divine reason for the approval of this latter man? It was his humility: "For every one who exalts himself will be humbled, but he who humbles himself will be exalted" (Luke 18:14).

Before we dismiss the advice of St. Benedict regarding the evils of the tongue, let us recall the strenuous words of St. James:

> If we put bits into the mouths of horses that they may obey us, we guide their whole bodies. Look at the ships also; though they are so great and are driven by strong winds, they are guided by a very small rudder wherever the will of the pilot directs. So the tongue is a little member and boasts of great things. How great a forest is set ablaze by a small fire! *And the tongue is a fire. The tongue is an unrighteous world among our members, staining the whole body, setting on fire the cycle of nature, and set on fire by hell.* (James 3:3-6, emphasis added)

In the age of social media, could we think of any better advice?

Finally, in his twelfth step of humility, St. Benedict says that we must be humble in our very posture. He describes the gaze of the monk with a bowed head and eyes looking downward. The exact details of this comportment will differ for each of us, and we must not merely affect a kind of false humility. (Indeed, that would be prideful!) The point is that all the details of our life, even how we walk around, should be stamped with Christian humility. To take up a metaphor from Fr. Ambroise Gardeil used early in this volume: from top to bottom, from head to toe, indeed, down to the tips of our toenails, we are called to be remade in Christ. We must recognize that we are sinners and that he is the redeemer. In this way, we no longer merely fear hell but, rather, speed forward on the pathway of love. As St. Benedict summarizes,

> Now, therefore, after ascending all these steps of humility, the monk will quickly arrive at that *perfect love* of God which *casts out fear* (1 John 4:18). Through this love, all that he once performed with dread, he will now begin to observe without effort, as though naturally from habit, no longer out of fear of hell, but out of love for Christ, good habit, and delight in virtue.[103]

Obviously, these reflections have been quite brief, and each of St. Benedict's steps deserves further commentary, given the immense riches in this lengthy chapter of his rule. However, a simple truth underlies the whole ascent that he proposes, and this truth is what I have wished to draw to the fore: to grow in humility is to grow *in the truth*. It is to see our true situation, our true place, our true calling in the circumstances of our lives. Above all, unfeigned humility leads us away from the dreadful pride that would place ourselves in the center of the universe and God upon its peripheries. To return to our opening metaphor: through humility, we are like a tree that is properly planted; we find that we can thrust down our roots into the life-giving sources of grace and can draw upon truly refreshing air. The soul of the prideful person is a dry wasteland with hard soil and suffocating air, filled with that which we can give ourselves without God: nothing! Thus, there is a kind of intelligence in being truly humble, an awareness of the true order of things: "There is nothing that bears witness to an intellect that is more informed and more aware of the true place of man in this universe, where God is first and man is second."[104] As we will see in a future chapter, this outlook is the entire generative source of the moral virtue of religion.

Through the theological virtue of hope, we receive the gift of a wholly supernatural trust in God *inspired by God himself, the source of salvation and of beatitude*. Through the virtue of humility, we express a particularly important aspect of the theological virtue of hope, for humility teaches us *not to stretch out* beyond our own power and circumstances. We must rely upon that strength which comes from God alone. This virtue is counterbalanced by another virtue, traditionally called magnanimity, meaning "to have a great soul." Through the latter virtue, we are ready to do what we are truly capable of doing.[105] However, this also implies that we have the humility to realize what we are not capable of doing. The most fundamental bent of truly Christian humility will be to acknowledge that at the deepest level, we *are not capable of doing* anything without God, who irrigates all of our actions, making them possible and also actualizing them—"for God is at work in you, both to will and to work for his good pleasure" (Philippians 2:13)—so long as we don't come along with the "nihilism" that is sin!

The prophet Jeremiah spoke inspired words that poignantly expressed this contrast between the arid soil of pride and the lush arbors of humility and trust in God:

Cursed is the man who trusts in man
  and makes flesh his arm,
  whose heart turns away from the Lord.
He is like a shrub in the desert,
  and shall not see any good come.
He shall dwell in the parched places of the wilderness,
  in an uninhabited salt land.

Blessed is the man who trusts in the Lord,
  whose trust is the Lord.
He is like a tree planted by water,
  that sends out its roots by the stream,
and does not fear when heat comes,
  for its leaves remain green,
and is not anxious in the year of drought,
  for it does not cease to bear fruit. (Jeremiah 17:5-8)

PRUDENCE

The virtue of prudence is perhaps one of the most misunderstood virtues. It seems rather cautious and fearful of adventure: "It wouldn't be prudent to take that risk." Such words represent a complete misunderstanding of this great virtue, which gives us a ready eye to see the way forward toward our moral goals. Through the virtue of prudence, we gain a well-formed conscience. It is like the gaze of the expert archer, seeking out his target, or like the charioteer, who knows how to travel the racecourse no matter the difficulties involved along the way as his horses pull this way or that way. Since this virtue is operative in all of our actions, these chapters on prudence are placed first among the subsequent sections dedicated to the various moral virtues. An entire book could be written about all the various subvirtues involved in the exercise of prudence. In this introduction, we will merely content ourselves with outlining this vitally important topic. Let others build upon this foundation!

CHAPTER FOURTEEN

Prudence, Conscience, and the Freedom of the Children of God

"Live as free men, yet without using your freedom as a pretext for evil; but live as servants of God" (1 Peter 2:16). By this point, I hope that I have made clear the fact that the Christian life is not a dense forest filled with signs which say no to this and no to that! The life of grace is not merely a shackle which limits our possibilities, merely another list of rules and laws, binding our freedom in chains. If this were the whole story, we would feel, as some indeed have, that it would be better not to believe. At least in that case, it is said, we might have the benefit of not knowing that certain things are wrong. We would at least arguably not be guilty for breaking rules that we do not know.[106] In the classical terminology of moral theology, we could at least have "invincible ignorance"—that is, nonguilty, "unconquerable" ignorance of moral truth. The next chapter will be devoted to why this idea is quite wrongheaded. In this chapter, however, I would like to extol the true freedom of the children of God. In particular, we now must discuss one of the greatest virtues in the Christian life, one that is often overlooked: the virtue of prudence.

The word "prudence" is surrounded by a bad odor. When we say, "That wasn't a prudent choice," we often mean, "That was too risky. If you were prudent, you would have been much more cautious." Well, that is good advice, in particular for those who would like to keep up a "respectable" appearance and to avoid the moral adventures of life. But do such words reveal the true character of the virtue of prudence? No, indeed not! In fact, traditional moral theology says that, after the theological virtues of faith, hope, and charity, prudence holds a central place. All our virtues first and foremost come together in charity, the divine love poured into our hearts (Romans 5:5). The song of this love is the main melody line woven through the whole symphony of the truly Christian life. However, in each and every circumstance of our lives, we must figure out how we are going to weave together the various requirements of morality, the various harmonies of the virtues. We must not merely *intend* to do good actions. We must know how to choose and do them! This task, which is great indeed, is the work of the virtue of prudence, the great composer of the divine melody of the moral life.

In fact, there is no such thing as a good action which is not, simultaneously, also prudent. Though this demanding standard may surprise secular minds, it should not surprise us as Christians. Christ has called us to a high calling. Think about the Sermon on the Mount, where the Lord calls us to reform even our *interior intentions* (see Matthew 5:21 and following). Moreover, recall the high bar that he set against the Pharisees, whose obsession with external actions led them to overlook the interior renewal to which they were called: "Not what goes into the mouth defiles a man, but what comes out of the mouth, this defiles a man ... For out of the heart come evil thoughts, murder, adultery, fornication, theft, false witness, slander" (Matthew 15:11, 19). If these intentions are important, why shouldn't we expect all the little details of how we perform our action to be equally weighty matters? Did not Christ say, "Unless your righteousness exceeds that of the scribes and Pharisees, you will never enter the kingdom of heaven" (Matthew 5:20)? Well, then, let us strive to learn how to be holy even in the way that we make our choices, even in the way we exercise our "conscience."

Now, we have an equally mistreated word to take into account here: conscience. Many speak of "freedom of conscience," and an equally numerous host will tell you, "Follow what your conscience tells you." These expressions are quite nebulous, and they will require a further chapter in order to dispel their deceptive charm. But, already now, we have a tool at hand to keep this word, "conscience," from meaning a little voice in our head that can allow us to make any decision whatsoever. In almost every case when we could use the word "conscience," we would find it even better to use the word "prudence." When someone says, "Follow what your conscience tells you," we should ask, "But is it a virtuously prudent conscience?" If not, there is only one path to follow: grow in the virtue of prudence![107]

Building on ancient philosophical traditions, St. Thomas Aquinas provides a very detailed catalog of virtues involved in prudence. There is a great task involved in coming to a moral decision. If we merely draw on an outline of his presentation, we will find that we will have a much richer concept of conscience than what we are told about when it is popularly depicted. However, we will also see that this classical theological and philosophical terminology, shared by many thinkers, is merely a reiteration of what common sense already could tell us in its own way.

When we exercise the virtue of prudence, we have technically already set ourselves in motion. When trying to choose what to do, we have some general *intention* about the action we wish to perform. If we are indeed truly virtuous, we will be inclined in some direction: to provide relief to a poor neighbor, to visit our parents, to courageously stand up to someone who is committing injustice in the workplace or in our community, or to deny ourselves so that we can provide something special for our children. However, setting up the target is only part of the task. We still must aim the arrow and ably shoot it. The end is *intended*, but will we truly reach it? For this, we need all of the *means* which can help us to achieve this goal. We must learn how to aim the bow, must choose the correct orientation for it, and then must actually pull the string. In other words, we need all of the various acts of prudence. This is what will help us to hit the target, and if we fail, we will miss it. In Greek, this failure is expressed by the word ἁμαρτία, *hamartia*, which is classically rendered in various biblical translations as "sin," missing the divine mark. Let us learn how to hit the target!

Prudence has three general kinds of actions. First, we must deliberate. Then, we must judge the best path for each of us to take. And finally, we must act. We must command ourselves to do the deed! Let us consider each of these actions in particular. Such reflection will be of use for all of us in our moral lives, for we will thereby emerge as better-informed people, now knowing a bit more concerning the day-to-day activity of choice which we perform in every single moral action.[108]

When we make a decision, we first must deliberate. Sometimes, in simple cases, little reflection is needed, and we quickly push on to the final decision. However, in tougher scenarios (and are they so rare?) we find that even our own memory is sometimes insufficient. We need to go to those who have an "eye to see" moral truths, most especially to virtuous people who have had much experience. We need to call our parents or elderly friends, who have seen the world and, hopefully, have lived a moral life. Everyone knows that Grandma or "Baba" often knows best! We need to be ready learners at their feet, yet also able to judge just how their advice does or does not apply *to ourselves*, for we are not they!

As Catholics, we are also aware of the great need to be informed by the treasury of the Church. And she gives us rich sources indeed: Sacred Scripture, the councils and catechisms, the declarations of the popes and bishops, the lives of the saints, their writings, and the writings of the Church's many theologians through the centuries. Moreover, in her monasteries and parishes, she has spiritual fathers and mothers who are like a living storehouse of all this wisdom. The practice of spiritual direction, in whatever form it may take, is merely a kind of "regularized counsel," ready to be deployed in our deliberation as we form our own consciences. The goal here is to find *our own path forward*, but given just how complex (infinitely so!) the world of morality is, it is always good to have a ready head and heart present to give us advice so that we too may deliberate concerning the path forward, weighing out all of these matters, pondering them in our own hearts.

But, ultimately, this decision is *ours*. It is not at all true that virtue and vice are going to look exactly the same in every person. A domineering "friend" may try to tell you that you *must* always do this or that. However, the Church is much gentler. She says: live virtuously, but your virtue will be unique, for God has a unique calling for you! The next chapter is dedicated to how this *does not* mean that all things are relative. There, we will see that the virtues are a firm bedrock for our moral life, and they are very demanding. Nonetheless, a great deal is left up to discernment.

A good example of this can be found in the practices of the Eastern Churches during the time of the Great Fast, called Lent in the Roman Church. For example, the Ruthenian Church has very basic norms for the Fast: no meat or meat products on all Wednesdays and Fridays; no meat, eggs, or dairy on the first day of the Fast as well as on Good Friday and Holy Saturday. In contrast with the stricter Orthodox practice, which would exclude all meat, eggs, dairy, wine, and even oil throughout the fast, this seems quite lenient. However, there is a tacit understanding that the faithful will have a spiritual director (or at least a ready pastor, along with each one's own personal experience) who will help them to establish an appropriate fasting regimen during the whole of the Great Fast. Moreover, the law itself makes it clear that a variety of medical reasons allow for the relaxation of these observances. Thus, prudence is needed! The "golden mean" must be chosen *for me*, in *my* current circumstances, given my character, my health, and so forth. This "mean" will not be a kind of "cool-hearted midpoint," like Goldilocks' porridge: just right, neither too hot, nor too cold. No, we know the Lord's own hatred of that kind of mediocrity: "Because you are lukewarm, and neither cold nor hot, I will spew you out of my mouth" (Revelation 3:16). Rather, we must find the mountaintop that stands between the two valleys of sin: excessive fasting and laxity in practice. A great labor must be expended here, and when the final judgment comes, it must be *my* judgment for *myself*.

Now, this does not mean that we cannot make moral judgments about others' actions. We can and must confront evils committed by others. Christ himself clearly said that we must go privately to our brothers and sisters to correct them when they are in the wrong (Mathew 18:15-20). However, he also cautioned us against judging small specks in others' eyes, for we have mighty oak beams in our own eyes (Matthew 7:1-5). And let us never forget his warnings about being too ready to pull up the weeds which are mixed all about with the wheat of the kingdom (Matthew 13:24-30). And St. Paul, a man who would not even judge himself (1 Corinthians 4:3-4), but who was also very well aware of the sinful nature of man, imbibed this Gospel maxim into his own teaching: "Therefore do not pronounce judgment before the time, before the Lord comes, who will bring to light the things now hidden in darkness and will disclose the purposes of the heart. Then every man will receive his commendation from God" (1 Corinthians 4:5; see Romans 2:6-8). This fraternal charity can indeed require us to go and confront our brothers and sisters when they are in sin, but when we do so, it must be solely for their own good. For our part, we should prefer being wronged rather than continuing the cycle of one personal lawsuit after another (1 Corinthians 6:1-8). Better to be reconciled with a brother than to come forward to the altar of the Lord with enmity separating us from our fellow brothers and sisters in Christ (Matthew 5:23-24).

In short, the ultimate judgment of prudence is utterly personal. It is *my golden mean* for achieving this or that virtue in *my current circumstances*. St. Thomas even assigned special virtues to this task of judgment, given how difficult it sometimes is to arrive at this ultimate sentence. Sometimes, there are cases that almost look like exceptions to the rule. They are not, of course, but we need a well-trained eye in order to see just what is morally required of *me, here and now*. Do we pray to God for continued growth in these virtues? Do we exercise them with great care? This is our calling!

Thus, the ultimate target has been set. I have taken up my bow, have settled on a choice, and my string is pulled back, with my eye fixed upon the target. All that remains is to let the arrow fly. I must command myself to do this action.

Here, too, we have a virtuous task ahead of us. We must not be dissuaded by our prejudices, petty desires, and weaknesses. We must not mistake evil for good along the way, and when someone else perhaps does something wrong right in front of us, we must try to find the right turn of phrase or deed in order to make good come forth from their evil. The ultimate goal of prudence is the accomplishment of this difficult task. Anyone who has needed to deal with a large family event knows just how difficult this can be. We must recognize the rights of others. However, we must likewise be flexible. Never ready to depart from good morals, we creatively push forward from person to person, trying to keep the peace and, let us hope, creating an atmosphere of familial love like the composer of an intricate musical piece. Even in comparison with Bach's greatest fugues, the work of such prudence is something great and profound!

Thus, we have the three great acts of prudence: deliberation (and all of the "counsel" we must undertake), judgment, and command. Sins against prudence will be discernible depending on how we fall short. We may refuse to listen to others, thus being insufficiently "docile." We may perhaps rely too much upon others, thus not actually taking up our own moral responsibility but, instead, merely parroting what others tell us to do without ourselves ever becoming mature. Perhaps we let ourselves forever deliberate without ever reaching a real decision, thus failing to fulfill our duties or even falling short in our own care for ourselves. We may worry more about worldly affairs and comfort than we do about the true moral requirements right before us in our moral life.

Who was more imprudent than the man spoken of by Christ as building a great barn to store his wealth so that he could finally enjoy it all at his life's end? What a man of business, what a man of abundance, how brimming a 401(k) and brokerage account! Now that all is safe and settled, he can finally live! And nonetheless, he is a fool, for he will die without having stored up true wealth in the eternal storehouses of God (Luke 12:16-21)! Or what of the rich man who refused even to allow Lazarus to have the scraps from his table (Luke 16:19-31)? These men are not only misers. They are also imprudent, for their "prudence" is nothing more than worldly craftiness! It perhaps looks like a virtue, but it surely is not. Just as the Pharisees were rightly condemned for their religious veneer, so too will this crafty man fall under the condemnation expressed in Christ's resounding words: "You are like whitewashed tombs, which outwardly appear beautiful, but within they are full of dead men's bones and all uncleanness" (Matthew 23:27). They attend to "business," but not to their true business. One is reminded of the line from Charles Dickens' *A Christmas Carol*, when old, dead Jacob Marley tells Scrooge that by focusing on work and money, he, Marley, had failed in his true life's business: "Mankind was my business. The common welfare was my business; charity, mercy, forbearance, and benevolence were all my business. The dealings of my trade were but a drop of water in the comprehensive ocean of my business!"[109] And let us never think that we are immune to worldly imaginings! The imprudent man slumbers within our breasts, and he has many awakenings. Let us pray that none of them bring us to the true shipwreck that is mortal sin.

The gospel message is one of true liberation: not mere economic liberation, nor social liberation, nor sexual liberation, but liberation from sin and, above all, *liberation for God*. Grace not only heals, it gives us this new freedom, our birthright as newborn children of God (Romans 8:21). This is true liberty, not libertinism. The Christian is free from all sinful attachment to the world, from all slavery to passing desires, so that through utter self-gift, we might live the divine life of friendship given to us through grace. We are free, yes. Free to make all of our acts contain a glimmer of the love of God: "For freedom Christ has set us free; stand fast therefore, and do not submit again to a yoke of slavery ... For you were called to freedom, brethren; only do not use your freedom as an opportunity for the flesh, but through love be servants of one another" (Galatians 5:1, 13).

And God does not leave us alone here! No, with open hands, the Christian can pray for the greatest of all help in times of need: "Lead me in your truth, and teach me, for you are the God of my salvation" (Psalm 25:5). The Father will not fail to give us the bread and fish we need to live our vocation (Matthew 7:9-10). And as Catholics, we know very well that we can turn for help to Mary, she who indeed deserves the title Our Lady of Good Counsel. In his final days among his disciples, Christ assured them, "I will not leave you desolate; I will come to you" (John 14:18). Now, while he reminded them in clear terms that if they, in fact, loved him they would keep his commandments (John 14:15), he immediately also assured them that their weakness would have a truly great auxiliary, the Holy Spirit, who would come with his counsel: "And I will ask the Father, and he will give you another Counselor, to be with you forever" (John 14:16). And when Christ foretold the fact that his disciples would be called before the Jewish authorities, he told them not to feel anxious, for his aid would be with them. These words hold true for us today: "The Holy Spirit will teach you in that very hour what you ought to say" (Luke 12:12).

Thus, the perfection of Christian prudence, like all things in the life of grace, hinges on prayer— that is, on an open hand turned upward to await gifts from heaven. Our conscience is guided, and our prudence perfected, by a light that comes from on high, the Spirit's gift of counsel. We merely need to think about so many holy but seemingly foolish saints to see how true this is. The saints make decisions which seem insane (and often despicable!) to worldly eyes, traveling the world for the sake of the gospel, giving up all things in poverty, trusting Christ and his Spirit with a radical, self-giving zeal. But all of this is merely an effect of one and the same vocation which we all share. How great is the perfection to which the child of God is called, and how great the aid given to all believers by so generous a Father! Catholics, whether of West or East, can pray and appreciate the wondrous words of the ancient Latin hymn *Veni Creator Spiritus*, "Come, Creator Spirit":

> Kindle our sense from above,
> and make our hearts o'erflow with love;
> with patience firm and virtue high
> the weakness of our flesh supply.[110]

May these words constantly be on our lips as we strive to form the virtue of prudence, to live with Christian conscience, and to await counsel from our all-wise God!

CHAPTER FIFTEEN

"Follow Your Conscience": Is Morality Relative?

"'All things are lawful,' but not all things are helpful. 'All things are lawful,' but not all things build up" (1 Corinthians 10:23). In this brief quote from St. Paul, we have the guiding principle for answering the question "Is morality relative?" In the first letter to the Corinthians, as well as in several others, St. Paul was concerned with pushing back against the Jewish legalism of his day. Thus, he wanted to be very clear: Christians should not get caught up in all of this; "all things are lawful." However, he was well aware of the opposite extreme which may tempt some Christians: "Anything goes!" Thus, St. Paul took care to balance the first phrase with a second: "but not all things are helpful ... not all things build up."

The temptation which St. Paul faced in his own day is not a mere relic of the Church's first century of existence. Throughout the history of Christianity, many have been tempted to think that Christian freedom implies absolute moral freedom. This represents a kind of perversion of the famous words of St. Augustine: "Love God and do what you will." Morality would be something for beginners, but when we truly love God, then, as spiritually mature people, we would leave behind our moral concerns. Such an error seems crazy, given all that we know from the gospel, but it is almost as ancient as the Church herself. In the fourth century, it was known as Messalianism. It is at least conceptually related to the famed Manichaeism from which St. Augustine himself converted. In the Middle Ages, it gave birth to Albigensianism, a movement which led to the founding of the Dominican Order, which was instituted in order to combat this error. And even in the Christian East, there was an influential instance of this error, known there by the name Bogomilism, a heresy which was at the center of the controversies surrounding the Orthodox mystical theologian St. Gregory Palamas.

Now, why mention all of this? I mention it because it helps to give some continuity to the world in which we find ourselves today. Old errors never seem to die, even if they take on new names. The human soul is not overly creative in finding mistakes to commit. Contemporary society speaks like a truncated St. Paul: "All things are lawful for me." Discussion ends there. The relativist whispers in our souls: "How could we say that morality is absolute? This seems too inflexible. Yes, yes, perhaps there are rules that are abstractly absolute, required *in general*. But, *in particular*, for each and every person? No, no! We cannot say what should be done. Are there any real moral *absolutes* in the *particular* situations encountered in day-to-day life? Is it not sometimes the case that our unique situation will require us to do something evil in order that some good may come out of it? It would seem that so long as we have a basic love for God, all will be well, with no danger for our souls. Does not perfect love cast out all fear (1 John 4:18)? Would this not include the fear of sin?" It would seem that as long as we have this one fundamental choice correct, "love God above all else," then all other potential courses of action would be permitted, depending on the situation.[111]

This relativist argument, though seductive, is sophistical. Yes, the love of God is primary. The theological virtue of charity is the "soul" of the virtues. Without this soul, the virtues lose their ultimate perfection, like a body which is well on the way to rotting like a corpse. To draw a metaphor from G.K. Chesterton, these "virtues" wander about quite dangerously without their unified, organic structure: "But [outside of Christianity] the virtues are let loose also; and the virtues wander more wildly, and the virtues do more terrible damage. The modern world is full of the old Christian virtues gone mad. The virtues have gone mad because they have been isolated from each other and are wandering alone."[112]

Nonetheless, "fundamental option ethics," which is so seemingly humane and yet also so speciously Christian, was condemned in clear terms by St. John Paul II in his encyclical letter *Veritatis Splendor*, On the Splendor of the Truth.[113] In that particular section of this lengthy text, he uses a selection from St. Paul's letter to the Galatians which makes a point similar to the words with which we opened this chapter. The relevant passage states, "For freedom Christ has set us free; stand fast therefore, and do not submit again to a yoke of slavery ... For you were called to freedom, brethren; only do not use your freedom as an opportunity for the flesh, but through love be servants of one another" (Galatians 5:1, 13). Christian freedom strives to make the virtues present in each and every one of our actions. Each of these actions has what moral theologians call "a moral object." We could call this the "essence" of what we do. Do we use our freedom in the service of putting moral goodness into every such essence, into every such object? Can we say of every action "That was an act of virtue"? Or do we allow ourselves to be enslaved to the passing desires we might have, giving in to fears, turning our view away from what would bring us true perfection—namely, virtuous love of God, self, and neighbor, not only in intention but, beyond this, in each and every one of our deeds?

In each and every one of our deeds ... This seems quite difficult and strenuous! In a little book, *On Conscience*, Pope Benedict XVI relates a story which has stuck with me through many years of reflection on this topic. When he was a young priest-professor, then-Fr. Ratzinger was approached by a fellow academic. This man was sensitive to the difficulties involved in the modern world as well as to the great demands made by Christianity. In view of these realities, he voiced a rather startling opinion: perhaps we should be grateful on behalf of all those who are unbelievers "in good faith"—that is, people who, through no fault of their own, do not believe in the gospel. Such people would be spared the burden of acting against the difficult injunctions of the morality of Jesus Christ. In their ignorance—which, as we noted in the previous chapter, theologians traditionally call "invincible" or "unconquerable" ignorance—they would not be guilty.[114]

The claim is at once astounding and yet, in a strange way, understandable. In fact, many years later, I ran across the same sort of thing in a footnote in the midst of translating a text by a different theologian, the great Dominican priest Fr. Réginald Garrigou-Lagrange.[115] He found himself faced with a slightly different, though ultimately similar, claim: when the world becomes so immoral that it is difficult to hand on Christian faith and morals, it would seem that people are more like unaware children than guilty parties. We might translate this claim into the language of our own days: Given how religion is not a central affair in popular culture, how prevalent pornography and sexual license are in entertainment, how the economy requires us to be somewhat selfish so that we and our children can "get ahead," etc. … can we really expect people brought up in this environment to know what the Catholic Faith requires, believing and practicing it in all of its strenuous details? This seems like too great a demand for most people, who are neither scholars nor priests nor, indeed, moral heroes! We all know the difficulties of the "rat race" of work and family life. Let us be merciful!

Both Ratzinger and Garrigou-Lagrange rose up in opposition to such claims, and so should we. How perverse it would be to say that ignorance is better than knowledge! In what other domain would we ever say so foolish a thing? We are made to know, and here we are given the suggestion that the person who is ignorant of morality is in the better position. We are told that men would be better off as children who have not yet achieved the "age of reason." Only one conclusion can be drawn, faced with such foolish claims: the very notion of morality has gone totally off its rails. Here, the law is viewed as a harsh mistress that binds our freedom, not a guide that enables us to forge onward by making the law of love our own perfection, our own fulfillment. Alas, we must drive out this demon!

Now, let us be clear: sin and moral error are dangerous and hidden things. They are much like a child who runs out in front of a bus coming down the road. Very often, they have some idea of what they are doing. And yet, the consequences will be fatal when the bus arrives! Something similar occurs in our moral life when we misinform our conscience. Obviously, as adults, we are far more likely to be guilty of the fault of ignoring moral good sense. In any case, when we turn away our sight from the danger of sin, we begin to stumble out toward the road. The direction is set, even if we convince ourselves otherwise. Moral truths remain inflexible. The basic claim of justice remains forever true, in all places and at all times: debts must be repaid within the limits set by their terms and right reason. Even if it is abstract, it is a kind of signpost pointing in the direction of justice, to which the virtue of prudence must then guide us onward.

This guidance, though, is no small affair. Here we have the whole difficult problem of "cases of conscience." In the sixteenth century, a great debate arose in Catholic theology, occasioned by the work of Fr. Bartolomé de

Medina (1528–1580). For centuries following upon this, well into the early twentieth century, the question of conscience became central to Catholic discussions, and many moral theologians asked these questions: Just how sure must our conscience be? Can I choose an action which may only *probably* be right? What is meant by this characteristic, "probability"? These were the great debates over "probabilism." Yes, that was the name of the movement! And these debates raged among the various religious orders, with Rome needing to condemn extreme errors, whether they be guilty of laxity or harshness. The discussion reached a fevered pitch, and thankfully some peace was reached when St. Alphonsus Liguori (1696–1787) helped to find a middle path through all the various solutions offered. For bringing holy peace to this turmoil, he rightly earned the title "patron of moral theologians."

Some have argued that, for the most part, this way of looking at things was based on a fundamental error in perspective. The "probabilist perspective" asks a question which is far too mechanical and algebraic: which is more probably right, what are the opinions on either side of this moral equation?[116] When teaching moral theology, I have found this critique to have some wisdom. Thus, I explain the formation of conscience in a slightly different way, drawing on sources from the followers of St. Thomas Aquinas, sources which are reflected in the *Catechism* (see CCC 1749–1761).

The most important aspect of every particular moral action is its *object*, the particular act that you choose to do. This *object* will have many *circumstances*, many *nonessential* elements. Now, merely because they are nonessential, this does not mean that they are completely unimportant. No, they affect an action's moral quality. If we consider something like *the act of giving a particular amount of money to a charity*, the question of *who* gives alms is not unimportant. If they are given by someone who is very wealthy, this may well mean, all things being equal, that this act is less good than that which is done by someone with less money but an equal desire to do good for this legitimate charity. The act itself remains the same. In the technical jargon, both of their acts have the same *object*. However, the *circumstances* differ, morally affecting the action by making it more or less good to the degree that these circumstances bear witness to a greater impulse on behalf of the good deed being done.

The same dynamic plays out if we consider the case of evil actions. Let us take a clear case such as murder. Even public law recognizes a kind of gradation among kinds of murder, assigning different degrees depending on the given circumstances of the action. Thus, when a person carefully premeditates the deed, this is assigned the worst degree of murder. When a person uses excessive force without premeditation, killing a person while trying to significantly harm him or her without killing, this person is perhaps guilty of second-degree murder. If further factors come into play, such as the presence of great passion, the use of a vehicle in a semi-faccidental killing, and so forth, then the accusation of murder is so diminished that most American locales prefer to call such acts "manslaughter." For our purpose, merely observe the fact that in all of these cases, the basic *object* remains the same: murder. However, the gradation is established by the given *circumstances* involved. They do not change the act's essential character, "the unjust taking of another person's life," though they can attenuate it greatly, especially as we approach cases of "involuntary manslaughter."

The deepest source of the object, however, is one's *intention*. This point is not always appreciated, but we must understand it aright. Recall what was said in the last chapter: the work of prudence always presupposes the intention of a virtuous end. We must have a target before we can aim at it. The target is the *intention*, and through prudence we aim to "hit" the *object*, the bullseye along with all of its *circumstances*.

In truly upright cases, we choose an *object* which is *virtuous*. The *intention* thus passes directly over into the *object* and gives it its moral character. Thus, if we look to *justly support our family*, we might choose to work as a carpenter or as a mathematics teacher. These activities are *morally indifferent* in themselves. However, in *our* particular circumstances, in view of prudence, along with all of its many considerations, they can become acts of *familial justice*. We look at the person who is working hard to support his or her family and say not merely, "He's teaching mathematics," but even more profoundly, "He is being a good husband and father."

But, let us not think that good intentions justify evil actions. Here, let's merely adjust the example we were already considering. Someone might choose to work in a job with exceedingly long hours, not allowing much time to be at home with his or her spouse and children. If this family does not need the extra pay that comes from this but, instead, the person is merely looking to achieve ever-increasing material comfort, it is quite arguable that we have here an example of an action which is, in fact, wrong—*morally evil*. Here, the desire to support one's family falls into excess, out of line with virtue. When someone begins down this path, he or she doubtlessly begins with good intentions: college must be paid for, retirement must be considered, possible illness must be taken into account, there are charities to which money could be given, and so forth. And yet, when the person aims for this *intention*, his or her hand slips on the bow. The target is missed, and the act no longer is *an act of familial justice*. Its very *object* is a sin. Somewhere off to the right of the target, there is another spot that has been hit: the vice of *familial injustice*. Perhaps the action is less bad, given the circumstantial fact that the person still half intends to do good. But the fact remains: the *object* is evil. And to the degree that this habit grows, one will gradually form a vice, increasingly setting the evil target up as though it were a good one. Thus, we have a fulfillment of the old maxim, "*Qualis unusquisque est, talis finis videtur ei.* The end to be achieved will appear differently to various people, depending on their respective characters." But if that character is evil, then we have the worst of all deceptions: "Woe to those who call evil good and good evil, who put darkness for light and light for darkness, who put bitter for sweet and sweet for bitter" (Isaiah 5:20).

The Catholic teaching on moral actions acknowledges all the possible truth that could be found in other systems of morality.[117] It is based upon the fundamental insights of Scripture concerning moral goodness and evil, articulated with tools drawn from the philosopher Aristotle, developed through the Middle Ages, and refined throughout the modern era. In this teaching, both *moral absolutes* and *personal uniqueness* are upheld. The term "Catholic" means "universal" or "all-embracing." Here, as in so many domains, the Church's solution is not "either / or" but, instead, is "both / and." She teaches that morality has a steady and rock-solid foundation: all of the moral and theological virtues, a bedrock which must be present not merely in each of our intentions but also in each of our actions. These virtues are the many-colored rays which radiate out from the perfection placed at the center of our hearts through the gift of grace. They are the many-hued reflections of the face of Christ, the rock upon whom the whole moral life must be built (see Matthew 7:24-27). However, the Church also speaks about the great and subtle virtue which directs this moral conquest, prudence, the imperious director of what Fr. Ambroise Gardeil termed "Our Personal, Supernatural Self-Government."[118] We must find a way to put these virtues *into all the details and circumstances of our lives*. Our virtuous intentions must pass over into *upright moral objects*.

In the previous chapter, I briefly used the analogy of a composer writing a musical piece as a way to illustrate the virtue of prudence. This image can help us here again too. While it is true that musical tastes and styles vary greatly, some of the greatest pieces of music are those which build on the rules of the craft of composition, pushing them to their extreme. Very often, when musical shows and magazines hold surveys and write articles considering who is the greatest musical composer of all time, they conclude in a way that gives my own preferences great pleasure: J. S. Bach was the greatest of all composers. I think this is very appropriate, for Bach drew into himself a whole tradition of music, combining the various threads of the renaissance and baroque eras with the profound simplicity of his Lutheran piety. Listen to one of his chorales or preludes, and you will see an example of this fact. All of the technical precision of his era, which he imbibed by copying many manuscripts of music written by others, is there combined with the simple songs sung in Lutheran services throughout his native German-speaking lands. At once, the great composer incorporates the past and the present, the simple and the profound, like an utterly free musician who is made free because he has so internalized the rock-hard elements from all of these traditions. What an excellent metaphor for our supernatural, personal self-government!

The moral conquest undertaken by our prudent consciences is a true composition by freedom. To use a different metaphor, here in the Christian life we have the solid foundation of Christ, like a hard diamond whose light radiates throughout the moral virtues, which are brought into existence in each and every particular action. To take up our music metaphor again: weaving together a host of circumstances, we create a moral fugue for the Lord, never departing from moral goods, while also never allowing ourselves to be conformed to our former ignorance but, rather, striving to be holy in all things (see 1 Peter 1:15-16). Here, we have the true meaning of the freedom spoken of by St. Paul: "'All things are lawful for me,' but not all things are helpful. 'All things are lawful for me,' but I will not be enslaved by anything" (1 Corinthians 6:12).

JUSTICE

All the various virtues related to justice perfect our will, enabling us to recognize the rights of other people and institutions. In every area where we find a question of *what is owed*, some kind of justice will be involved. In this section, we will see that many surprising things are involved in this particular domain of morality: religion, our duties toward parents, parents' duties toward children, the duty to be generous, the duties involved in politics, and many other such duties! The domain of justice is quite broad, for it involves all the various social bonds that link people together. For this reason, this will be the longest of all our sections. We will begin, however, with something which must color all of the believer's justice: mercy.

CHAPTER SIXTEEN

Mercy Triumphs over Judgment

"The work of divine justice always presupposes the work of mercy. Indeed, God's Justice is founded upon His Mercy."[119] No Christian account of the virtue of justice could be true to its object if it did not begin with this *central* principle. Justice presupposes that things exist and have their particular natures. We owe something to someone because of who that person is or is not, because of the contracts we have established with him or her, and so forth. Most especially, we owe a debt to other people because they are persons. They have rights merely because of *what they are at their most fundamental level*. Now, they must exist as persons before anything else is owed to them. This is very clear in the case of children or parents. We owe a debt of justice to our children (namely, to rear them and love them as parents) and to our own parents (because they brought us into existence and nurtured this life in us). But in order for all of this to be the case, they must *exist*, and can we really act as though we were the source of our own existence, as though existence were something ho-hum that we could take for granted? No indeed! Our very existence is a gift. Each and every one of us stands here today even though *we did not need to*!

In this fact, we glimpse a "secret" name of God, a name which is hidden in one of his most well-known titles: Creator. He is indeed the Creator of all things, visible and invisible. He is their source and also their goal. All things come from God, and through the deep love which animates all things, they strive in some way to return to him. Read the Canticle of the Three Young Men in Daniel, and you will see this praise spring forth from all of creation: "Bless the Lord, all [you] works of the Lord, sing praise to him and highly exalt him for ever. Bless the Lord, you heavens ... sun and moon ... rain and dew ... mountains and hills ... all things that grow on the earth ... all birds of the air ... you sons of men ...” and so forth (Daniel 3:29-68). Throughout the Church, both East and West, these words are echoed in the Liturgy of the Hours every week on Sundays and on feast days. They are words that mysteriously ring forth from the whole universe in praise of the Creator for the primordial gift, something freely given: existence. When we say that God created “ex nihilo,” *from nothing*, let us not misunderstand the word “nothing.” Nothing isn’t *something*. He didn’t create all things “from” some kind of preexisting “nothingness-glop.” Rather, with nothing at all presupposed, with nothing whatsoever at hand, he called creation into existence, and in his providence he continually guides it until the end of time.

In short, he bestowed the gift of existence *out of pure largesse*. He did not need creation. God does not *need* you in order that he might be fulfilled. His life is pure life, and his joy is a joy that is eternal, rejoicing in the purest of all goods: God himself. And yet, for all of this, God is not cold. He is not a kind of isolated philosopher’s deity, contemplating himself and thinking, “Wow, I’m so great! I’ll keep watching myself like an eternal football game!” No! Out of a pure desire to share his own goodness, he created the universe and, in the case of spiritual beings, extended to them the greatest of all gifts, the gift of supernatural grace. He wished that his own joy might also be ours, and he pressed on so far as to come in person in order to reveal this fact to us: “These things I have spoken to you, that my joy may be in you, and that your joy may be full” (John 15:11).

Do we realize that there is this great gift at the heart of what we are? We did not *need* to exist, yet here we are. The thought should be overwhelming. It should make our heads spin with joy. Down to the most foundational fibers of our souls, the words of St. Paul hold true: “What have you that you did not receive? If then you received it, why do you boast as if it were not a gift?” (1 Corinthians 4:7). In fact, even our actions depend totally upon God: “God is at work in you, both to will and to work for his good pleasure” (Philippians 2:13). Indeed, Christ himself says, “Apart from me you can do nothing” (John 15:5).

The English author G.K. Chesterton was a man of great joy, aware of the giftedness of all things. He had a light heart, along with a keen and childlike awareness of the gift of creation. Very often in his writing this theme comes up, with his pen communicating his vibrant awareness of the overwhelming joy that we should feel merely because we exist. Our souls are marked by this fact, and if we silently reflect on ourselves, we will be startled awake by a shocking but wondrous truth: our existence is a gift. What a source of true joy! As Chesterton remarked so well in his autobiography:

> At the back of our brains, so to speak, there was a forgotten blaze or burst of astonishment at our own existence. The object of the artistic and spiritual life was to dig for this submerged sunrise of wonder; *so that a man sitting in a chair might suddenly understand that he was actually alive, and be happy.*[120]

Faced with this great fact, there is only one possible response: gratitude. "Rejoice always, pray constantly, *give thanks in all circumstances*; for this is the will of God in Christ Jesus for you" (1 Thessalonians 5:16-18, emphasis added). This is not something that makes us slaves in the negative sense. We do not become servile by recognizing what is truest about us. In fact, gratitude is something we only offer to someone who is greater than we are, someone who has given us something that we did not have on our own. We issue commands to those who are beneath us in the chain of command. Our attitude toward those who are above us is different: we praise them for their particular greatness, we ask them to help us as is appropriate, and we offer them words of gratitude for the kindness which has spilled down over us.[121] Human reason finds its fulfillment here, and our hearts find their greatest joy. Only humans can formulate prayers, *beseeching* and *praying* for things above their own abilities, and only those who can *recognize* gifts have the wonderful ability to express that gift's goodness in joy-filled words of gratitude. To quote Chesterton one more time: "Thanks are the highest form of thought; and ... gratitude is happiness double[d] by wonder."[122]

All of this is hidden in the name "Creator," which we often use to describe God almost as though he were fashioning the world out of dough. He is much more than a careful baker making up a great loaf of bread. He is the ever-bountiful God who gives with utterly free largesse. He bestows gifts where *nothing is owed*. Before there ever is justice, there is bounty, there is free gift, and therefore, in a way, there is a kind of "mercy," the giving of the gift to the undeserving nothingness from which all things are called into existence! Left to our own devices, we are a mere breath:

"Men of low estate are but a breath, men of high estate are a delusion; in the balances they go up; they are together lighter than a breath" (Psalm 62:9); "Surely man goes about as a shadow!" (Psalm 39:6). The English historian-monk and saint the Venerable Bede recalled a tale told by an Anglo-Saxon king. This ancient English ruler compared human life to the flight of a sparrow through a large hall: it flies in from the dark winter and back out into the dark and cold night.[123] Yet, here we are. We are, in fact, *in the hall*, and we know, unlike the poor little bird, that this hall is, in fact, through grace, the beginning of the great wedding feast of eternity if only we remain free from sin!

Now, when our first parents lost this grace, God nonetheless set to work to restore to all people the bounty already given. As we already noted in an earlier chapter, the work of salvation launched forth from the moment of the Fall, when the Savior's coming was prophesied in the promise spoken to Eve, who was told that her offspring would crush the head of the snake. And the whole of the Old Testament is a kind of tale of God's merciful designs, his utter bounty to his people. We tend to think of the Old Testament as the story of the vengeful and angry God. Yet so many texts—from the first books of the Bible through the history texts, the Prophets, and the wisdom texts—all bear witness to the keen sense that God is forever seeking out man, no matter how unfaithful he might be. Thus, the great twentieth-century Jewish author Abraham Heschel wrote a text whose title encapsulates the whole of Judaism (and, ultimately and most truly, Christianity) in one poignant phrase: *God in Search of Man*.[124]

All of this was fulfilled when the New Lawgiver came, though as someone who gives more than just a new external law. He is the new law *in person*: the incarnate Christ, the *gift* of the second Person of the Blessed Trinity. He is mercy *incarnate*, the greatest act of giving and of salvation, drawing us from the pits of sin into which we had plunged ourselves (and into which we, alas, continue to plunge ourselves). Indeed, in the Sermon on the Mount, he proclaims to us a perfection which calls for the greatest of mercy. We have already reflected upon the words of Christ calling us to perfection: "You, therefore, must be perfect, as your heavenly Father is perfect" (Matthew 5:48). But let us not take this to mean, "Click your tongue like a perfectionist," nor, to steal a phrase from American vice-presidential history, "You, therefore, must be a nattering nabob of negativism." No, indeed. The scriptural context tells us a different story.

The old law proclaimed, "An eye for an eye and a tooth for a tooth" (Matthew 5:38; Leviticus 24:20). This injunction actually was not as bloodthirsty as many think it was. The human temptation is quite harsher than this, forever risking an attitude that says, "You dishonored me and my family by hurting my eye. I will kill you and your family," devolving into the violence of Don Corleone. The Old Testament injunction is merciful by limiting a devastating escalation of merely human "justice" which, through lack of mercy, is in fact injustice.

Nonetheless, Christ comes with a new message:

> But I say to you, Do not resist one who is evil. But if any one strikes you on the right cheek, turn to him the other also; and if any one would sue you and take your coat, let him have your cloak as well; and if any one forces you to go one mile, go with him two miles. Give to him who begs from you, and do not refuse him who would borrow from you. (Matthew 5:39-42)

It is as though he had said: "Never stop your engagement with your enemies, never stop trying to win the souls of those who would harm you. If it takes two thousand steps in order to help them, expend four thousand in order to guarantee success! Repay debts beyond the count of 'strict' justice, for, in the end, you are all debtors. You all have been granted your life at a great cost. Who are you to mistreat your fellow servants?" (See Matthew 18:21-35.) Yes, indeed, there is no limit to the amount of mercy we must show, forgiving not merely seven times but "seventy times seven" (Matthew 18:22).

Now, the harsh keepers of justice may well now step forth to make their proclamation: "We cannot be so indulgent! We cannot overlook the injustices of the world." But let us note so many of Christ's examples. He does not say, "Abandon those who are overlooked and mistreated, for you must be merciful to their persecutors. Do not worry about those who take the spoils while failing even to look after those who are closest to them." This is far from Christ's sentiment and utterly distant from his preaching! He gives to his followers a stiff requirement, the demands of the Cross: suffer with those who hate you, for in this way alone will you be as perfect as God, who himself became incarnate, suffered, died, and rose again for mankind, though mankind spurns his love countless times each day! The brief formula is in fact quite readily known and easily summarized: deny yourself and take up your cross every day and follow Christ (Matthew 16:24; Mark 8:34; Luke 9:23), for no disciple is above his master (Matthew 10:24).

Our God has many enemies who he wishes would be his friends! *We* make ourselves God's enemies. *He* continually comes to us with grace, for he "desires all men to be saved and to come to the knowledge of the truth" (1 Timothy 2:4). Although the world is filled with evils, and while God's heart is indeed moved to sorrow for his creation, nonetheless he does not destroy the work of his hands. Even if his merciful justice must let loose the floods of water, he wishes all were like the godly man Noah (Genesis 6–9; Hebrews 11:7), to whom we can apply the words of the psalmist: "Therefore let every one who is godly offer prayer to you; at a time of distress, in the rush of great waters, they shall not reach him" (Psalm 32:6).

How merciful a figure Christ cuts! He eats with sinners and tax collectors, coming to save them, not the self-deceived "righteous" (Matthew 9:10-13). He heals crowds who come for healing, likewise feeding them with physical and spiritual food (Matthew 15:30 and following). He is the shepherd who goes after his one lost sheep even if it means leaving the other ninety-nine behind (Matthew 18:12-14). He pays full wages to the first and to the last who labor in his vineyard (Matthew 20:1-16). When he critiques the Pharisees' shortcomings, he does not overturn religious observance but, rather, makes clear that they had "neglected the weightier matters of the law, justice and mercy and faith" (Matthew 23:23). The picture he paints shows a justice which is tightly intertwined with mercy. He calls the poor to the kingdom (Luke 14:7-24), is like the father of the Prodigal Son (Luke 15:11-32), and washes the very feet of those who would soon cover them with the dust of desertion as he prepares to be put to death (John 13:1 and following). Many more passages could be cited, but this suffices to make the point: he cuts a merciful figure, this God of ours!

And his figure is our figure, his perfection our perfection. "But I say to you, Love your enemies and pray for those who persecute you, *so that you may be sons of your Father who is in heaven*; for he makes his sun rise on the evil and on the good, and sends rain on the just and on the unjust" (Matthew 5:44-45, emphasis added). Let these words ring in our ears: "So that you may be sons of your Father who is in heaven." Be merciful if you wish to be like him, for the great secret of all of his relations with creation is the fact that he is merciful and superabundant, to the point of the Incarnation, Cross, and Resurrection. If you merely repay tit for tat, what is divine in that? If you always are so careful to worry about "getting what is owed to you" and "doing the minimum," how is that something impressive? No, Christ draws a conclusion which is very important. At the end of the texts we have just now been discussing, he speaks words which are cited so often but which are perhaps not well enough understood in our homilies and in our own hearts: "You, *therefore*, must be perfect, as your heavenly Father is perfect" (Matthew 5:48, emphasis added). "Therefore": it is a kind of conclusion! Let your mercy abound! Then, you will be worthy of your new birth. Then, and only then, will you be true sons of the Father. Only then will you truly live the life of Christ-conforming grace given to you, for only then will you fit the description of him whose entire existence is tied up in the great merciful mission of redemption.

In short, no Christian account of justice can be full and complete without this central and guiding truth: *if justice is to be truly divine—and our life is a divine life—then it must be second to mercy*. This mercy is a kind of radiation of the theological virtue of charity over the whole of our relations with others. Because we are filled with the very love of God, we then must diffuse this love to others. We must work to "Christify" them through mercy, by taking a page out of the great divine story, which shows us the great truth that must forever temper and elevate our relationships, a truth with which we opened this chapter: "The work of divine justice always presupposes the work of mercy. Indeed, God's Justice is founded upon His Mercy."

CHAPTER SEVENTEEN

Justice: Blind and Cold or Warm and Humane?

"He has showed you, O man, what is good; and what does the LORD require of you but to do justice, and to love kindness [or, mercy], and to walk humbly with your God?" (Micah 6:8). Through the centuries, the Old Testament prophets spoke out with increasing clarity: the renewal God wishes for is of the whole person, especially of the heart. Such was the point of the declaration by Ezekiel proclaiming to the people that God would give them the new heart they needed (Ezekiel 18:31, 36:26). But can the heart be renewed without society being thereby renewed as well? "By this all men will know that you are my disciples, if you have love for one another" (John 13:35). The tree is known by its fruits (Luke 6:43-45), and the heart renewed by grace spills out in good deeds; indeed, it even marks our countenance: "A man is known by his appearance, and a sensible man is known by his face, when you meet him" (Sirach 19:29). Because of the new order in the soul, new relations arise among people and institutions, and this domain of interpersonal relations is the vast sphere of life shaped by the virtue of justice.

Justice seems like such a harsh word. We imagine the statue of Lady Justice, holding her scales in hand with her eyes covered, pictorially declaring the message that the fair measure must be meted out without paying any attention to the parties involved. Law treats all people equally. There are no distinctions between people. It is as though one were to say, on the level of social life, "Let your yes be your yes and your no be your no, always and everywhere." Justice seems not so much concerned with what is interpersonal as with what is *impersonal*. In any case, this is what many think about these matters!

We can begin to rehabilitate the notion of justice by considering what is meant by saying that it binds us to each other by the repayment of what is *due*, what is *owed* to others. There are many ways that things are owed, not all of which are a mere question of strict contractual repayment. Just repayment is not merely tit for tat, nor are all debts things that we freely will to take on by way of black-and-white contract. The virtuous response to the reception of a gift blasts apart the cold idea of justice as a kind of strict agreement: "I *owe* you a *debt* of gratitude." Common language conceals great wisdom. Here it contains a glimmer of the broad vistas envisioned in the truly Catholic account of the virtue of justice. In this land of many different biomes, there are the lofty heights of religious practice and the foothills of recognizing our parents and acknowledging the great gift of the stable political order in which we live. There are plains filled with the flowers of the debts of gratitude and forests full of the majestic trees of reverence, whereby we publicly recognize truly great people, whose virtue and skill must be recognized *as a matter of justice*. A cold virtue of contracts? This is not the story of the virtue of justice, along with its many sibling virtues! All of these various forms of justice are concerned with recognizing what is owed to other persons, institutions, or even other things (such as animals and the environment). These are the bonds that hold us together in love and friendship, and they will be the subject of a number of chapters to come.

Kneeling in confession, someone says to the priest, "Father, I was uncharitable to my relatives at a recent gathering. I should have been friendlier, but they're just so difficult to deal with!" A moment of silence follows, filling the penitent with dread. He thinks, "Oh no, what is he going to say? Am I going to get a lecture?" Well, a lecture is coming, but not an upbraiding regarding sins against charity! The priest finally responds, "Actually, that is the sin of being quarrelsome, a sin against virtuous friendliness. Your problem is that you were unjust, not that you were uncharitable!"

This comment is quite shocking in comparison with our customary use of language. So often, many faults of unkindness, ingratitude, and selfishness are all blanketed with the word "uncharitable." Now, as we saw in an earlier chapter, there is indeed a sense in which the virtue of charity applies quite directly to our brothers and sisters. It is called "fraternal charity," and it requisitions all of the divine energies of grace so as to make the divine love itself settle down upon others. It is an imperious virtue, the divine love itself, inspiring self-sacrifice as described in the gospel. It is a sharing in the divine love, by which we commune with our brothers and sisters *in the very love of God*. Strictly speaking, this is not a question of debt. It is a question of wholly free and spontaneous largesse, so that we may be bound together with one and the same love, the love of charity, sharing together in the single divine friendship given to us through the new birth of grace. Recall the story of St. Benedict and St. Scholastica recounted in our earlier chapter on the theological virtue of charity. There, we saw a free and spontaneous sharing in divine gifts, and this is the essence of fraternal charity, not the repaying of a debt.

Nonetheless, love needs its instruments, including the many virtues of the moral life. One such instrument is the repaying of what is, strictly speaking, owed to others, and however surprising it might sound, we *owe* others respect and kindness precisely because they are persons. Let us not, therefore, confuse charity and justice. Charity is the divine love itself, calling for a supernatural, "Godlike" self-gift for the sake of our brethren and spilling over in mercy, along with all the acts of divine friendship that bind us together in God through grace. But where there is a debt to be repaid, we there have a form of justice. We must make distinctions between various virtues even though, in the end, all of them are woven together in our activity.[125]

The rich nature of the virtue of justice is reflected quantitatively if we look at St. Thomas Aquinas' *Summa Theologica*.[126] With all of his careful analysis, drawing together many strands of tradition, he dedicates sixty-six questions to this virtue! This quantity of topics is greater than what we find in any other treatise in his very lengthy theological work. Now is this because he is worried about "keeping the rules," legalistically listing all the ways we can transgress the law? No indeed! He is sensitive to the fact that we have many debts—owed to each other, to the communities in which we live, and above all to God. All of these must be addressed if we are going to lay out the fertile and rich domain of justice.

Yes, St. Thomas is aware of "tit for tat" justice, by which we pay back clear debts to each other. However, he also points out at length the many other forms of justice which exist as well. Some of these debts are to our political community and society, where we owe allegiance to the common good expressed in just laws. Likewise, society must be just to its members, not playing favorites but, rather, recognizing how we should distribute public recognition, and even material goods, to the members of society. To each other, we owe the debt of being truthful, grateful, friendly, and generous. Indeed, to people who are truly excellent, we owe signs of honor and reverence. We were never consulted in choosing our parents, but we owe a special debt to them too, one which we cannot truly repay. Yet, as a matter of strict justice, we should do what we can. The same is true of our relationship to our nation, to which we owe countless benefits no matter how frustrated we may at times be with its limitations and imperfect character. And above all, giving stability to this whole network of justice, we owe God the debt of our recognition and devotion. In fact, we even owe him our trust, as we pray to him, turning our minds toward him in order to ask for goods which exceed our own powers. This is the virtue of religion, the soaring mountain peak in the domain of justice.

Thus, we can see the risk of deception involved in the classic image of Lady Justice. Yes, in the administration of written law, Aristotle's maxim seems to hold true: "The law is reason unaffected by desire."[127] However, even in Aristotle's own work, he is very clear that there is something almost superhuman and quasi-divine about this high bar. The pettiness of rulers and magistrates must be kept in check, so the letter of the law must rule. Yet, what is really needed is a virtuous ruler's discerning eye. A book of medicine may be necessary if someone suspects that his or her doctor is suggesting treatment merely for the sake of getting rich. However, it would be even better for such a person to call in true and competent doctors who are not swayed by their own personal gain. Medicine is not an exact science, for it requires the touch of someone who has much experience, not merely book knowledge. The same is true of the law, for even in public life, we have a confirmation of St. Paul's words: "The written code kills, but the Spirit gives life" (2 Corinthians 3:6). A virtuous judgment is needed, indeed a unique virtue, επιείκεια, *epieikeia*, which is sometimes translated as "equity" or "fairness," though it could also be understood more broadly as "indulgence" or "leniency." One needs to have a ready eye to see what the legislator meant, for human circumstances are countless in number. An "exception" to a law is, in fact, a way of respecting the law itself—but such exceptions must actually be called for and not merely be random favors bestowed by lawmakers. Virtue is needed here too!

The topic of justice could take up an entire book. It would present us with an image of the human soul spread throughout the world, with persons and institutions connected to each other by bonds which are at once visible and invisible. It is everywhere: in truthful actions, in families wherein the generations are tied together as children recognize their parents and parents form and rear their children, in our political associations, in generous actions by which we use our wealth in a truly just way, and even in the worship we give to God, to whom we owe our entire existence and our new birth in grace.

Yes, indeed, the virtue of religion is an example of *justice*, not solely "piety" in the sense of "religious sentiment." When questioned about taxes, Christ responded with the well-known words "Render therefore to Caesar the things that are Caesar's, and to God the things that are God's" (Matthew 22:21). Certainly, the second half of this expression includes the whole of the Christian life, all of the virtues. Nonetheless, we may, at least in part, read these words as meaning "Repay unto God what is owed to God." The very first debt of justice which we owe is a debt of devotion, recognition, gratitude, and prayer to God. This response is "our side" of the relation that we have to his merciful and generous action. We see here a confirmation of what we discussed in the previous chapter. Merciful bounty pours forth the gifts of existence and of grace. We respond, yes, out of love, but also out of a true kind of justice, given that we owe all things to God. Then the whole order of justicc spreads throughout the world and will flow from this primordial relationship of gift and recognition. And where it is not recognized, the order of things is shaken. In the words of Hippolyte Taine, who was no believer himself, in those eras when society wished to do away with Christianity, "it became an evil and cut-throat place."[128] This situation was, of course, seen quite well by St. Paul: "Since they did not see fit to acknowledge God, God gave them up to a base mind and to improper conduct" (Romans 1:28).

Christ reassured his followers that God provides for all our needs, just as he provides for the birds of the air and the flowers of the field: "Seek first his kingdom and his righteousness" or, as some versions render this, "his justice," "and all these things shall be yours as well" (Matthew 6:33). These words find fulfillment in many ways, one of which is the way that the entire order of justice cascades downward from our own recognition and attempt to repay the infinite debt we owe our Creator. It is to this topic that we will now turn in the next chapter.

CHAPTER EIGHTEEN

Religion: What Do You Owe God?

What is the greatest virtue? Charity. What is the greatest *moral* virtue? Well, in a sense, it is prudence, for every action must be prudent. We need its light to guide our way along the pathways of morality. As regards the *means* for living the moral life, the virtue of prudence is the servant helping us to forge forward. However, in relation to the *ends* which should inspire our morality, the virtue of religion is the greatest of the moral virtues.

Like everything in the life of grace, the virtue of religion is subordinate to the theological virtues. Faith, hope, and charity are the great supernatural sources of our life as children of God. Recall once more a capital truth in Catholic moral theology: the theological virtues are uniquely divine, directly "tuning" us to the knowledge and love of God. They are like a transplant of the divine life into our souls. Or, to put it more along the lines of Christ's own words, by the theological virtues we are grafted onto the divine life: "I am the vine, you are the branches" (John 15:5). Through them, we really and truly participate in God's life. We must continually remind ourselves of this principle if we are to understand the Church's moral teaching.[129]

By contrast, the moral virtues perfect *us*; they help to put *us* in line with the lofty divine life of grace. Through justice, our wills are turned away from egoism and made ready to recognize the rights of others. Through courage, our fears and anger are put in line so that they might be instruments of virtuous living. And through temperance, we are no longer slaves to our passions but, rather, use our passions as instruments for the good, the divine good. All of these virtues help to renew *us*. They make the divine life of grace permeate into the deepest corners of our being, into the most bodily, animal parts of who we are. The divine life radiates even there:

"Do not yield your members to sin as instruments of wickedness, but yield yourselves to God as men who have been brought from death to life, and your members to God as instruments of righteousness" (Romans 6:13). The whole of our being can shine forth the divine life, each part with its own unique hues.

Now, among these virtues, religion plays a unique role. As created beings, we must be ready to recognize that we are not the source of our own existence. And, as reborn children of God, we must be ready to recognize the gift of grace which has given us the divine life. Through the theological virtues, we contemplate like God (through faith), we rely upon God the Savior (through hope), and we love with God's own heart (through charity). Through the virtue of religion, however, our wills are made ready to perform acts of interior devotion and prayer, along with exterior sacrifice and praise. This distinction is very subtle, but it is important: through charity, we quite literally love with God's own love; through the virtue of religion, we have a character that is ready to give homage to God. An analogy could be drawn to Christ: as God, he owes no religious duty to the Father, but precisely as incarnate, he is "a merciful and faithful high priest in the service of God" (Hebrews 2:17), "the apostle and high priest of our confession" (Hebrews 3:1).

No doubt, this distinction is surprising, but it is very important. We must forever remember that the gift we are given in grace and charity is the divine friendship: "No longer do I call you servants ... I have called you friends" (John 15:15). The Christian life is not *merely* about morality nor even about religious observance. Yes, of course, it includes both of these. However, it is something infinitely more as well: it is a new and divine life. Mere philosophers could say that the highest fulfillment for humans would be found in religious observance. Through religion, we recognize that there is something higher than we are, someone to whom we owe all that we have. But the Christian message tells us that we are truly children of God. We are so profoundly connected to each other and to Christ that we are indeed members united together in *his mystical body*: "For just as the body is one and has many members, and all the members of the body, though many, are one body, so it is with Christ" (1 Corinthians 12:12). Do not be tricked by the word "mystical." This doesn't mean "paranormal," nor "metaphorical." The term is meant to designate the fact that we are more really members of Christ's body than we are members of the nation in which we are moral members. We truly are *his* body. We might say, his sacramental body. And the theological virtues make this truly divine life possible.

Nonetheless, we remain humans, and in order for us to be perfected, we must be ready to recognize these marvelous gifts which have been offered to us. Through every fiber of our being, from head to toe, we must be made perfect in every respect, even in our most human aspects: "And let steadfastness have its full effect, that you may be perfect and complete, lacking in nothing" (James 1:4). This process of human perfection begins with the highest and most perfect of all our virtues—namely, the virtue of religion, a virtue which is characteristically human, the most perfect aspect of a truly rational and free creature.

However, I can immediately feel our secular prejudices rising up in protest: "Now wait! Religion is the most perfect aspect of a truly *rational and free* creature?" If anything, religious observance seems to involve sentimentalism and subservience. How could it be truly rational? We call man Homo sapiens. Is it really correct to call him also *homo religiosus*? To many, religion seems like a kind of deformation of character or, at best, a form of subservience that helps the ignorant and gives confidence to the uninformed. It would seem to help prevent society from falling into debauchery and selfishness. But, in the end, it would be merely a tool which is useful for keeping the "masses" in check. Is this sentiment all that unknown? Does it not risk polluting even our own souls?

Nonetheless, we must insist on this point: religion bears witness to the fact that we are *rational beings*. Human reason is a kindled spiritual light deep within us. It is powerful, illuminating all of our actions: we rule our bodies and even our own wills, at least if we have strength of character. If we have the virtue of prudence, we have the power of command, a kind of self-government. Our attitude is imperious, exercising our freedom of conscience. However, at the core of all of this, we realize that all that is good ultimately comes from God: "Every good endowment and every perfect gift is from above, coming down from the Father of lights with whom there is no variation or shadow due to change" (James 1:17). Thus, the highest thing that the human creature can do is turn his or her eyes upward. Even the pagan Roman world was aware of this sublime aspect of the human character. The poet Ovid writes of Prometheus fashioning human persons: “While other animals turn their gaze toward the ground, he gave man an upright countenance, commanding him to look toward the heavens, raising his eyes so that he might gaze upon the stars.”[130] If we truly seek to avoid delusion, to recognize our place in reality, then there is nothing more rational, nothing more sane, than a ready and devout heart: “There is nothing that bears witness to an intellect that is more informed and more aware of the true place of man in this universe, where God is first and man second.”[131]

When we call man Homo sapiens, we are not saying “man the best calculator” or even “rational man.” *Sapiens* means “wise.” Man is not merely the maker of tools (*homo faber*), nor merely concerned with getting ahead in the marketplace (*homo economicus*), nor even merely a social being (*homo socialis*). All of these other aspects of man are explained first and foremost by our capacity for wisdom, our ability to know the right meaning of reality and to set our life in order in light of this meaning. Now if St. Augustine’s words, cited in our opening chapter, are true— “Behold: the heavens and earth exist, crying out that they were made”—then we see that the only way to acknowledge the right order of things is to recognize our religious duty toward him who is our source. In short, in order to be truly rational, we must be wise (Homo sapiens), and the wise person, he or she who truly recognizes the order of things, will be stamped by this religious character (*homo religiosus*).[132]

Now, all of this seems very abstract. How are we to put it into practice? Thankfully, the Church is eminently practical, helping us to inscribe our religious devotion in religious practices. The *Catechism* tells us of the traditional notion of the five “precepts of the Church” (CCC 2041–2043). These five requirements are quite basic, stating that all the faithful must attend Mass on Sundays and holy days of obligation; confess their sins at least once per year; receive the Eucharist at least during the Easter season; and observe prescribed days of fasting and abstinence. Moreover, the baptized have a duty to help provide for the material needs of the Church.

All of these actions are, in fact, related to the virtue of religion. They are intermingled with other virtues, yes. The Eucharist is not merely *our* act of worship but rather, first and foremost, is Christ’s own sacrifice, present today through the sacramental action of the priest. In the words of St. Thomas Aquinas, the Eucharist is the "sacrament of charity."[133] And Byzantine Catholics pray before the reception of Communion, drawing from St. John Chrysostom, "Accept me today as a partaker of your mystical supper." It is food for the divine life, flowing like blood and water from the Cross of Christ (John 19:34). Likewise, when we observe the fasting requirements of the Church, we are slowly but surely perfecting the virtue of temperance, becoming free from the bonds of passionate attachment to created things. Nonetheless, each of these actions can also be considered as a strictly religious action as well: sacrifice, worship, and prayer on the Lord's Day and holy days of obligation; prayer of penitence for our sins; and sacrifice of our bodies not merely for health but for God himself. And the same holds true for the offering of material support for the Church as well. The virtue of religion helps us to readily perform acts of devotion, prayer, and sacrifice for God.

Let us be clear, however; these "precepts of the Church" represent a very low bar. As the *Catechism* states, they are a "necessary *minimum*" (CCC 2042). They are indispensable, but they are really just a beginning. If a Christian merely observed these few rules and never sought to push on further, he or she would gravely risk performing nothing more than external ritual without the actual spirit of religion. Ultimately, the religious impulse should inspire us to offer our entire selves in homage to God. This is the greatest thing a mere creature could do, turning himself or herself, to the degree that this is possible, toward the divine heights, recognizing that every single fiber of his or her being, every one of his or her actions, is a gift coming from God: "What have you that you did not receive? If then you received it, why do you boast as if it were not a gift?" (1 Corinthians 4:7). This is the core of the religious impulse.

Let's consider our "Sunday obligation," which should be a kind of wellspring from which many other religious deeds flow. Again, at the risk of being repetitive, we must be clear concerning an important point: the requirement to observe Sundays and holy days of obligation is not a matter of charity or even of faith. It is something that we owe to God *in justice*. There are only two *positive* orders issued among the Ten Commandments given to Israel. Eight of these commandments are phrased as prohibitions: "Thou shalt not ..." However, in the third commandment, a positive decree is made: "Observe the sabbath day, to keep it holy, as the Lord your God commanded you" (Deuteronomy 5:12; see Exodus 20:8-11). And as we will discuss in the next chapter, the fourth commandment, concerning the honor owed to parents, is likewise positive. We owe such recognition as a matter of justice.

Now, how great and merciful is God! Even for ancient Israel, this obligation was not meant to be a burden. Instead, it was a renewal of the original covenant of Creation itself—"So God blessed the seventh day and hallowed it" (Genesis 2:3)—and indeed a recognition of the great saving deeds of God, freeing the people of Israel from bondage in Egypt (Deuteronomy 5:15). This gives the deepest meaning to Christ's words: "The sabbath was made for man, not man for the sabbath" (Mark 2:27). This does not merely mean, "God gave you a day on which to get extra sleep," even if physical and emotional rest are part of Sabbath observance. More importantly, the Sabbath is a gift in time, providing us with the space to recognize the great and marvelous things of God—that is, to recognize the most profound truths about ourselves: that we were bounteously created "from nothing," that we were saved from sin and reborn as children of God, and that even now we stand upon the doorstep of eternity, "awaiting our blessed hope, the appearing of the glory of our great God and Savior Jesus Christ" (Titus 2:13), for "he who does the will of God *abides for ever*" (1 John 2:17, emphasis added).

As Christians, we are the inheritors of the profound tradition of Jewish religion and ritual. If you ever wish to see the great spiritual depths of Jewish thought, consider reading *The Sabbath* by the Jewish author Abraham Heschel.[134] I knew an elderly priest who was a convert to Christianity from Judaism. This book was dear to him, and I still retain the copy that he gave me once upon a time, inscribed in the front with his words to me: "May all of life become your Sabbath joy." Although the Christian can push further onward, for we now celebrate the day of the Lord, the day of Christ's victory over death, and the true dawning of eternity in time, still the Christian cannot fail to be inspired by a truly devout Jewish account of the Sabbath, there seeing at once the recognition of God and the fulfillment of the human person.[135]

The celebration of the Sabbath structured the entire life of the Jewish people. In fact, it alone was able to sustain them throughout their exile when the temple sacrifices were not possible, and the Sabbath still to this day remains their most distinctive act of religious observance. The same should be true for us as Christians, who every Sunday participate in the renewed offering of the fulfillment of all sacrifices, Christ's self-offering on the Cross: "O sacred banquet, in which Christ is received, the memory of His Passion renewed, the mind filled with grace, and a pledge of future glory given to us."[136] This Sunday observance should mark the whole of our week, for it is a partaking in the center of history: the Easter mystery. Do we go forth offering each morning to God, praying to him throughout the day, and thanking him each evening for all that we have received that day? And even when all seems to go ill, when life crushes us with sorrow, do we still turn to him alone who is the source of all things? In the words of the Psalms, "Evening and morning and at noon I utter my complaint and moan, and he will hear my voice" (Psalm 55:17). The Church's Liturgy of the Hours represents a wonderful devotion which can be tailored even to the busy life of lay Christians. Every day, praise and prayer ascend from the monks, nuns, and priests who pray this daily cycle of the Church's official prayer. However, great riches may be drawn from it by parents and children who thereby turn their whole day into a great cycle of self-offering to God. Such prayer can indeed be the occasion for great acts of faith, hope, and charity. However, it also is a chance to be truly just toward God, to recognize even how each of the hours of our day is dependent upon him.

A practical atheism would have us go to church on Sundays and holy days but then live like unbelievers every other minute of our lives. However, if we take the most basic precepts of the Church seriously, we should feel an impulse to push further on, to recognize our God in all things, to offer even our "bodies as a living sacrifice, holy and acceptable to God," thereby giving him true "spiritual worship" by dedicating to him all that we have and are, even our time (see Romans 12:1). We, in fact, *owe* this to him, and that is why the virtue of religion is a form of justice. If we fall short, we are not merely uncharitable; we are guilty of injustice!

It is easy to talk about how God has been removed from public life in America and throughout the Western world. There is no small truth to this, but when we talk about "the world" or "society," we tend to talk in abstractions. How much can *we* personally do to change national politics?

We can do small things around the edges, and perhaps a few of us will be able to do "great" things. However, we must be careful not to forget duties that are far more real. We will talk about family duties in the next chapter, but here we have the most personal of all duties: our personal duty to recognize, to the degree possible, God—our creator, redeemer, and giver of every grace and good thing. We have our own garden to tend, and often when we set out to change the world, we risk leaving our garden to wither and become covered with weeds, while likewise also failing to change the world. Even the anti-Catholic French author Voltaire spoke, in *Candide*, of this wisdom of "tending one's garden," but Christ spoke far more truly still when he said, in the parable of the talents, "Well done, good and faithful servant; *you have been faithful over a little, I will set you over much*" (see Matthew 25:14-30, emphasis added).

When first things come first and second things second, justice prevails. Here, in the domain of justice, we have yet another application for Christ's words, "If your eye is sound, your whole body will be full of light" (Matthew 6:22). If we do not serve God, we will find that we are all too ready to serve ourselves. In the end, there really is no other choice: God or ourselves, whom shall we serve? When we see that the service of God is nothing other than the loving recognition of the merciful and all-good source of all things, we will then also recognize the rights of others, who are all children of one and the same God who created and redeemed us (Malachi 2:10; Ephesians 4:6). Although not every argument is religious in nature, all our actions ultimately depend on the answer to the religious question: who is first, God or ourselves? The words may seem harsh to our contemporary ears, but the early Christian message was not upbeat concerning the prospects of an irreligious world: "For men will be lovers of self, lovers of money, proud, arrogant, abusive, disobedient to their parents, ungrateful, unholy, inhuman, implacable, slanderers, profligates, fierce, haters of good, treacherous, reckless, swollen with conceit, lovers of pleasure rather than lovers of God, holding the form of religion but denying the power of it" (2 Timothy 3:2-5). And this represents the Church's traditional teaching through the centuries. True recognition of God is the mark of the wise human person, Homo sapiens. This will give us the strength to change the world, for good deeds befit all those who "profess religion" (see 1 Timothy 2:10). In the words of St. James, whose religious ideal is at once stern and quite practical, “If any one thinks he is religious, and does not bridle his tongue but deceives his heart, this man’s religion is vain. Religion that is pure and undefiled before God and the Father is this: to visit orphans and widows in their affliction, and to keep oneself unstained from the world” (James 1:26-27).

Here, too, we find that God comes to our aid to a supreme degree. As Christians, our religious exercise must look different from “merely human” religious expression. Our devotion does not just recognize a kind of “unknown god” (Acts 17:23), a nameless source of being. We recognize *our Father*, in a true and strong sense, for we are true brothers and sisters of Christ and thus likewise share in his divine sonship, ourselves being remade in the Spirit. God inspires our religion with a particular gift of the Holy Spirit, traditionally called “piety.” The “pious” are truly meek, not like little fearful sinners in the hands of an angry God but, rather, as sons and daughters who know that they are not the center of all things. The “pious” are well aware that, in order to truly recognize our dependence upon God, we must “get out of the way” and allow the Spirit to enable us to acknowledge and praise our heavenly Father, for we have “received the spirit of sonship. When we cry, ‘Abba! Father!’ it is the Spirit himself bearing witness with our spirit that we are children of God” (Romans 8:15-16). Let us pray for this gift of piety from the Spirit, so that each of us may be truly human, not merely as Homo sapiens but, more profoundly, as homo religiosus.

CHAPTER NINETEEN

Family Life as a Virtue

In the previous chapter, we discussed the virtue of religion as the primary form of justice to be acknowledged. By acts of religion, we recognize the fact that we owe all things to God. We thereby give some small degree of internal and external recognition of this "excessive debt." There is nothing that we can do to "repay" it, but we must attempt to do what we can. In such a domain, where a true and profound debt does in fact exist, *some* recognition is better than none at all. And, indeed, when the religious impulse is full and strong, it will give rise to the intricate, gilded liturgies of the Byzantine Church, to the soaring grandeur of a Roman High Mass, and to a spirit of devotion which strives to serve others in order to thereby render service to God, who is recognized in such activity. In fact, religion is the ready instrument of the divine love. It is the loftiest peak of our morality *as humans*, forever prepared to be deployed in service to the wholly divine theological virtues of faith, hope, and charity.

Well, what if I were to say that we could look upon our parents as little gods? This seems perverse, perhaps! We must not replace God with any other being, not even our parents; God commands, "You shall have no other gods before me" (Exodus 20:3; Deuteronomy 5:7). Nonetheless, the great Greek philosopher Aristotle, himself a pagan (though perhaps on the pathway to a kind of philosophical monotheism), saw this connection quite clearly. In fact, he emphasized that our recognition of our teachers is likewise similar to the dynamic at the heart of religious observance. In his *Nicomachean Ethics*, Aristotle observes how we must attempt to repay our teachers, parents, and God (he says "the gods") in some way, *precisely as a matter of justice*, even if we can never repay the benefits they have bestowed upon us:

> And so too, it seems one should make a return to those with whom one has studied philosophy, *for their worth cannot be measured against money*. In fact, *they can get no honor which will balance their services*, but still, it is perhaps enough, *as it is with the gods and with one's parents*, to give them *what one can*.[137]

But, we need not turn to a pagan for such insights, though the great Greek and Roman philosophers have provided many philosophical riches which have been used by Christians through the ages. The contemporary Jewish intellectual Leon Kass expresses a similar connection, doing so in language that reads as though it were written by a Catholic:

> The teaching about "father and mother" comes right on the heels of the reason offered for sanctifying the Sabbath day: God's creation of the world and His subsequent setting apart and hallowing a time beyond work and motion. It thus extends our attention to origins and "creation," now in the form of human generating. God may have created the world, and the whole human race, but you owe your own existence to your parents, who are, to say the least, copartners—equally with each other, equally with God—in your coming to be. For this gift of life—and, one may pointedly add, for not aborting you or electing to [contracept] the possibility of your existence—you are beholden to honor them, in gratitude.[138]

Moreover, Kass notes a connection here to God himself, implicitly showing a connection to the virtue of religion: "They also, in their unmerited devotion to our being and well-being, serve as the embodiment of, and our first encounter with, the gracious beneficence of the world and of its bountiful Source."[139]

Let's dwell on the connection which Kass points out as existing here between the commandment to keep the Sabbath and the commandment to honor our parents. Consider the structure of the Ten Commandments. In both scriptural accounts telling us about the giving of the commandments (Exodus 20:1-17; Deuteronomy 5:6-21), they are arranged into two "tables." According to the harmonized numeration generally used in Catholic tradition, following St. Augustine's approach to the two slightly different texts, the divine injunctions are split into three and seven commandments, the first group being devoted to God and the latter seven being devoted to our relations with others. The entirety of the Ten Commandments opens with the need to recognize God, turning then to our duties to our parents, then to the actions, words, and thoughts that we must not perform in relation to our fellow men (i.e., murder, adultery, theft, lying, or coveting). The structure is quite beautiful, cascading from God downward to our very inner thoughts.[140]

The two *positive* commandments are found at the hinge point between the two tablets: "Remember the sabbath day, to keep it holy ... Honor your father and your mother, that your days may be long in the land which the Lord your God gives you" (Exodus 20:8, 12). All of the other commandments follow the language of "thou shalt not," but here we have two requirements in the language of "thou shalt." In them, we are given the structural beams for the whole of our internal and external order. Place first things first: God and parents. St. Thomas (and others too) will come to note that this commandment truly extends to all those who are connected to us by birth, like a series of concentric (or at least intersecting) circles: parents, relatives, and country.[141] We could add as well that everyone who has played a fostering role in our lives participates in the requirements spelled out the fourth commandment. However, it all starts close to home—with Mom and Dad.

As inheritors of this ancient norm of family life and morality, we tend to miss the fact that there is something quite important (and, to a degree, radical) involved here. Obviously, we have a kind of native impulse to love our own, and tribalism is at least somewhat wired into us.[142] However, as regards societal principles, the great temptation for humanity is to mingle alongside the gods people who are "great and important movers and shakers," *heroes*.[143] Why should we afford so special a place to *parents* and ancestors, as indicated by the fact that the divine commandment concerning them is so closely connected with the very day upon which we are to worship God? Parents and ancestors are connected to us merely by birth, whereas truly great people—be they politicians or philanthropists—would seem to be deserving of more attention, given how much good they do *for the world* and not merely *for us*. Moreover, it seems quite irrational to be attached to the "mere accident of birth." We are a rational people, after all. These kinds of inherited bonds to the past seem to be so secondary in comparison with the forward march of progress, which must be orchestrated through planning and *reason*.

The Church's teaching about family life, however, is nothing more than a sane expression of a point of anthropology which is undeniable: we are not merely *reason*; we are *embodied* spiritual creatures, at the borders of matter and spirit. Our bodies mean something, and the fact that we happen to exist *here and now*, as particular men and women, is filled with meaning.[144] The Judeo-Christian mind cannot help but see romance and drama everywhere. Scripture does not present us with a God who merely blinks salvation into existence after the Fall, everywhere once and for all. Perhaps a religion dreamed up by a technocrat or by a philosopher would employ this kind of *immediate* universalism, telling us to love "the brotherhood of mankind." However, God acts in a *mediated* fashion. He calls *one* man (Abraham) to form one people (Israel) so that Christ may come to be incarnate and thereby throw open the doors to a true universal brotherhood. The story of salvation history can look scandalous to those who do not have faith, for God seems to play favorites time and again. Nonetheless, through all of this drama, allowing particular persons and peoples to play their roles freely in this tale, he brings about the salvation of the world. In fact, the tale looks so calamitous that it seemed to fail, with Israel being whittled away; then, with so much failure and sin, God saves us in the very person of the Son. This mysterious meandering of salvation history brought St. Paul to his knees in awe: "O the depth of the riches and wisdom and knowledge of God! How unsearchable are his judgments and how inscrutable his ways!" (Romans 11:33).

God mediates his plan for us through the particular vagaries of our lineage and parents. We are not born of Humanity. We are born of two parents, into a particular family, in a given nation, at a particular time, with particular abilities. Our whole life is tied up with this nexus of circumstances. To an unbelieving technocrat, they seem like unwieldy and irrational points of data to be overcome. To the eyes of a believer, they are the marks of a divine calling, a vocation. By showing honor to our parents (and others like them who have variously reared us), we recognize the activity of God's providence in our lives.

There are some who speak of "chosen family," replacing their blood relations whom they believe to have fallen short (and perhaps who have). No doubt, we all have a circle of friends and associates to whom we can say, "You are like a brother," or, "You are like a sister," or, "You are like a second mother." However, the tragedy of the expression "chosen family" is precisely the fact that, in the end, the two words clash with each other. The nature of family is precisely the fact that it is *not* chosen. Anyone who has had a difficult relationship with a sibling or parent has doubtlessly said, on many occasions of frustration, "Yeah, but she is my sister … I know; I know; but still, she is my mother." At a deep level, we feel that the *unchosen* nature of family ties is the reason for choosing to love our relatives, in spite of their shortcomings.

In fact, we could say that family life provides each of us with a ready aid for overcoming the vice of acedia. Recall, acedia (or, as many call it, sloth) is not merely a vice of "laziness." Very often, we can hide this vice in activity, becoming busybodies who, in fact, procrastinate in relation to our *true* duties. Acedia involves a cooling of love, a kind of sorrow in the face of what we truly should love, above all God, but also whatever—and *whoever*—God's providence has placed in our lives' pathways. Our families are a great example of this first level of God's providential provision, something we have not chosen but, rather, which *he* has chosen. We could apply to our families the words which we drew on from G. K. Chesterton in the chapter on acedia: "We make our friends; we make our enemies; but *God makes our next-door neighbour*." We may add the words "and he also makes our families."

St. Paul did not hesitate to draw a very strong conclusion from this connection: "If any one does not provide for his relatives, and *especially for his own family*, he has *disowned the faith and is worse than an unbeliever*" (1 Timothy 5:8, emphasis added). These words are incredibly striking! They are nonetheless justified, given the close bonds between religion and the duties which we have toward our parents and family. In fact, in classical moral vocabulary, the word "piety," from the Latin *pietas*, referred to the duties we have toward our family, our nation, and toward God.[145] Although we must be sensitive to the needs of humanity at large, we nonetheless cannot equate the "human *family*" with our own *actual* family. A kind of cosmopolitan ethics would have us worry first and foremost about worldwide problems, whereas a Judeo-Christian ethic will not fail to reflect the fact that God himself brings about universal salvation through the particular choice he makes on behalf of a particular people and, ultimately, in the utterly particular case of the incarnate

Word. This is part of the logic of the Incarnation, and it is reflected in our very morality.

Now, there may be an objection. Did not Christ say, "If any one comes to me and does not hate his own father and mother and wife and children and brothers and sisters, yes, and even his own life, he cannot be my disciple" (Luke 14:26)? Yes, indeed. But we here have a situation akin to when, after his mother and relatives approached him, he said to his disciples, "Here are my mother and my brethren! For whoever does the will of my Father in heaven is my brother, and sister, and mother" (Matthew 12:49-50). Though some have wished to look at this saying as though Christ were insulting his mother, what he has in view here is quite simple: put first things first. If the Mother of God is going to have a unique place among humanity, this will be judged in accord with the fact that she has a unique holiness, a unique conformity to God's will.[146] So too, when Christ tells us to "hate" our relatives, he is pointing out, by means of hyperbolic rhetoric, how our supernatural vocation must come first in our lives. Our *new* birth through grace takes precedence over our *first*, physical birth. Nonetheless, nothing prevents our families from being part of the drama of grace in our lives. In fact, one of the great duties of Christian parents is to raise their children in the Faith.

Now, obviously, family situations are not always perfect. Because of the sins of parents against their children or the sins of children against their parents, these bonds can be severed. No matter how frequent, however, these cases remain exceptions, not the rule, and those who experience these sad circumstances know all too well that this state of affairs represents a loss. For them, there will be surrogate figures who will fill this role, and for them too, the fourth commandment will exert its requirements.

Such "piety" is reflected in our nostalgia for our homeplaces as well. Although I grew up on the edges of Appalachia, my immediate peers were not fans of country music, even though many of my fellow students in middle school and high school listened to one of the many country stations in our poor little county on the borders of West Virginia and rural western Maryland. As a young smart aleck, I would poke fun at what I took to be undue attention placed upon "Mama" in such music. (We all know the stereotypes about country music: trucks, mama, train wrecks, beer, dancing, and heartbreak.) It took leaving the area and then returning in order for me to appreciate much of the Appalachian experience, which in fact was the experience of my paternal family, especially those bearing the classically Scots-Irish name Mitchell. In the music of Appalachian bluegrass, there are a number of songs which give voice to the desire to return to one's home and parents, having left the hills in one's youth in order to strike out on one's own.[147] And even when one never can return, a nagging voice will remind the person who grew up in the simple life of the hills: "Don't get above your raisin'."

Now, obviously, family life is not merely a static "thing," nor is our home merely a place in the hills. It is an activity, a way of being together with others. It is precisely because of this activity that we owe something to our parents. They are not mere "progenitors," nor are we mere "offspring." We are children of parents, who spend years—indeed, the rest of their lives—passing on the wisdom of culture and of the Faith to us. The Church speaks of this relational fact in terms of the obligation of parents to "educate" their children. In order to avoid thinking of this obligation as being merely about learning facts and skills, we could perhaps translate the term and say that parents have the duty to fashion the full identity of their children.

It is so easy to ignore the fact that the profound roots of our identity are tied up with the knowledge that parents and relatives have of us and with the love they have expressed for us. "Yes, yes," we say, "Mom knows me best," but we usually end up plunging back into the business of the day. It becomes tempting to live as though each of us were solely our own man or woman. Obviously, we are each free and unique, not the mere "instruments" of our parents, relatives, friends, and neighbors, and each of us has his or her own unique moral destiny. Nonetheless, the fact that we exist in the knowledge and love of another person is actually quite important to our identity and to who we are in the world today. We cannot help but think of ourselves as persons who are *known and loved* by another person. And although friendships and spousal relationships lead us to form utterly close bonds of knowledge and love, there is something unique about familial relationships. I recall words spoken to me once when I expressed condolences to a friend whose brother had recently died. As we were talking, she observed that this was a more difficult loss for her than the relatively recent loss of her husband of forty years. Although her brother lived geographically far away, the two of them shared many unique experiences, meaning that she alone would now remember them—an entire childhood, a part of herself, gone for the rest of her life here below. And when a parent dies, the full story of *how we became who we are* seems to now be left solely in our hands, for dutiful parents will have fashioned the very person who we are. We owe such a debt to them that we feel that neither this debt, nor even ourselves, will be understood by anyone else, something poignantly expressed in the bluegrass song "I'm a Stranger Here," which I recommend to the interested (and, perhaps, indulgent) reader.

Parents' duty to "educate" their children gives birth to such intimate bonds. As I already noted above, the word "educate" can be deceptive. If we quickly pick up a book of Catholic moral theology, we will see that the primary end of marriage as a human institution is directly tied up with the "procreation and education of one's offspring." All of this is very true![148] (Inasmuch as Christian marriage is a sacrament, it is also a living sign of Christ's union with the Church.) However, the word "educate" has a much broader meaning than mere intellectual education. It refers to all of the activity of rearing that takes place in the family—all of the explicit and implicit ways by which parents form the characters of their children and help to integrate them into the broader social network of the immediate family, the extended family, the Church, and the social community. We live in a nexus of many relationships, and the center from which this web is spun begins with our parents, who themselves have a kind of "flip side" duty included in the fourth commandment.

And beyond such moral, cultural, and intellectual education, Christian parents must look even further. They live out the life of the Church in family life itself. They are the heads of a "domestic church":

> Christian parents must also understand that they are destined not only to propagate and preserve the human race on earth, indeed not only to educate any kind of worshippers of the true God, but children who are to become members of the Church of Christ, to raise up fellow-citizens of the Saints, and members of God's household, that the worshippers of God and Our Savior may daily increase.[149]

This does not merely mean, as a cynic might think, that parents need to give birth to children in order to keep the pews filled. Rather, it means that *as parents* they are the first educators of their children in the life of grace. Imagine what it was like in Nazareth for the incarnate Christ to be taught by Mary, who no doubt was herself also taught by so great a son!

A truly moral society will recognize all of these bonds. It will not treat the previous generation as something to be cast aside, a mere accessory to the plans and aspirations of the up-and-coming generation. Rather, it will encourage the *strict justice* requiring parents to rear their children and the *strict justice* which requires children to recognize and care for their parents: "If a widow has children or grandchildren, *let them first learn their religious duty to their own family and make some return to their parents*; for this is acceptable in the sight of God" (1 Timothy 5:4).

Obviously, each situation is unique. Nonetheless, the fourth commandment remains in force: "Honor your father and your mother, that your days may be long in the land which the Lord your God gives you" (Exodus 20:12). St. Paul drew attention to the fact that this commandment was quite unique. In the sixth chapter of his letter to the Ephesians, as he lays out all the various relationships among the members of the household, he notes at the start, while citing the fourth commandment, that "this is the first commandment with a promise" (Ephesians 6:2). Let us take these inspired words seriously, and whether as parents or as children (or as aunts, uncles, cousins, and so forth), let us look upon the requirements of family life as being a place to exercise the virtue of "piety," a kind of reflection of the virtue of religion, anchoring the whole social order through unchosen but, God willing, unbreakable bonds. Let us see that the family provides a ready place to store up treasures for heaven: "Whoever honors his father atones for sins … and whoever glorifies his mother is like one who lays up treasure" (Sirach 3:3-4).

CHAPTER TWENTY

"Render unto Caesar …"

We should begin by connecting this chapter to the previous one on the family. It is tempting to fly off into the skies when talking about politics. We are all too ready to speak in great and lofty abstractions: country, party, government, universal human rights, tax policy, and so forth. However, the classical (and Catholic) teaching concerning society starts much closer to home. It starts with human nature itself: man is a social and political animal. In fact, human nature has this "political orientation" precisely because we are rational animals. Our ability to reason and reflect is not merely a private affair. All throughout our day-to-day lives, we reason together with others, solving shared problems, trying to accomplish things that we could not accomplish on our own.

In this kind of *shared* activity, we have an instance of what is called "the common good." Very often, this expression is quite ambiguous. Some politicians and pundits use it to imply the idea of "thinking about all of us together," of not being merely self-centered in what we do. Often, we translate "the common good" as "the greater good," and we generally mean something like "the greatest good for the greatest number of people." We must be careful with such language, for the common good is not a kind of greatest possible sum of individual goods. The common good is not merely achieved when a group of individuals gets "maximal output." The achievement of the common good is, in fact, something *more than the mere benefits accruing to the members of a group*. Here, we have a clear application for the expression "The whole is greater than its parts."

For the sake of clarity, it is perhaps better to speak of *a* common good or *this* or *that* common good, not *the* common good. For example, consider four people who come together to sing a song in four-part harmony. Each person brings a particular strength to the group: a dulcet Irish tenor, a booming Russian bass, a mellow alto with the beauty of someone like Karen Carpenter, and a soprano with a voice as clear as a bell. Each voice has its own beauty on its own. However, when the four voices come together, something—beautiful harmony—happens *between* the notes that they each sing. The soprano by herself or the tenor by himself may sing a beautiful solo. However, when they sing a song together, they take part in something *new*, which they can only accomplish together. They are doing something truly *common*: each is *singing this harmonious song*, even though each is "only" doing his or her part. Yes, they are parts; however, they are parts of a *new whole*. We could say that this shared melody "lives" in each of them, though it can only do so for as long as they are united in this one aim, in this shared end, in this good. This example helps us to grasp the meaning of the expression "the common good" in a very down-to-earth situation. This same dynamic of the *whole* and the *parts* will play out everywhere that the common good is found.[150]

Now, Catholic social teaching always says, "Begin local." This is sane advice, and it helps us to keep our minds on the straight and narrow, lest we fly off into great and grand abstractions. The most "local" common good is *family life*. Whether in our particular household or in our extended family, we perform many tasks *together*, tasks which could not be accomplished if we were merely individuals doing our own private activities. We learn how to *be together* by first *being together* with our family (as well as with our most immediate neighbors). Shared celebrations of holidays, mutual help given to relatives experiencing hard times or merely needing a hand with a home-improvement project, shared prayer as a family, all the energy expended by parents to educate their children—all of these sorts of activities are what we could call "first-tier social activities." None of them are abstract political notions like defense policy, education policy, or tax law. Nonetheless, they are all real expressions of social life together, and in each of them we live out real virtues and duties. Something so simple as physical procreation, giving rise to family bonds, creates an entire network of social relationships which are among the dearest, most enduring, and most important to us: mother, father, children, grandparents, cousins, and so forth. What a testimony to the fact that, yes, human beings are *political animals*!

However, to see the full meaning of this word "political," we need to expand our circles a bit. After the family, there is the local community, then the larger county, then the state, then the whole nation. With each and every one of these larger spheres of community, we have an increasingly broad social and political order. There are certain things that each level cannot do merely by itself. For example, a given person may have skills as a carpenter. However, he can only ply his trade with other people in the local area, not merely because he needs customers but also because, in order to make truly useful products, carpentry itself requires many hands and various trades: fellow carpenters, masons, roofers, electricians, and so forth. Likewise, trade unions and other associations help to train future generations of carpenters, ensuring that these skills are handed on from one generation to the next. Moreover, there needs to be a general system of exchange that is agreed on, along with a taxation system that acknowledges the ways that profits don't exist in a vacuum but, instead, are related to the common society as well as to the individual who has justly earned such money through his or her work and ingenuity. The carpenter must be able to presume that goods can easily be sold from one state jurisdiction to another and even abroad, thus requiring national economic policies in addition to a general assurance that international unrest will be addressed through diplomacy and, if necessary, military power.

We must keep track of all of these concentric circles! None of them is unimportant, and we must strive to keep what is local at the local level. For example, it would be foolish to go seeking after a new federal system to manage all the various interactions of building trades in a given locality. However, it may be helpful to set universal standards so that the various trades may meet a certain minimum bar, thus helping them to work across various state lines and also helping to ensure the basic quality of work taken for granted by the society as a whole. It is sane, however, to think that these kinds of standards will largely be negotiated *by the trades themselves* and not merely by government fiat. Government does not replace everything "beneath it." Rather, it coordinates these groups where coordination is needed.

Obviously, drawing the lines between government and nongovernment is part of the very task of politics. There is great room for debate, and differences here will separate various political parties and factions from each other. But the basic principle remains: if something truly belongs to a "lower level" of governmental activity, it *must* be left there and not replaced by some higher level. This is what the Catholic Church has come to refer to as the "principle of subsidiarity," something already implied long ago in words written by St. Paul, cited in the previous chapter: "If a widow has children or grandchildren, *let them first learn their religious duty to their own family and make some return to their parents*, for this is acceptable in the sight of God ... If any one does not provide for his relatives, *and especially for his own family*, he has *disowned the faith and is worse than an unbeliever*" (1 Timothy 5:4, 8, emphasis added). His point is quite clear: fulfill your duties to your family and community! Don't be like Ebenezer Scrooge in Dickens' *A Christmas Carol*. When he was asked to help a local charity, he appealed to the tax dollars that he already had paid:

> "Are there no prisons?" asked Scrooge.
>
> "Plenty of prisons," said the gentleman, laying down the pen again.
>
> "And the Union workhouses?" demanded Scrooge. "Are they still in operation?"
>
> "They are. Still," returned the gentleman, "I wish I could say they were not."
>
> "The Treadmill and the Poor Law are in full vigor, then?" said Scrooge.
>
> "Both very busy, sir."
>
> "Oh! I was afraid from what you said at first, that something had occurred to stop them in their useful course," said Scrooge. "I'm very glad to hear it." ...
>
> "I wish to be left alone," said Scrooge. "Since you ask me what I wish, gentlemen, that is my answer. I don't make merry myself at Christmas, and I can't afford to make idle people merry. *I help to support the establishments I have mentioned—they cost enough; and those who are badly off must go there*."[151]

We have spoken of trade unions and building trades. However, let's take something that hits closer to home: education. In the end, the *duty* and *right* of education belongs to parents. Precisely by virtue of being parents, they are the ones who *must* provide for their children's education, using the various means available to them. While we might (and indeed can) argue that it is the duty of the community to help in this task, the obligation first and foremost falls to parents, who thereby work with the broader community in order to fulfill the task of socializing and educating their children. There are many ways that this can be accomplished, and this coordination is a task falling to the virtue of prudence. The Church is not opposed to public schooling, but she *is* opposed to a state monopoly on education, something she has condemned as being unjust:

> The task of educating belongs fundamentally and primarily to the family. The function of the State is subsidiary: its role is to guarantee, protect, promote and supplement. Whenever the State lays claim to an educational monopoly, it oversteps its rights and offends justice. It is parents who have the right to choose the school to which they send their children and the right to set up end support educational centres in accordance with their own beliefs. The State cannot without injustice merely tolerate so-called private schools. Such schools render a public service and therefore have a right to financial assistance.[152]

Balancing out these rights and duties is a very important aspect of a nation's politics.

Now, all that we have said up to this point functions as a kind of primer of political philosophy. Though very brief, it was necessary so that we might see that politics is not something at odds with human nature, a necessary evil. Our political activity answers a profound need in human nature, for we are social creatures, forming bonds with others and working together on many shared tasks, all throughout each and every day. There will never be some imagined "perfect future" when the state will wither away. Politics is not corrupt by its very nature. It is corrupt because we are corrupt, because we humans are sinful. The common good—that is, not a tyrannical rule of the many over the few but, rather, common and shared activity, making all of us more perfect and fulfilled—will forever be something immensely good. Even in heaven, the common good will remain—no longer the common good of political society, which will have passed away but, rather, the vision of God, shared as one commonly experienced eternal life by all the blessed. Without doing away with the individual lives of those who see and love God, the beatific vision and beatific love will be a true *communion* (i.e., *common union*), in a single shared supernatural life of knowledge and love, the full *communion of the saints*. Here, we see the truest sense of Aristotle's words in his *Nicomachean Ethics*, cited warmly by many Catholic thinkers: the common good of the city is better and more divine than the private good of one man alone.[153] We Christians know the truest sense of these words: the common good of the divine city of God is the most divine good of all!

Let us now push on a little bit further, for we must recognize the fact that Christ did indeed radically relativize the Christian's relationship to the state. The Pharisees approached Jesus, trying to get him to say something that might land him in trouble: "Is it lawful to pay taxes to Caesar, or not? Should we pay them, or should we not?" If he answered no, Christ would have found himself in the crosshairs of the Roman authorities. If he simply answered yes, many of his fellow Jews would have been angered, for this would seem to affirm the unjust treatment of them by the Romans. Christ, however, had a ready and balanced response: "Bring me a coin, and let me look at it." When they handed over a Roman coin, he asked them to look at the image on it. They frankly admitted, yes, that Caesar's image was on the coin, and Christ responded with well-known words: "Render to Caesar the things that are Caesar's, and to God the things that are God's" (Mark 12:14-17).

In other words, we are to fulfill our duties to the state while not neglecting the duties we owe to God. St. Paul would express this as follows:

> Let every person be subject to the governing authorities. For there is no authority except from God, and those that exist have been instituted by God. Therefore he who resists the authorities resists what God has appointed, and those who resist will incur judgment. For rulers are not a terror to good conduct, but to bad. Would you have no fear of him who is in authority? Then do what is good, and you will receive his approval, for he is God's servant for your good. But if you do wrong, be afraid, for he does not bear the sword in vain; he is the servant of God to execute his wrath on the wrongdoer. Therefore one must be subject, not only to avoid God's wrath but also for the sake of conscience. For the same reason you also pay taxes, for the authorities are ministers of God, attending to this very thing. Pay all of them their dues, taxes to whom taxes are due, revenue to whom revenue is due, respect to whom respect is due, honor to whom honor is due. (Romans 13:1-7)

Obviously, neither Christ nor St. Paul were saying that the state is *completely* independent from the law of God. In fact, St. Paul says quite the opposite: "Those that exist have been instituted by God ... The authorities are ministers of God." However, given all the possibilities of human sin, there is such a thing as an *unjust* law, which in fact is *no law at all*, for it has no basis in the natural law, whose most important requirement is that we recognize God and true morality. In slightly older theological language, this subordination of the state to God was reflected in the Catholic Church's emphasis on what she referred to as her *indirect* authority over the state. She did not claim that the Church should meddle in the day-to-day affairs of politics. The Church and the state have two different goals: eternal salvation and the temporal common good. However, we cannot treat politics as though it were indifferent to morality and to our divine vocation.[154] This is why an unjust law is no law, for an unjust law fails in one of the most basic functions of the government—namely, the upholding of the rights of its citizens, the first of which is to be free to live a moral life: "Therefore, the principal freedom that we must defend is that of doing our duty, above all, our duty toward God, a duty that is founded on the rights of God, who is our principle and our end."[155]

However, the state must be very careful to strike the right balance here, not running roughshod over human freedom, for our moral life, along with our religious observance, must be freely exercised. The Second Vatican Council's Declaration on Religious Freedom spelled out that the state cannot coerce faith in its subjects. However, in this document, the Council Fathers made it clear that this limitation does not mean that the state is indifferent to religion and morality:

> Religious freedom, in turn, which men demand as necessary to fulfill their duty to worship God, has to do with immunity from coercion in civil society. Therefore, it leaves untouched traditional Catholic doctrine on the moral duty of men and societies toward the true religion and toward the one Church of Christ.[156]

This is why secularization is not something innocuous. Religion cannot be placed solely into the sphere of "private life," for our religion makes moral demands which will affect the way society should be structured, not only in questions of life and death but also in questions of economy and culture.

In a general text like this, we cannot get into all of the intricacies of the Church's social doctrine. We must be clear about the most-important, principal operative in this domain: our life as citizens is something of immense moral importance. If we pay attention to all of the various rights and duties of families, communities, states, and countries, we realize that there are real questions of morality involved here. It might be tempting to get caught up asking questions about how to judge whether various laws are unjust. However, the virtue of "piety" (or *virtuous patriotism*) is not merely devoted to *how to avoid sins*. That is barely a beginning! As has been emphasized throughout this book, sin must be defined in light of virtue. Darkness is a *lack of light*; light is not a lack of darkness.

Among the greatest achievements of human justice, we must include the work of establishing and maintaining a just political order. Thus, we have the *moral duty* to be active citizens, well-informed regarding the political questions of the day and how it is that we may reasonably influence politics through voting, communication, organizing, and, where appropriate and necessary, through peaceful protests.[157] However, we should not allow the word "duty" to make this seem like a harsh requirement. The rough-and-tumble of politics is, in fact, something of immense importance. We are all very fortunate to live in a political system which enables us to participate actively in this process in a way that is informed by our faith and articulated by our reasoning, which here applies the natural law in one of its most important domains. Pick up a book by someone like Robert P. George, a faithful Catholic professor of jurisprudence at Princeton and a founder of the Witherspoon Institute, and you will see one example (among many others) of how powerful Catholic reflection on politics can be![158]

The inspiration for our political activity, for all the various acts of "general justice" and "distributive justice" in which we may be involved, is the virtue of "piety," *pietas*, virtuous patriotism. And there is no sin involved in this! We are not nationalist jingoists because we love our home country, and even when we must react to unjust laws, seeking to overturn them, we do so in order that we might make our nation truly better. Indeed, the person who ends up losing his or her life for not following an unavoidable, truly unjust law, can proclaim that the unjust law itself is injurious to the nation, thus meaning that he or she must die *for* his or her country by being killed for refusing to follow this law. A true, though paradoxical, martyr's courage was expressed in the words of a Soviet dissident who said: "I will always be ready to die for my country, but I cannot lie for it."[159]

We should feel an immense debt to our home country. Writing in the United States, I feel that this is an incredibly important thing to emphasize and appreciate. Today, there are a number of powerful voices which would like to minimize the positive tale of our nation and all the great good we have done for the world. Obviously, the people and leaders of our nation have committed sins and must continue to overcome our country's faults and weaknesses. However, we would be disastrously naive if we did not think that this were true of every nation. The philosopher Immanuel Kant observed rather pessimistically but with no small truth, "Nothing entirely straight can be fabricated out of such crooked wood as that from which the human being is made."[160]

Our job is to try to make good with what we are given, and in our case as American citizens, there are many true goods that have been given to us. We are a nation of castoffs who have found a true home in which to flourish. My own ancestors are representative of a number of second-class citizens who all benefited from the great opportunities given to them in our nation. They were poor Scots-Irish farmers who came to own a good deal of land (used for mining and logging), which they eventually donated in whole to a local state park; poor German farmers who established a solid family of hardworking descendants; and poor Slovak miners and steelworkers with descendants who have gone on to public office but, more importantly, to independent family life, no longer tied to the "coal patch" and the company store. I grew up in a blue-collar family in Appalachia (and live there now) but have been educated to the point of having a doctorate and have traveled to places none of my poor ancestors ever could have imagined going. I have experienced an endless list of benefits which are staggering to someone who grew up in one of the poorest counties in Pennsylvania. I cannot help but feel an immense love for the land of my birth.

Those who are given such great things should, in turn, recognize them and then work to make so blessed a nation a greater and more moral place. It is a fine thing to love one's nation more than any other nation, just as we should love our family more than those who are more distant from us.[161] Some fear that such an attitude might lead to nationalistic prejudice. Far from it! Let the French have their wine and cheese and the Germans their beer and schnitzel! Our task is to take part in the life of our particular nation, recognizing the goods that we have received from her. Recent immigrants no doubt feel this sentiment most powerfully. However, even native-born citizens should as well, for just as they are the children of their beloved parents merely by "happenstance," so too are they children of their nation by a happy chance. Even such "unchosen" relationships require us to recognize the fact that we have received much from those whom we now must choose to love! Thus, we can see, I hope, how it is that the classical tradition could tie together religion, family duty, and the state, laying out quite clearly the lofty requirements involved in all three of these domains. In the words of St. Thomas Aquinas, "thus just as religion involves giving worship (*cultum*) to God, so too, in the second place, piety involves giving worship (*cultum*) to one's parents and one's country."[162]

CHAPTER TWENTY-ONE

Abortion and the Dignity of Persons

The topic of abortion is an emotionally difficult subject. From the start, we must here acknowledge that many bear the wounds of this great tragedy, either in their own lives, in their family's lives, or in the lives of their friends. I have had friends whose parents told them that they were going to abort them but decided not to do so. I know people who themselves, prior to religious reversion, had abortions and later regretted it. I have had relatives, now deceased, who were involved in helping someone else get an abortion, thus precipitating family divisions. It is a topic of great psychological and moral weight, and I do not take it lightly. My goal in this chapter, laying out the Church's perennial teaching, is not to ride roughshod over those who have been faced with this tragedy. God's mercy is immense. Let us recall the theme of chapter sixteen above: "The work of divine justice always presupposes the work of mercy. Indeed, God's Justice is founded upon His Mercy." In the end, my goal is to show the *positive* meaning for the Church's constant declaration of the intrinsic evil of abortion.

In order to understand this teaching, we must begin with a point of philosophical and theological anthropology: the unique nature of the human person. If we do not have some understanding of this fact, it is very difficult—in fact, impossible—to render an account of the Church's perennial proclamation on behalf of the dignity of human life from conception to death. This approach also shows why it is that dogmatic theology is so very necessary for moral theology. The two cannot be disconnected.

The whole of our day-to-day experience is filled with material realities. We live in the midst of things, plants, and animals. Sitting in my home office, I see the stones in the planter outside of my bay window; I see the pine trees out of the window behind my desk; and I hear the chirping of birds and the clicking of insects. All of these beings have their matter-bound existences and activities. Rocks obey gravity. Trees go through their life cycles, using inorganic material so as to live organic lives. The birds have knowledge and experience of the world which they use in their mating and migration cycles each year. The cycle of material nature is full of color and life. However, all of these beings have a limited "horizon": the world of physical, sensible experience. Ultimately, they are all bound to materiality.

Humans, however, contain a secret that does not allow itself to be constricted to the "here and now" and to the "there and then": the spirituality of the human soul. There is a sense in which plants and animals have souls, principles of organization which enable them to live in a way that is more than merely inorganic. However, unlike the plant or animal soul, the human soul is also spiritual. Unlike the highest ape, we have certain activities that are not intrinsically conditioned by matter: intellectual understanding and spiritual love. However, unlike the angels, we do require our bodies, brains, emotions, and imaginations in order to achieve such spiritual activity.[163] The human person is really and truly a microcosm, the meeting place of spirit and matter. Other material beings have a material horizon. We *are* the horizon between the two worlds of spirit and matter. We stand upon earth but look toward the Infinite One.

This fact is reflected throughout everything in our experience. All the books in my office are not merely physical things—wood pulp and dark markings. No! They are *incarnate ideas*, waiting to be discovered anew, putting the reader in touch with truths which often span the centuries. A flower placed in a jar for my wife is not merely a flower. No! It is the declaration of a truly interpersonal, spiritual love of one person for another, the same sort of love which spouses have been showing each other for millennia. Music is not merely sound floating through the air like a babbling brook. No! It is like the spiritual soul of the composer reaching out to touch the ear of the hearer. In all of these domains, spirit splatters itself throughout the material world, making the material world richer than mere matter. But how easy it is to forget the spiritual core of all these things, to think that our activities were ultimately limited to our current life, passing away with death, "as though the sun, which gilds the clouds with its fiery glow, did not continue its radiant course after passing over the horizon!"[164] However, the Church teaches (and, in fact, sane philosophy teaches) that there is more than matter involved in the world. There is, in fact, man's spiritual soul, which is more precious than every nonspiritual being in the universe combined.

What is more, at the deepest point of our human nature, we are open to God in a unique way. All things obey God, for he is our creator. We, however, obey God in a knowing and free manner. In fact, at the heights of what we can know merely by our natural reasoning, we can turn to God (if we are not turned away by sin) and say, "God, I know that you exist, that you are the greatest good, and that I myself desire goodness with every fiber of my being. If it were possible, I would will that you give yourself to me completely. How I wish this were possible!" But it is possible, for God has made it so through his grace! He answers the deepest wish of our soul by giving it an answer greater than we could ever have anticipated. He gives us himself. We might say that "human life and the Divine Life are made to be united."[165]

Certain classical theologians used to emphasize our direct and close bond with God by saying that in his or her most profound spiritual depths, the human person is actually elevated above all of the universe. Yes, our emotions can be affected by a bad dinner, and we experience the sensation of pain at being physically hurt, but the spiritual secrets of our hearts are things which even the angels cannot know. They are not strictly connected to the universe. They are only connected directly to God, who alone can know our most profound thoughts and loves.[166] Only of him can we say:

> O Lord, you have searched me and known me!
> You know when I sit down and when I rise up;
>   you discern my thoughts from afar.
> You search out my path and my lying down,
>   and are acquainted with all my ways.
> Even before a word is on my tongue,
>   behold, O Lord, you know it altogether.
> You beset me behind and before,
>   and lay your hand upon me.
> Such knowledge is too wonderful for me;
>   it is high, I cannot attain it. (Psalm 139:1-6)

This is what each little embryo is called to live: a truly spiritual life, something greater than all the stars, a life which will, in fact, be lived as a relationship with God, with the Father, through the Son, in the Spirit. Each person is a little microcosm, potentially capable of containing within himself or herself anything at all within the universe, doing so through knowledge and love, which are spiritual activities. As the philosopher Pascal wrote, all the bodies in the world would not add up to one single thought or one single spirit. And what is more, we are called to the life of grace. Thus, he also added: all of our thoughts, all spirits, considered solely in their natures, could not add up to one little act of grace and of charity.[167] How great and marvelous the vocation to which we have been called by God!

Obviously, though, all of this must develop over the course of one's life. Nonetheless, the human person has this orientation from the start. The life that he or she lives is the same life that he or she will live throughout his or her whole existence. As the acorn shoots upward with the life of the oak tree, so too does human life unfold even in the embryo, who already begins knitting together the entire organism who will grow and develop as a baby, all the way through adulthood and, God willing, to eternal glory. Thus, the early Church Father Tertullian put it quite well when he said, "To prevent birth is anticipated murder; it makes little difference whether one destroys a life already born or does away with it in its nascent stage. The one who will be a man is already one."[168] We could say that the object of the action is the same: to end *this human life*. The only thing that differs is the circumstance of time: the deed is done to someone who is *very* young.

Or to be more positive, we could take up the Psalm cited above, which celebrates the way that the mystery of the human person begins through the Creator's activity even from the time of his or her life in the womb:

> *For you formed my inward parts,*
> *you knitted me together in my mother's womb.*
> I praise you, for I am wondrously made.
> Wonderful are your works!
> You know me right well;
> my frame was not hidden from you,
> *when I was being made in secret,*
> *intricately wrought in the depths of the earth.*
> Your eyes beheld my unformed substance;
> in your book were written, every one of them,
> the days that were formed for me,
> *when as yet there was none of them.* (Psalm 139:13-16, emphasis added)

Thus, the Church has forever been inflexible in what she teaches regarding abortion precisely because she remains inflexible about the nature of the human person. She has so high an opinion of human nature that she cannot help but proclaim that it is infinitely better to exist and experience the divine life of grace than not to do so. No other society, no other religion holds the human person to the same high standard as does Christianity, above all as does the Catholic Church, for she proclaims a supernatural vocation: we are to live the very life of God through knowledge and love, through the gift of grace and the life of the theological virtues.

Contemporary societies have not maintained anything close to this rigid assertion of human dignity. There are likely many reasons for this backsliding: general sinfulness, a loss of common awareness of the special status of human life, fear of overpopulation, social control, and so forth. This state of affairs should not surprise us. When the Christian faith permeated the Greco-Roman world, the Church had to face practices of abortion and infanticide, alongside other evils as well. The early Fathers of the Church had to push back against this deformation of society and of the human spirit. It is a tragic fact, for technically this teaching is something that can be known by reason alone, something belonging to the natural moral law. However, bad customs and sin can blot out much of morality from our awareness. The Church has, nonetheless, forever maintained one and the same doctrine concerning the moral evil of abortion.[169] She comes with her grace and teaching to illuminate our darkened minds and to straighten our crooked hearts.

Obviously, there are mitigating circumstances which reduce the guilt of those who choose to have abortions: abandoned mothers, fearful youths, cases of rape, and so forth. (Obviously, too, Christians have a *duty* not only to prevent such abortions but also to aid these troubled cases, providing for their physical, mental, and spiritual needs.) However, a reduction in guilt is not the same thing as changing the action into something that is morally acceptable. Moreover, when contemporary society speaks of the case of "the mother's health," most politicians and commentators are far too inexact, for there are indeed cases in which certain medical procedures are permitted, even if they *indirectly* risk the viability of the life of the child. The Church is aware of such scenarios, in which case she sees a tragedy but not an abortion. This matter is very nuanced and somewhat difficult, requiring the application of what moral philosophers and theologians call "the principle of double effect." This principle does not provide a way to discover an exception to the rule but, instead, helps us to a case wherein someone is not actually performing an abortion but, instead, is performing some other medical procedure which has the termination of the pregnancy as a foreseen but unintended effect. I will provide resources concerning this topic in a note connected to this paragraph. Further discussion must be left to other books.[170]

Moreover, there is a close connection between the mentality that accepts abortion and the general consumeristic mentality that plagues modern first-world societies. Being a parent makes great demands on one's life. No longer can you go kayaking and skiing whenever you want! Likewise, one's career is never the same after having children, and sleep becomes a rarer commodity than gold and platinum! And a free moment of quiet at home is something only remembered like an ancient myth, a tale that we can hardly believe was ever true. The great virtues of family life and parenthood in fact make up for all these losses, and the activity of being a parent ultimately can bring great joy. Nonetheless, it is somewhat like a marathon, like taking up a healthier diet, or like learning a language: for a long time, it's painful and difficult.

Faced with such difficulties, a kind of self-satisfied consumerism can convince us only to want to have children when it is convenient or *only* if it fulfills our desires. This is incredibly dehumanizing for the child to be born, who is not a means for fulfilling our needs and desires but, instead, is an end in himself or herself, a spiritual person, uniquely willed into existence by God, someone more unique than all the universe. (Look through the faces in a crowd. St. Thomas says each individual angel is a unique species. This almost seems true for each human person too, each marked with a unique countenance and character.)

Moreover, one of the increasing dangers of this consumeristic attitude toward birth is tied up with the questions of in vitro fertilization and genetic modification technologies. Books on bioethics discuss these topics at great length.[171] However, the Church's prohibition on the former and her concerns regarding the latter are based on her sure conviction that the human person deserves to be recognized as an *embodied* person who has a unique *spiritual* destiny. A person is not a product, not merely the something that we create. Our human origins are tied to the at once procreative and unitive nature of the sexual bond, something we will discuss in a later chapter, when we take up the topic of contraception.

But, alas! We humans convince ourselves that *this* world is all that matters, that comfort in *this* life is of the utmost importance, and that the lives of our own children are not what they in fact are—spiritual lives which therefore are naturally immortal and, through grace, called to participate in God's eternal life. The sin of abortion denies all of this of human nature. It is, in the end, murder, even if it nips off the bud of life while it is still young and small. As the prolife club at my undergraduate college used to print on their shirts, "A person is a person, no matter how small." This is not meant to be a flippant attempt to appropriate the language of Dr. Seuss. Instead, it is merely one moral application of all the riches contained in the notion of personhood: a spiritual being, tightly bound to God in knowledge and love, with each such person having a unique, eternal destiny. Yes, when we understand what the Church teaches about abortion (something which, moreover, reason itself teaches), we must bear in mind the teaching of the fifth commandment, which holds true here: "You shall not kill"; that is, you shall not murder (Exodus 20:13). However, this "you shall not" is based upon something more affirmative and positive, upon a much more powerful affirmation and upon a much more powerful "shall":

> When I look at your heavens, the work of your fingers,
> the moon and the stars which you have established;
> what is man that you are mindful of him,
> and the son of man that you care for him?
> Yet you have made him little less than the angels,
> and you have crowned him with glory and honor. (Psalm 8:3-5)

> They *shall* see his face, and *his name shall be on their foreheads*. ... To him who conquers I will give some of the hidden manna, and I will give him a white stone, with a *new name* written on the stone *which no one knows except him who receives it*. ... I have called you *by name*, you are mine. (Revelation 22:4, 2:17; Isaiah 43:1, emphasis added)

CHAPTER TWENTY-TWO

Generosity Isn't Optional: "Freely You Have Received, Freely You Must Give"

"No servant can serve two masters; for either he will hate the one and love the other, or he will be devoted to the one and despise the other. You cannot serve God and mammon" (Luke 16:13). What could these words of Christ mean? How seriously, *really*, should we take them? It is quite easy to find reasons to attenuate his proclamation. How often do we all—and here, I include myself!—find a way to soften the words of Christ and the apostles when it comes to questions of wealth: "Well, obviously, it's not mean to be taken literally. He means that you can devote your life to money, so long as you remember God on occasion as well."[172]

But how can such a reinterpretation be squared with the early Church's sentiment? We read in the letter to the Hebrews, "Keep your life free from love of money, and be content with what you have; for he has said, 'I will never fail you nor forsake you.' Hence we can confidently say, 'The Lord is my helper, I will not be afraid; what can man do to me?'" (Hebrews 13:5-6). In reality, this is nothing more than a faithful echo of Christ's own words: "Therefore I tell you, do not be anxious about your life, what you shall eat, nor about your body, what you shall put on ... Consider the ravens: they neither sow nor reap, they have neither storehouse nor barn, and yet God feeds them" (Luke 12:22-24). And St. Paul writes to his disciple Timothy:

> There is great gain in godliness with contentment; for we brought nothing into the world, and we cannot take anything out of the world; but if we have food and clothing, with these we shall be content. But those who desire to be rich fall into temptation, into a snare, into many senseless and hurtful desires that plunge men into ruin and destruction. For the

> love of money is the root of all evils; it is through this craving that some have wandered away from the faith and pierced their hearts with many pangs. (1 Timothy 6:6-10)

Many are ready to say, "Notice what St. Paul says. He does not say, 'Money is the root of all evil,' but rather 'the *love* of money.'" And obviously the philosopher and the theologian will rightly come along and say, "Of course, *self-love* is the root of all evil, for the angels did not fall through a love of money." And this is true. However, let us not suck the marrow out of the words of Scripture. Let us keep both *this* and *that*: self-love in contempt of God is the root of sin, but for humans there is a great temptation to store up self-confidence in wealth and things of this world, so much so that we must exercise great care in this domain.

Money is a means. We all know this, of course, at least at certain moments when we reflect on the matter. This point is quite clear in contemporary America, where our currency is fiat, backed solely by a good-faith trust in the government. However, even when currencies are tied to things like gold, silver, or some other commodity, we have turned those commodities into a means, at least for as long as they are used as a mode of exchange. Gold and silver have their own properties and uses. Gold is used as a conductor in electronics, and silver likewise is an excellent conductor, finding much use, for example, in the manufacture of solar panels. But, when gold and silver are used *precisely as a currency*, we are not directly worried about these properties. We are only concerned with their exchange value. Currency's role is *to flow*, to run along through the veins of industry and exchange, a fact that is captured well in the analogy used by the early modern political philosopher Thomas Hobbes, who called money "the blood of a commonwealth."[173]

It is a great tragedy when someone spends his or her life pursuing fortune for fortune's sake. It is like letting water run without using it for anything meaningful! Such people extend a melancholy warning about what happens when we pursue mere means: we become like a dog chasing its tale, or even more grimly still, like a snake eating itself and causing its own death. Of course, nobody merely pursues wealth for its own sake, with no further explanation. There is always some other, all-devouring motive beneath the surface: emotional insecurity, desire for power and status, and so forth. However, it remains the case that, for as long as one is chasing wealth, one is not running after something which is good *in itself*. One is running after a flow, something which is good solely *as a means*—as something whose value is completely derived in relation to some other use—ultimately, some human use.

When this order of things gets turned upside down, we end up with a world in which everything is for sale. The contemporary social philosopher Michael Sandel has written and lectured on this topic with great clarity. Though not everything that he writes is one hundred percent in line with Catholic teaching, on many points in political philosophy his basic insights harmonize well with the sane presuppositions which are part of the Church's teaching on wealth and society. His book *What Money Can't Buy: The Moral Limits of Markets*, reflects with great clarity and insight on the problem of how market *economies* can degenerate into market *societies*, where it seems like everything has a price tag. It is not an antimarket book, but it is a text which meaningfully reworks the old maxim used (and, arguably, abused) by Mastercard: "There are some things that money can't buy." Sandel's point is simple: There are some things that money *shouldn't* buy, some things that it is *immoral* for money to buy. If we treat everything as though it were measured by money, we lose touch with an important fact: money's value is derivative and secondary. In short, we must avoid falling afoul of what Aristotle saw even prior to the coming of Christ. If our soul is not in order, we will forever look to fulfill our spoken and unspoken desires and ambitions, turning everything into a means for procuring wealth:

> Given that they are excessive in their desire for enjoyment, they seek out an art which produces an excess of enjoyment, and if they are not able to provide for their pleasures by means of the art of getting wealth, they try other arts, in turn using every faculty in a way that is contrary to nature. For example, the virtue of courage is not intended to make wealth but, rather, to inspire confidence. Nor is wealth the aim of the general's art, nor that of the physician, for the first aims at military victory and the latter at fostering health. Nonetheless, some men turn every character trait or art into a means for getting wealth, conceiving that this is the purpose of life, striving to make all things contribute in promotion of this goal.[174]

It is in pursuit of *intrinsic goods* that we must spend our money, and those goods measure how much money we need. This is obvious when it comes to our family life. We convince ourselves, yes, that we are doing well by saving for retirement and for our children's future education. And, truth be told, this is something admirable when done in a virtuous manner. However, Providence has not placed us on this earth merely to save up for the rat race of the next generation, building barns from generation to generation in which our dynasty can store up their money. Christ was quite clear: store your treasure elsewhere; store it in heaven (see Matthew 6:19-21; Luke 12:13-31). God's grace gives you a wonderful gift. By his own power and bounty, your deeds can themselves merit eternal reward! Why would you store up your coins here when your love can expand for all eternity? Virtue, merit, living the divine life—these are the reasons for having and using money. It is beautiful to build a home that is welcoming for your family and friends without, however, feeling the need to engage in an endless pursuit of wealth without true time for reflection and the shared life of love and virtue! Business is a negotiation with what is most important in our life. Business and work is *nec-otium*—the Latin roots of the word *negotiation* literally mean, "not leisure." Leisure (properly understood as reflection and virtuous living), not the marketplace, is the foundation of life and culture.[175]

However, we need not return to political philosophy and to Aristotle. We need only turn to the words of the early Christian community. The matter was quite clear to the apostolic era of the Church. Consider, for example, the words of St. John to his community: "But if any one has the world's goods and sees his brother in need, yet closes his heart against him, how does God's love abide in him?" (1 John 3:17). In fact, this injunction is made on the heels of a quite exacting requirement: "He laid down his life for us; and we ought to lay down our lives for the brethren" (1 John 3:16). This self-sacrifice and service led to the formation of a community wherein the needs of others were placed directly in the foreground: "And all who believed were together and had all things in common; and they sold their possessions and goods and distributed them to all, as any had need" (Acts 2:44-45). And the preaching of the Gospel aroused conversion in faith alongside generous action on behalf of others:

> And with great power the apostles gave their testimony to the resurrection of the Lord Jesus, and great grace was upon them all. There was not any one needy among them, for as many as were possessors of lands or houses sold them, and brought the proceeds of what was sold and laid it

> at the apostles' feet; and distribution was made to each as any had need. (Acts 4:33-35)

The great movement of monasticism that swept through the Church as Christianity became more socially respectable in fact saw itself as nothing more than a return to these early communal values. Do our parish communities live up to this standard?

And this is not a mere matter of "charity." The virtue of "liberality," or what we could call "generosity," is a question of justice! We owe it to others to be generous with our time, our abilities, and, yes, our money. All of this must be decided in view of our own particular needs and requirements. This is why the virtue of prudence is active everywhere, even in questions of justice. Moreover, we need the guidance of God's Spirit, for it is indeed quite difficult for the rich to enter the kingdom of God! Let us not explain away the loftiness of our Christian calling by applying a minimizing interpretation to Christ's words: "Truly, I say to you, it will be hard for a rich man to enter the kingdom of heaven. Again I tell you, it is easier for a camel to go through the eye of a needle than for a rich man to enter the kingdom of God" (Matthew 19:23-24). We who live in the first world must take consolation that all things are possible for God! Nonetheless, let us remember that the apostles left all things to follow Christ, and it is not merely to them that he preached his gospel. The call to holiness—to *eminent, loving, self-giving holiness*, a holiness that is greater than that of the scribes and the Pharisees (Matthew 5:20)—is a calling made to all Christians! We are all called to perfection in charity.[176]

But take care not to misinterpret my words. A Christian understanding of wealth is neither Marxist, nor socialist, nor capitalist. It is none of these, for it contains what is true in these systems of thought while far surpassing them. All of these economic theories were born outside of the Church in the secular rapacity of the modern era.[177] The Church thinks in centuries, for she is old and wise, having seen the coming and going of many kings and kingdoms, of many nations and empires. Thus, it took some time for her thought to germinate concerning the modern social order, even though there were indeed many medieval, renaissance, and baroque theologians who fought against the excesses of markets and of governments. However, the most pronounced beginning of Catholic social theory came in the mid-nineteenth century with the Italian Jesuit

Luigi Taparelli, whose influence would irrigate the thought of a man who would come to play an important role in the late nineteenth century: Vincenzo Pecci, Pope Leo XIII. Through Taparelli, it was the Catholic Church who minted the notion of "social justice," though in a sense quite different from the nebulous contemporary use of this expression. In its original meaning, the expression indicated how all the various groups in a society (families, various free associations, local governments, larger governmental associations, and so forth) all related to each other in a truly just way, recognizing the rights of each kind of association. Catholics have the intellectual rights here, and we should exercise them! However, that is a matter for another book![178]

Continuing the reforms of his illustrious predecessor, Blessed Pius IX, Pope Leo XIII inaugurated a number of great renewals in the Church during his papacy, which lasted from 1878 to 1903. In the area of social doctrine, he took up the Church's condemnation of communism and socialism (already condemned in a decisive fashion during the papacy of Pius IX). The message communicated in his 1891 encyclical *Rerum Novarum* was so clear and resounding that this text is often accounted as the official beginning of Catholic social teaching. Of course, it is not, for the roots for this teaching go back through the centuries, all the way into the Old Testament, which itself contains a vast wealth of social teaching in the Law, the wisdom literature, and the Prophets. However, in the modern era, Leo's encyclical represents a major step forward, for it addressed the problems of the new economy, insisting that there does not need to be a class struggle, while also, however, recognizing the need for change in the social order. Much of the later papal teachings on the economy and on society would come to be formulated in explicit relation to Leo's own proclamation.

Now, in one sense, the Church is not revolutionary. She does not call for the tearing down of the wealthy, nor does she call for the crushing of the worker. Instead, she merely says, live virtuously in your surroundings and fulfill your duties, those which are closest to you. We are called to this kind of faithfulness in small things (Luke 16:10-13), like stewards over the little corner of history that has been given to us for the time being (see Matthew 25:14-30; Luke 19:11-27). If someone were to say to you that you should truly neglect your own children or relatives so that you could do good for someone far away, in another country, you would be justified in being aghast at this request. Obviously, wealthy nations and their citizens must help other nations. However, if we start there and solely focus our attention there, we will find that we are merely writing checks to unknown people while, perhaps, not paying any attention to those near us to whom we owe, in justice, a true debt of generosity.

As the son of Slavic immigrants who worked in the mines and steel mills in western Pennsylvania, I cannot help but look on the network of libraries and public works projects undertaken by the great coal and steel barons with a somewhat jaundiced eye. The great titans of that era of American industry had the good sense to be publicly generous with their money, and no doubt there was sincerity in such giving. However, their first duty was to their workers, who were in fact often treated as convenient and cheap Eastern European labor. I was blessed to grow up in the shadow of my great-grandparents' generation, who survived well into my childhood, and they were of great influence on my own mother, as well as on her father. Their tales, echoed by many who lived through the last days of the old order of coal mining, ring all too clearly and truly in my ears, forever giving me pause when reflecting on these matters, as do the words of Scripture themselves, where St. James thunders, as is his wont, against the excesses of the wealthy: "Has not God chosen those who are poor in the world to be rich in faith and heirs of the kingdom which he has promised to those who love him? But you have dishonored the poor man. Is it not the rich who oppress you, is it not they who drag you into court?" (James 2:5-6).

While public expenditure is good and admirable, it is hard not to remember that traditional Catholic moral teaching has a rather short list of sins that cry out to heaven, all drawn directly from Scripture. These are murder ("the blood of Abel"); the "sin of the Sodomites"; mistreatment of the oppressed and "the foreigner, the widow, and the orphan"; and "injustice to the wage earner" (CCC 1867). Many become uneasy with one or another sin placed on this traditional list. In this book, we reflect on the first two, at least to a degree, in our discussions of abortion and contraception. The others are touched on indirectly in our other chapters, for they are better handled in a text on Catholic social teaching. Here, though, we must heed again just how stern Scripture is concerning matters of wealth. The final member of the list of sins just recounted—"injustice to the wage earner"—finds its basis both in the Old Testament

(Deuteronomy 24:14-15) and in the New Testament in the letter of James, where very strong words are stated deserving of full citation:

> Come now, you rich, weep and howl for the miseries that are coming upon you. Your riches have rotted and your garments are moth-eaten. Your gold and silver have rusted, and their rust will be evidence against you and will eat your flesh like fire. You have laid up treasure for the last days. Behold, the wages of the laborers who mowed your fields, which you kept back by fraud, cry out; and the cries of the harvesters have reached the ears of the Lord of hosts. You have lived on the earth in luxury and in pleasure; you have fattened your hearts in a day of slaughter. (James 5:1-5)

Thunderous words! But we who live in the first world, wealthier than any others throughout the whole of human history, should all get nervous when we hear them. A concern with wealth-obsession is not merely something which applies to the "one percent." It should apply to almost all of us in one way or another, depending on our particular circumstances. Otherwise, we will find ourselves like the prosperous, lukewarm people who are condemned in the book of Revelation:

> So, because you are lukewarm, and neither cold nor hot, I will spew you out of my mouth. For you say, ["]I am rich, I have prospered, and I need nothing["]; not knowing that you are wretched, pitiable, poor, blind, and naked. Therefore I counsel you to buy from me gold refined by fire, that you may be rich, and white garments to clothe you and to keep the shame of your nakedness from being seen, and salve to anoint your eyes, that you may see. Those whom I love, I reprove and chasten; so be zealous and repent. (Revelation 3:16-19)

Yet, we must be clear, for many bend these points to their own particular political agendas. The Church does not therefore say, "The government must handle all of this. Send it to the feds." No, indeed not! There is something which, in fact, is quite revolutionary in her teaching. She condemns all excesses, and Christ's calling resounds to each and every one of us. The gospel first and foremost calls each of us to *personal* conversion and to perform our duties, without being concerned with fixing the faults of others. Our own faults are quite enough to deal with! They make up one part of the anxieties spoken of by our Lord when he said, "Therefore do not be anxious about tomorrow, for tomorrow will be anxious for itself. Let the day's own trouble be sufficient for the day" (Matthew 6:34).

Our first duties are not to the whole world, nor to the broad swathe of the nation taken as a whole. It's all too easy to write a check and send it off to a charity or to pay the tax man in order to fund some program of use to citizens in a city or state that is far away from us. But as we already considered in our discussions on the family and on taxes and our duties as citizens, the Church's teaching on "subsidiarity" reminds us that we are actually first defined by our closest relations. We must be generous to our own family, to our neighbors, and to our community. Yes, Christ announced the Great Commission so that the whole world might receive salvation: "Go therefore and make disciples of all nations, baptizing them in the name of the Father and of the Son and of the Holy Spirit, teaching them to observe all that I have commanded you" (Matthew 28:19-20). However, he did not commission *each* of us to save the *entire* world. Rather, he sends us forth to help in the salvation and temporal well-being of those who are closest to us. Let us recall that heaven rejoices when even one sinner repents (Luke 15:10), which we might extend to meaning that heaven rejoices when truly meritorious and generous deeds burst forth in the humble matrix of our day-to-day life.

How could we fail to be inspired by St. Paul's own great eagerness to raise money for the poor in the Church, something he admits that he was most eager to do (Galatians 2:10; see Romans 15:25-32; 1 Corinthians 16:1-4; 2 Corinthians 8–9)? And when the apostle says, "So then, as we have opportunity, let us do good to all men, and *especially to those who are of the household of faith*" (Galatians 6:10, emphasis added), he is not saying, "Forget all outsiders and don't waste your money on those sinful scum." No! He is merely voicing a sane point of counsel: These are your brothers and sisters, your truly closest relatives, for they share with you the divine life. How could you not be willing to help them in their need? It is no small wonder that an ancient letter was attributed to his apostle, Barnabas, making this very point: "Share with your neighbor whatever you have, and do not say of anything, 'This is mine.' If you both share an imperishable treasure, how much more must you share what is perishable."[179]

Let us attempt to end on something of a positive note, for generosity should not be presented as something negative. No, it is an aspect of the self-giving, self-diffusive character of the great goodness to which we are all called. Now, among the various virtues enumerated alongside courage, St. Thomas numbers "magnificence," an interesting virtue having to do with the topic we have been discussing. The virtue he is describing under this name (following observations made by Aristotle) deals with readiness to undertake large expenditures in a virtuous way. An overly great attachment to money must not prevent us from spending greatly when this is appropriate, as it is appropriate, with an attitude that is appropriate, and so forth. (Virtue balances many scales!)

This seems, perhaps, a bit strange, though. Is there not a particular vice which plagues those who overspend—the vice of prodigality? Isn't being "magnificent" a bit garish, showing off one's wealth? The daydream of Tevye in *Fiddler on the Roof* as he sings "If I Were a Rich Man" comes to mind; he describes his dream house with three staircases built just to show off. Did not Christ say, "Beware of practicing your piety before men in order to be seen by them ... When you give alms, sound no trumpet before you ... [rather,] do not let your left hand know what your right hand is doing, so that your alms may be in secret" (Matthew 6:1-4)? Is there any possible way we could hide away great acts? Is not the idea of magnificence all too much like a great trumpet, ready to "toot our horn"?

The solution is quite easy: we must "hide" our deeds in virtue! Make something else shine with the gilding of our money. Celebrate something which deserves to be celebrated, in a way that is appropriate, and then our money will become what it truly is: an instrument, a mere means. Perhaps to the Greek philosopher, magnificence was only a virtue for the great and the wealthy, but we have many opportunities to do great and magnificent things. The garish showiness of American weddings does bear witness (through excess ...) to a very important fact: this event is highly important for symbolizing the union of two people and of two families. Instead of giving in to the impulse of the selfish self-aggrandizement that plagues the world of American weddings, Christians can use weddings as an opportunity for a beautiful liturgy and for a meal that will somehow uniquely bring together these two families. Likewise, every holiday presents an opportunity for setting aside a bit of financial fear so that many can be served from our table and at our hearth. In fact, God in the flesh, Jesus Christ, tells us quite directly to hold banquets! But they are to be banquets which are clothed in virtue with a love which does not look for repayment. In this way, we will take on the appearance of God himself, who calls all of us poor sinners to the great banquet of heaven: "When you give a dinner or a banquet, do not invite your friends or your brothers or your kinsmen or rich neighbors, lest they also invite you in return, and you be repaid. But when you give a feast, invite the poor, the maimed, the lame, the blind, and you will be blessed, because they cannot repay you. You will be repaid at the resurrection of the just" (Luke 14:12-14). Let us make use of the great feasts of the Church to store up such merits for heaven—all the while making the love of God descend upon our neighbors.

Still, let us not forget that the widow's mite was worth more than all the abundant funds offered by the wealthy (Luke 21:1-4). The little way of St. Thérèse of Lisieux is the pathway for all of us to walk. In the end, God will look upon all the splendors of the material world and say, "In one hour all this wealth has been laid waste" (Revelation 18:17). However, for the time being, with all our wealth, we have a task set before us:

> As for the rich in this world, charge them not to be haughty, nor to set their hopes on uncertain riches but on God who richly furnishes us with everything to enjoy. They are to do good, to be rich in good deeds, liberal and generous, thus laying up for themselves a good foundation for the future, so that they may take hold of the life which is life indeed. (1 Timothy 6:17-19)

We can radiate an eternal and divine light in all kinds of small acts of generosity. Thus, take up this virtue of justice—namely, the virtue of liberality or generosity—and brandish it like a sword in the service of love! What small thing can you do for a neighbor, your spouse, a friend, or a relative today—small to the eyes of the world but soaked with the eternal splendors of divine grace? In this way, justice becomes something more than justice. It becomes a tool in the service of fraternal charity. But even when applied in such noble service, this particular virtue remains something that we, strictly speaking, *owe* to our brothers and sisters: the readiness to give generously from our abundance, the virtue of liberality or generosity. May our virtue of prudence be ready to serve this impulse, giving us a quick eye to see those moments when the smallest of generous acts might also radiate a blinding light, the light of the divine love. Then, we can truly say that our righteousness exceeds that of the Pharisees and scribes (Matthew 5:20).

COURAGE

With the virtues of courage and temperance, we find ourselves entering into the domain of the passions and emotions. Everything in our being—our joys and delights, our fears and sorrows—must be elevated to the divine level of our vocation as reborn children of God. Through courage, we refashion our fear and anger so that we are forever ready to spring into action for what is truly moral, virtuous, and indeed divine. This is a virtue which belongs to all Christians, for we are all soldiers—not warring *against* others but, rather, vigorously pushing forward under the banner of Christ's love. This section is devoted to this virtue and to what it means for us as we live out our vocation in an increasingly post-Christian world.

CHAPTER TWENTY-THREE

Courage: Getting Fear and Anger Under the Control of the Golden Mean

With the virtues of courage and temperance, we are turning more and more toward what is most human in our morality, what is most "earthy," we could say. The theological virtues of faith, hope, and charity divinize our minds and wills, enabling us to know and love God supernaturally. Prudence and its related virtues perfect the mind, the "intellect," so that we can make right moral choices and, indeed, perform actions when it is appropriate to do so and in a truly virtuous manner, taking all the various circumstances into account. Finally, the virtue of justice perfects the will, the spiritual power of desire and activity which is unique to humans, our "rational appetite" as it was traditionally called. Our wills must be ready to observe rights where they are truly found, ready to recognize everywhere that something is truly *owed* to another person or institution.

Obviously, all of these virtues touch on our lives as humans, as embodied creatures. We have faith in the *incarnate* Lord. We love our brothers and sisters, not mere abstractions. What would prudence be without unbiased moral memory, which must make use of all the synapses in our brains? What would familial justice be without bodily relationships? So, of course, we must not overly spiritualize the virtues that we have discussed thus far. Nonetheless, in traditional Catholic moral terminology, what these virtues perfect are our mind (or, "intellect") and will, our spiritual powers of knowledge and of love. Faith, hope, charity, prudence, and justice are all lodged in the spiritual heavens of the soul.

In the cases of the various virtues related to courage and temperance, we find ourselves considering matters that directly touch our desires and joys, our fears and sources of anger. Grace must take up the entire mass of who we are and transform it. We are works in progress, with passions and emotions that are doubly unruly. They are unruly merely because of the frailty of human nature but also because of the congenital moral defect from which we all suffer—namely, the effects of original sin, which will remain in us all of our lives alongside the effects of sins which we have ourselves freely committed. We limp along as humans, and our souls quiver with the effects of sin, which place us out of harmony with the life we are called to live.

Thus, we must, so to speak, tune these discordant strings. We often love things which we ought not to love; we allow fear to dissuade us from doing what is right; and with a prideful heart, we rush forward into action, following our anger unreflectively, often to our own detriment as well as to the harm of others. Indeed, how often do we speak ill words of our family, friends, and neighbors merely because we are angry and feel self-justified. The words of St. James are aimed at us like a keen arrow: "Let every man be quick to hear, slow to speak, slow to anger, *for the anger of man does not work the righteousness of God*" (James 1:19-20). We must take all of our passions of desire and joy, of fear and anger, and make them instruments of grace: "Do not yield your members to sin as instruments of wickedness, but yield yourselves to God as men who have been brought from death to life, and your members to God as instruments of righteousness" (Romans 6:13).

Based on a long tradition, going back at least to the Greek philosopher Plato, the human passions have been divided into two major camps. There are those which deal with matters of love, desire, sorrow, and hatred. Traditionally, in Western Christianity, these are called "the concupiscible appetite." However, since the expression is quite clunky, we could call them the "passions of desire." These are the passions which are "tempered" by the virtues associated with temperance. Traditionally, these passions numbered as follows: love (as a feeling, not as a theological virtue), desire, joy, hatred, aversion, and sorrow. On the other hand, there are passions which deal with our response to the difficulties experienced in life, giving us our "fight or flight" response. Traditionally, these have been called the "irascible appetite," but we could also call them, in clearer language, "passions of fear and anger." These passions are hope (as a feeling, not as a theological virtue), despair, daring, fear, and anger. These passions are put in order by the virtues related to courage. All of these passions, both “of desire” and “of fear and anger,” could be discussed at great length; however, such detailed teaching must be left to other books, some of which I will list in a note.[180]

For our purposes, let us take a moment in order to note something about the more general term we are using, “passion,” which we are treating as being roughly equivalent to “feeling” or “emotion” for the purposes of this introductory text. In the *Catechism*, we are told, “In themselves passions are neither good nor evil. They are morally qualified only to the extent that they effectively engage reason and will” (CCC 1767). In other words, if we merely consider love, hate, joy, anger, or fear, we really can’t say whether or not something morally good or morally evil is involved. We will need to ask, for example, “Are you actively (i.e., *with your will*) loving something that *truly* should be loved? Are you shrinking back in fear (i.e., *with your will*) from something that is *truly* your duty?” The passions are tools, we might say. We sin by misusing them, by allowing them to throw us off the path of virtue, but by themselves, they are indifferent.

Now, you should take care when you read some traditional Christian authors, who use the term “passion” in a slightly different sense. Many early monastic writers (and those who have been influenced by them) use the term “passion” where the *Catechism* would use the term “vice.” This can make such authors sound like they are haters of emotion or of the body. However, this is somewhat deceptive, given the difference of language involved here.

The language that they use comes from philosophers who are called Stoics. We use the word “stoic” today to describe someone who does not show much emotion. This contemporary meaning is derived from these philosophers’ own particular moral teachings, or at least from the way that these teachings have been popularly understood. The name “Stoic” historically comes from a mere historical fact: the first Stoic, the Greek philosopher Zeno of Citium, taught in Athens at a building known as “the painted porch”—in Greek, ποικίλη στοά, or *poikílē stoa´*. They are the front-porch philosophers!

You have perhaps encountered people who say that they are Stoics. This has become a fashionable thing to claim nowadays. Such people often read works by the Roman political figure and philosopher Seneca (known as “the Younger”), by the Greek ex-slave Epictetus (who lived in

Rome during his time of servitude), or by the Roman emperor Marcus Aurelius, finding wisdom in their very sober approaches to life.[181] These men are later Stoics, whose writings are more complete and more easily understandable than the earlier Greek Stoics, whose philosophical teachings come down to us in fragmented form. All of these various Stoic philosophers have had an immense influence, above all through their claim that we must not act in accord with our emotions but, rather, must act "in accord with nature" and "in accord with reason."

This idea of "tempering" our emotions or of not letting the emotions guide us often has left-over residue from Stoic philosophy, which has exercised a great influence on our culture through the centuries. The contemporary "Stoic," reading popular self-help books based on Stoic texts, will tell you that you must not follow your emotions, that you must learn to set your emotions aside so that you can do what is truly "rational." This popular conception of Stoicism emphasizes the supposedly negative side of the passions. Reason must rule, not passion. And this is very true! But Stoic vocabulary always tends to tilt toward a more extreme claim: the passions must be done away with, so that our reason may rule as a lone mistress in her kingdom!

Now, such Stoic language *was* very influential on early Christianity. Many of the writings in the Orthodox collection of monastic texts, the *Philokalia* (compiled in the eighteenth century but based on ancient sources), use language about emotions and the passions in a way that reminds the reader of Stoicism. The collection *The Sayings of the Desert Fathers*[182] also bears the marks of Stoic verbiage, and the monastic goal of "apatheia," meaning "freedom from the passions, *a-pathos*," is Stoic in provenance. This language comes down to our own day, and it tends to make the passions seem like something bad, something to be overcome, so that we might be ... well ... apathetic!

Obviously, you should be *feeling* a kind of revulsion at that idea. There is nothing unknown to Christ, neither joy nor sorrow, neither love nor anger. All of these emotions can be encountered in the Gospels; all of them can be divinized in our own lives. Christ wasn't merely speaking about a kind of disembodied, unfeeling state of soul when he said, "These things I have spoken to you, that my joy may be in you, and that your joy may be full" (John 15:11). Yes, through grace, we have the greatest *spiritual* joy. However, as we have stressed so often in this book, grace needs to descend down into every nook and cranny of who we are. We must be fully divinized in every corner of our being! The spiritual joy of charity must change our emotions, or passions, too. In the vision of God in heaven, the resurrected will have their beatitude spill over onto all of their being, including their sense powers and their passions. They will not be destroyed but, instead, will then find their noblest form of exercise.

The Stoic language of "apatheia," taken up by the Fathers, can be harmonized with the language drawn from the Catechism above. When we say that "reason" (that is, prudence, illuminated by faith) must rule our moral life, this is very true. But the "rule" that is exercised does not need to be tyrannical. The Church teaches that although reason (illuminated by faith) does indeed rule the realm of Christian morality, it does so by means of a kind of "politically just" rule. Through the exercise of the virtues, we help to put the passions *in order* so that we can find true joy and so that fear and anger can be deployed in the *true* battle that must be waged for the sake of justice and truth. To be "apathetic" in the truly Christian sense means not to allow passion—emotion, or *pathos*—to have the ruling role in our lives. To draw an image going all the way back to Plato, prudence, like a charioteer, must steer the strong horses of our passions so that they may help us win the race. In the words of Fr. Gardeil,

> With his gaze fixed on the course that he must travel, he holds his horses in hand. He has an eye for everything: for accidents on the road, for the advance of his rivals, and for the smallest movements of his animals, whose unique character he has come to know in every detail. This one rears up, that one acts freely, and the other strains against the reins. Nonetheless, the chariot driver pulls his harness, and by his voice—and, if necessary, by the whip—he tempers, stabilizes, and excites them, ceaselessly implementing his initiatives in the midst of the circumstances facing him, knowing how to modify its conduct along the way and how, so to speak, to shape his interventions onto the life of his team.[183]

The charioteer is not merely exercising his horses for their own sake. No, he guides them toward victory. He has a race to win. In a similar way, the virtues related to temperance and courage are not something that we generally pursue for their own sake. They *help* other virtues as instruments.[184] It's quite difficult to imagine the situation in which we merely would be temperate *for the sake of being temperate* or would be courageous merely for the sake of being courageous. These virtues help us to have the tools needed so that we might exercise loftier virtues, the many virtues related to justice and, above all, the theological virtues of faith, hope, and charity. We are careful about drinking alcohol *because we do not wish to endanger ourselves either physically or morally*. We watch what we eat *for the sake of our health* or *in order to avoid spending money wastefully on food*. On days of fasting, we forgo foods *in order to give even our bodies to God as part of the sacrifice which we offer as a form of religious observance*. And when we are courageous, we are such *because we are standing up for something or for someone*. In all of these cases, temperance and courage are *for the sake of something* else, dynamic tools used in the service of higher virtues, a fact that is reflected in the language above: "because ... for the sake of ... in order to ..."

Now, let's consider the dynamic that is involved in courage, as we try to hit the mark of this virtue. My very first teaching job, while I was still completing my dissertation, was in a night school program tailored to nontraditional students, who were very insightful and a joy to teach. However, I was always surprised at how much time I had to spend describing to them the difference between *courage* and *rashness*. Clearly, our culture had taught them the notion referred to by the term "courageous" primarily described people who are ready to run headlong into battle with their swords drawn, no matter the circumstances!

This misconception called for an important correction. I needed to make clear the old maxim "*In medio stat virtus*": virtue is found in the golden mean! Now, what is this "golden mean"? It sounds like something very serene and very Greek, measured and carefully cut like a marble statue which is beautiful but not all that daring, indeed, not bold like Christian boldness! What is meant by the claim that we must aim for the "mean," the "middle path"? For Aristotle and then for the Church, who took up his language, the idea of the "golden mean" refers precisely to something we have already referred to in terms of *hitting the mark of virtue*. It is the "point of perfection" which avoids all vice and backsliding. The golden mean stands like a mountain peak between *two different* vices, which are akin to deep pits of failure!

In the case of courage, we have the two failures of *rashness* and *cowardice*. The former falls short of virtue *by being excessive*, the latter *by being deficient*. The rash person rushes forward, whether merely in anger or because of fear of inaction, toward something that should not be done right now. How often have we rushed into a decision because we did not want to sit and think things through? How quickly have we spoken ill about someone only to find out that we misunderstood his or her motivations or actions? The coward, by contrast, shrinks back in fear, refusing to act or even fleeing from action when he or she should act. Do we avoid conflict because we do not want to face the difficulties that might come with confronting someone about his or her self-destructive habits? It might seem a bit strange, at first glance, to say it, but are not many cases of procrastination nothing more than a kind of cowardice, a fear of "getting the ball rolling," of starting our work which might involve no small difficulty? The person with courage finds a way to face fears while also avoiding rashly running forward. He or she finds the *golden mean*, the peak between the valleys of vice—here, the vices of rashness and cowardice.

Notice, therefore, that this "golden mean" is not merely, as a certain early modern philosopher wrote, "a mediocrity of passions." It's not a question of being like Goldilocks, looking to have porridge that is "just right," lukewarm and easily slurped down. Christ has called us to live a life of *extreme* holiness: "I came to cast fire upon the earth; and would that it were already kindled!" (Luke 12:49). Finding the perfect aim between rashness and cowardice is a truly difficult task! And living out this courage is quite difficult as well, requiring a well-trained eye and fingers to guide the bow string to launch the arrow at the target.

Now, how do we find this perfect aim and pull the string? The answer is obvious, for we have already said it above: by means of the virtue that gives us the "clear moral eye," the virtue of prudence. It is the chariot driver spoken of in the quote above. By means of prudence, we set the middle path of courage, turning left when we must turn left and turning right when we must go off to the right. In matters of courage and temperance, prudence has a very important role to play, for each of us has a different character, different circumstances, different duties, different strengths, and different weaknesses, all of which must be weighed out so that we may stay on the "straight and narrow," the path of virtue. As we said in our earlier chapters on prudence, there are indeed moral absolutes. *Never* will it be morally good to be intemperate, rash, or cowardly. But we must find the path forward in our own unique circumstances. How important, therefore, it is to have a spiritual guide through the mountain passes which lead us to the peak of virtue. Here, we should hear the words of Christ echoing in our ears: "Enter by the narrow gate; for the gate is wide and the way is easy, that leads to destruction, and those who enter by it are many. For the gate is narrow and the way is hard, that leads to life, and those who find it are few" (Matthew 7:13-14). Prudence is needed so that we might find the golden mean in these virtues![185]

As we draw this chapter to a close, it should be clear that if we are courageous, we do not lose our passions. No! If we are courageous, we find that we are ready and able to use our fears and our feelings of anger and "verve" in order to push forward toward whatever it is that we must accomplish. If we are married people, we are prepared to face the possible difficulties of having children, able to look fear in the eye and nonetheless remain undaunted. When we see an injustice at work, in our own family, or in our community, courage will prevent us from merely slinking away from doing our duty to help overturn this injustice. And sometimes even in small things, we will learn to overcome the insidious and crippling power of fear. How many exercise programs, which would help our mental and physical health, are avoided out of fear of the pain which they will cause? Even something as minor as healthy living is part of the battlefield of morality, requiring a courageous heart!

The courageous person will almost certainly not lack feelings of fear. In fact, what would courage be if we weren't facing *truly fearful* circumstances, standing up and (most importantly) *courageously enduring them* in spite of the difficulties to be faced. Yes, indeed, our anger and bold daring must push us forward, but throughout all of this forward motion toward our moral goals, we will still be *facing up* to our fears. This powerful endurance is the primary act of courage. Through such courage, we will work to put our passions in their rightful place so that we might serve God in all the movements that jostle about within our souls, placing the chariot in order so that it may push forward in small and large things, never dissuaded by the passions of fear and anger but, instead, holding fast to what is good, never flagging in zeal, aglow with the Spirit, serving the Lord (see Romans 12:9-12).

CHAPTER TWENTY-FOUR

Courage in the Midst of a Post-Christian World

The virtue of courage has a particularly important role to play as we Christians strive to live in the midst of a world and culture which is increasingly out of step with traditional Christian faith and morality. Yes, we could talk about the need to exercise virtuous kindness in our relations with others, or temperance in the face of the seductions of advertising and of television programming, or humility in the face of the temptation to get ahead in worldly terms. And this would not be a wrong direction for our reflection to meander. All of these virtuous tools must be requisitioned in the service of God and of all that is good. Here, let us look for some light by considering how the virtue of courage must be deployed as an adjunct to train our fear and anger in the exercise of all of these other virtues which are needed in our lives and relationships.

What we will say in this chapter will bear witness to an important fact which we discussed in the previous chapter: virtues like courage and temperance are not good *merely for their own sake*. They put us "in order" so that we can do truly human and virtuous things. We are not merely courageous for the sake of being courageous. We are courageous because there are certain duties that require us to stand up to our fears: protecting our family, refusing to lie even if this might bring us woe, and so forth. Thus, courage and temperance both get mixed up with the other virtues, something that will be clear in the examples we use in this chapter and in those that follow.

In the contemporary West, we live as the heirs of over fifteen hundred years during which Christianity has played a central role in public life. Of course, the world during this time was far from uniformly faithfully Christian. From the very start, during the period when Christianity was made legal, Arianism, denying the divinity of Christ, was held by many (including no few bishops). The Latin Middle Ages were filled with upheaval between rulers and bishops, between kings and popes, between throne and altar. The modern era saw many battles between nation-states and the various Christian communities. Nonetheless, the framework was Christian, and the mainstream was Christian. It was only with the continued advanced of the so-called Enlightenment[186] and the consolidation of its total critique of Christianity that the West finds itself facing the possibility of a truly post-Christian world, one in which the broader culture is actively set in opposition to Christianity, which is increasingly viewed as a relic of a more barbarous, bigoted era.

Persecution is nothing new to Christianity, but we should not take the word lightly. In contrast with first-world claims of persecution, there are *true* persecutions occurring throughout the developing world right now as I write these words and as you read them, so much so that the BBC (an agency which is not looking to grind conservative axes) ran a story in 2019 entitled "Christian Persecution 'At Near Genocide Levels.'" The article pointed to a study concerning the worldwide persecution of Christians.[187] These suffering men, women, and children throughout the world deserve to have the words of Tertullian applied to them: "The blood of the martyrs is the seed of the Church." Concerning them, we must feel, in the depths of our own hearts, the words of the letter to the Hebrews: the world is not worthy of them (Hebrews 11:38).

As Americans, we must be very careful not to equate our difficulties with this true martyrdom happening around the world. Indeed, in recent American memory, everything seems quite different from all of this worldwide persecution. Readers who are members of the baby boom generation will have warm memories of listening to recordings of Bing Crosby singing "Christmas in Killarney" and will recall the days when John F. Kennedy's election signaled to some that American anti-Catholicism had at last come to an end. Even today, no doubt, many will note, as well, the fact that (upon publication of this book) six of the nine of the United States Supreme Court justices are Catholics (over double the representation of Catholics in the general population), along with the current president. There seems to be no conflict between being a contemporary American and being a Catholic.

However, a brief survey of the culture does throw some water on this hopefulness. The end of blue laws that prevented work on Sundays has tempted all of us to turn the Lord's Day into one more day of consumption and work. A ramble through television and movies would prove to us that contemporary morals are quite different from those of the gospel. Our public schooling system actively excludes meaningful religious education from our children's day-to-day academic instruction, often implicitly and directly handing on anti-religious narratives or, at the very least, making religion seem quite secondary to the positive achievements of Western culture and science. (How often do we hear about the Galileo affair without, however, being told about the ways that the Catholic Church has positively influenced the whole of scientific history? Merely to take two examples: Fr. Georges Lemaître proposed the big bang theory, and, even more importantly, the very notion of a university comes down to us from the Western Middle Ages.)

In fact, a number of political changes during the past fifteen to twenty years have led certain conservative commentators, whether Catholic, Orthodox, or Protestant, to emphasize how quickly our culture is getting out of step with a traditional Christian outlook.[188] Indeed, these commentators often emphasize the rapid pace of these changes as the culture careens over the edge, quickly falling away from traditional Christian (and Orthodox Jewish) moral teachings. We see indifference to abortion, a complete cultural acceptance of contraception and a free-flowing sexual culture, the placement of same-sex unions on the same cultural and legal level as heterosexual marriages, a vociferous activism surrounding LGBT issues to the point of silencing anyone who is not in line with the reigning zeitgeist, and the use of medical and insurance regulation laws to force Catholic hospitals to do certain immoral procedures. We also see the mainstreaming of socialism (regularly condemned by the Church as being at least as injurious to right social order as is unfettered individualism),[189] the enslaving of the next generation to the spending of the current generation through debt (whether public or private in the form of student debt, which helps to prop up the special interests of the higher-education establishment), and so forth.

My desire is not to inflame partisan quarreling, nor to consider this dynamic in detail. (Obviously, too, I am not calling for any kind of hatred of *any* group of people—this should be all too obvious from what has been said up to this point in this book and also what is going to be said later in this chapter.) We merely must note these facts, which are obviously not conducive to Catholic life and culture, a claim that should be quite obvious to the eyes of any Catholic with a *Catechism* in hand, let alone faithful works of theology and philosophy.

The commentators mentioned above make various recommendations, from more active engagement in the public sphere to withdrawal into a kind of conservative Christian subculture waiting out the storm and preserving the right order of things for later generations. I am neither a cultural critic nor a politician, so I have little ability to offer prudential prescriptions. However, as a professor of moral philosophy and theology, I can tell you about one thing that will be necessary no matter what path Catholics must take in the coming years: the virtue of courage.

Let us think, for example, of the issue of prolife activism. Each year, the March for Life in Washington, DC, draws large crowds (quite larger than what most media outlets allege, when they bother to recognize it at all). For the *vast* majority of those who attend, it is a peaceful and even joyful protest. These hosts of people—teenagers, families, elderly people, priests, religious, and laity alike—coming from a variety of Christian churches and communities, gather together to make sure that the country does not forget the rights of the unborn, giving voice to the voiceless. I have warm memories, year after year, of attending this event, even of joining with a group of Missouri Synod Lutherans to sing traditional Lutheran hymns as we marched along.

For all these warm memories, however, I must admit that each year when I go to the March, I fear that some act of violence might target the marchers who gather in Washington, DC. Obviously, this would have no historical precedent. Yet, with each passing year, the difference between the general culture and the traditional Christian teaching on abortion grows wider and wider. Courage is needed, each year, in order not to decide, "It's better to avoid the potential danger."

Let us choose another example from the same pool of controversial issues. I have mentioned, in passing, the whole web of controversial topics surrounding the contemporary "LGBT movement." This phenomenon presents seismic changes concerning our human self-understanding as male and female; however, a vociferous part of our culture (frequently backed by corporate and media power) often silences anyone who steps out of line from the prevailing narrative about this topic. There are faithful voices raising their concerns without malice,[190] but I can personally say that more than once I have thought, "Someday I am going to face the 'cancel mob,'" who will readily shout me down without knowing anything meaningful about me other than the fact that I did not one hundred percent agree with the new morality and new vision of humanity proclaimed by this cultural moment. Nonetheless, I must have the courage to teach the Church's position concerning these matters, though doing so in charity and kindness.

This charity and kindness is important, however, to *true* courage. The person who is courageous is not a brash and rash person, who is always ready to "fly off the handle." In fact, such an intemperate person falls into sin. Thus, when discussing this topic in my bioethics courses, I always keep readily in mind the many human complexities involved in these issues. Indeed, they have even touched my own family, so woe to me if I forget the human struggles (above all the sad struggle of sin where it is, in fact, involved) felt by so many people who are actively or passively taken in by the revolutionary assertions of this movement today. While remaining *wholly* faithful to the Church's teachings concerning sexuality and gender, never wishing to muddy the clear water of her doctrine, I also never wish to be a kind of Christian caricature, loudly pronouncing condemnations, casting stones all too readily, despite the fact that we have been warned against doing so by a Person of rather high standing (John 8:7). Between fear and falsely righteous anger, we must find the golden mean. How necessary is the virtue of courage here as well!

We may consider another example which has come up on and off throughout the chapters in this book: education and our children. How difficult it is to raise our children in a way that is, at once, authentically Catholic and yet also not extremist and isolationist. No matter what path we choose—public education, private schooling, or homeschooling—courage is needed so that our spines might not turn to jelly. If we send our children to public schools, we will need to be ready to defend the

Faith—without sounding defensive!—when our children come home with questions raised by teachers or fellow students whose worldviews are quite different from a Catholic one. If we send our children to a faithful Catholic school, we will almost certainly face months where it is tempting to say, "I know we said that we could afford this, but it is so expensive!" Finally, if we choose to homeschool, no matter how much help we receive from fellow parents and relatives, the daily grind with our children will tire us out, the likely need to be a single-income family will cause many pressures, and we will feel nearly exasperated at continually trying to convince our friends and relatives that our children won't grow up to be antisocial. In the latter two cases, even if we are sure that we are performing our parental duties toward our children, we will constantly be reminded that very few people, even our relatives perhaps, care at all about the injustice of the public-school taxation system in the United States. (See the quote above in chapter 20, drawn from official Church sources, concerning this issue.) How much easier it would be just to float along and let "the system" do most of the work so that we can live a comfortable life with our fulfillment in our work and enjoyment afforded to us by the things of this world that we can buy for our amusement! However, if this is the only reason we are sending our children to public school, we have moral problems which we must not fear to face!

We can draw one more example, a quite important one, if we are to truly understand how the Christian must live Christ's staggering humility and courage. How ready we are to think in terms of "market benefits," not merely in financial matters but also in our social interactions. From our youngest days, we are very sensitive to whether or not we fit in with the "in-crowd." As young professionals, we feel the need to "network" with "important" people so that we can have "the right friends." We tell ourselves that we don't want to be viewed as being a "loser." However, is this truly Christian?

I cannot help but think of someone whom I know who moves in very wealthy circles and has done very well for himself. He rubs elbows with important people from all around the world, with the great "movers and shakers" of our day. And yet this same person often spends time with the blue-collar people he has met throughout his life. He makes sure they have a place to go on holidays so that they are not abandoned because of their sad financial and family circumstances. And I remember once when he shared with me how comfortable he felt at a very humble wedding, full of the boisterous dancing and raucous celebrations reminiscent of the working-class wedding celebration which opens up *The Deer Hunter*. When his peers wonder at his character, he reminds them of his humble upbringing. How encouraging it is to see someone who seems to remember the old maxim "Don't get above your raisin'." It calls to mind the closing lines of Rudyard Kipling's poem "If":

> If you can talk with crowds and keep your virtue,
> Or walk with Kings—nor lose the common touch,
> If neither foes nor loving friends can hurt you,
> If all men count with you, but none too much;
> If you can fill the unforgiving minute
> With sixty seconds' worth of distance run,
> Yours is the Earth and everything that's in it,
> And—which is more—you'll be a Man, my son![191]

We are all called to this kind of conduct. I am reminded of a simple scene in the television show *The Chosen*, which presents a dramatized account of the Gospels. Early in the series, Jesus unexpectedly shows up at a Shabbat being held at Mary Magdalene's residence, after he had miraculously healed her. The series portrays Jesus with a perfectly even and human demeanor, soft-spoken without being awkward and introverted, friendly without that cloying "friendliness" we have all experienced in certain people who want to be popular.

Moreover, the men and women who gathered at table are a mixed bag of characters. Christ did not look on them as deplorables. He looked on them as weak and sinful humans in need of salvation—that is, in need of divine friendship. In contrast with the splendid Shabbat being held by the local Pharisees, here he was eating with sinners, something for which the Pharisees would eventually question him (Matthew 9:10-13). In Christ, we see a full and true reflection of St. Paul's words:

> Rejoice with those who rejoice, weep with those who weep. Live in harmony with one another; do not be haughty, but associate with the lowly; never be conceited. (Romans 12:15-16)

> I therefore, a prisoner for the Lord, beg you to walk in a manner worthy of the calling to which you have been called, with all lowliness

> and meekness, with patience, forbearing one another in love, eager to maintain the unity of the Spirit in the bond of peace. (Ephesians 4:1-3)
>
> We who are strong ought to bear with the failings of the weak, and not to please ourselves; let each of us please his neighbor for his good, to edify him. For Christ did not please himself; but, as it is written, "The reproaches of those who reproached you fell on me." (Romans 15:1-3)

This is true Christian courage, a courage that is informed by a supernatural love giving us the readiness to bear all things, to believe all things, to hope all things, and to *endure all things* (1 Corinthians 13:4-7). How much does this fulfill the basic insight of ancient philosophy and classical theology, as summarized under the quill of St. Thomas: "Therefore, the principal act of courage is endurance, that is, to stand unmoved in the midst of dangers, rather than to attack them."[192] And what is the greatest danger but to sin against the virtues and to be unjust or, infinitely worse, to lack charity, merely because we give in to fear of losing our supposed high "status"?

The disciples James and John were the zealous "sons of thunder" (Mark 3:17), who wished to call down fire from heaven to consume a Samaritan village that did not welcome them (Luke 9:52-55). No doubt they said to themselves, "Here we are truly courageous!" However, Christ rebuked them for their rash zeal. The Christian path of courage is far quieter: turning of the cheek, giving of a second cloak when one is requested, and walking two miles when asked only to walk one (Matthew 5:39-41). Let us recall, also, how Christ, the great bringer of true justice, was described in advance by the prophet Isaiah: "He will not cry or lift up his voice, or make it heard in the street; a bruised reed he will not break, and a dimly burning wick he will not quench; he will faithfully bring forth justice" (Isaiah 42:2-3; Matthew 12:19-21).

When we strengthen the virtue of courage, our fears will not go away, but they will not rule us. Nor will courage do away with our anger. Rather, instead of leading us to lash out in self-righteous anger against the "godless," our anger will become a tool enabling us to keep our spines hard and straight in the face of a frustrating and foolish culture. This virtue will help us stand firm—all the while perhaps being quite silently overlooked—in the midst of a world which increasingly (and unjustly) believes that Christianity is a bigoted and ignorant religion. Such Christian courage will help us to reflect, in our own lives, the beautiful description of the early Christian community presented in the second-century text "Letter to Diognetus":

> Christians love all men, but all men persecute them. Condemned because they are not understood, they are put to death, but raised to life again. They live in poverty, but enrich many; they are totally destitute, but possess an abundance of everything. They suffer dishonor, but that is their glory. They are defamed, but vindicated. A blessing is their answer to abuse, deference their response to insult. For the good they do they receive the punishment of malefactors, but even then they, rejoice, as though receiving the gift of life. They are attacked by the Jews as aliens, they are persecuted by the Greeks, yet no one can explain the reason for this hatred.
>
> To speak in general terms, we may say that the Christian is to the world what the soul is to the body. As the soul is present in every part of the body, while remaining distinct from it, so Christians are found in all the cities of the world, but cannot be identified with the world. As the visible body contains the invisible soul, so Christians are seen living in the world, but their religious life remains unseen. The body hates the soul and wars against it, not because of any injury the soul has done it, but because of the restriction the soul places on its pleasures. Similarly, the world hates the Christians, not because they have done it any wrong, but because they are opposed to its enjoyments.
>
> Christians love those who hate them just as the soul loves the body and all its members despite the body's hatred. It is by the soul, enclosed within the body, that the body is held together, and similarly, it is by the Christians, detained in the world as in a prison, that the world is held together. The soul, though immortal, has a mortal dwelling place; and Christians also live for a time amidst perishable things, while awaiting the freedom from change and decay that will be theirs in heaven. As the soul benefits from the deprivation of food and drink, so Christians flourish under persecution. Such is the Christian's lofty and divinely appointed function, from which he is not permitted to excuse himself.[193]

TEMPERANCE

The final set of virtues that we will consider are those related to temperance, by which our desires and joys are put into line with the moral and divine goods we are to pursue as children of God. Too often, these virtues are mischaracterized. Some spurn them as being unimportant and say, "Charity and justice are greater." These words are not false. However, in order for the life-giving water of charity to flow, we need solid riverbanks, lest our passions flood forth! Some, however, present these virtues as though they were merely negative: don't eat too much; don't drink too much; don't have too much sex. This section aims to correct both such errors, showing the beauty of Christian temperance and how it enables the divine light of grace to shine even in the lowliest human corners of our being.

CHAPTER TWENTY-FIVE

Temperance Versus Teetotalism

In the general chapter on courage above, we discussed some important basic points about the virtues of courage and temperance, as well as about the passions in general. There, we mentioned the idea of the "passions of desire," which traditionally have been referred to using a term that is somewhat awkward in English—namely, the "concupiscible appetite." Technically, these passions of desire involve everything in the spectrum of love and hate: love (as a feeling, not as a theological virtue), desire, joy, hatred, aversion, and sorrow.

In the moral philosophy inherited from Aristotle, questions of desire tend to be classified into two categories: food and sex. We could slightly expand food to include, perhaps, alcoholic beverages as a subcategory. However, it would seem that in the end, for the Greek philosopher, these basic desires tell the tale of the virtue of temperance. It is understandable why Aristotle thought this. He was thinking only of those desires, and so forth, that we share with the animal kingdom, what we might call "the lower part" of the soul. Dogs and apes feel their own kinds of aversion and hatred, their own sorts of joy and love. For us humans, all of this neurological wiring and emotional reaction must be elevated by virtue so that it may serve in the overall life of grace which, as has been said on many occasions now, looks to find every small crevice in our character, making all things serve the new life we are given by God. We must spiritualize all of these desires through morality and through grace.

Pleasures of food and sex are the most necessary desires for our basic survival as individuals and as a species. Thus, they exercise a unique power over us, as we all know. However, it is helpful to add some further virtues related to temperance, all elevating other desires involved in human life, such as the desire for knowledge ("studiousness") and attachment to clothing and external appearances ("modesty in dress").[194]

When it comes to matters falling to courage and, in particular, temperance, we find that it is increasingly difficult to describe the moral absolutes involved. Justice can be much easier to explain. You merely need to figure out what is owed and then, once this is put into words, repay that debt. Obviously, as we discussed earlier, there are many forms of justice which are not quite strict tit for tat: the virtues of religion, of "piety" (or "virtuous patriotism," as well as the virtue of recognizing the debt we owe to our parents), and of generosity, merely to name a few. Nonetheless, it is much easier to put into words the basic debts involved even in these broader forms of justice: we owe all things to God as Creator and Redeemer; we owe a debt to our parents and to our country for all the good they have brought us; we owe it to others and to society at large that we use our money for the good of others and not just for ourselves and our families. Because justice is a virtue of the will—a virtue of the "*rational* appetite"—it is highly intelligible, highly *rational*.

Turning to temperance, however, we find it far more difficult to explain just what the boundaries of desire are. The nutritional needs of a physical laborer are different from those of an elderly woman. The limits to be placed on alcohol consumption are quite different for the ex-alcoholic (not one drink!) in contrast with the person who does not suffer from such temptations. Moreover, even in the latter case, how different it is to have several drinks over the course of the evening at a wedding, in contrast to the more problematic case of drinking alone! When it comes to sexual relations, all of this seems very private, and when people give us advice in this domain, we are tempted to say, "Get out of my bedroom!"

However, despite the seeming relativism involved here, there are very basic and universal norms involved even in the virtue of temperance. Though it is quite mundane and obvious, we can come up with a guiding principle that universally applies to every man and woman of goodwill, to every moral person, let alone to the Christian: "Your desires shouldn't merely run wild. They should be organized in view of true human flourishing." Well, then …! That does not seem to go very far. The cynical person will say, "Duh, of course." But what are we to do about all of the details? How will they all be painted out? Indeed,

> how can I determine with certitude, here and now, in matters that directly concern me (and not you) the golden mean to preserve in matters of temperance, meekness, humility, courage, patience—all while this golden mean depends on many particular circumstances that are still known only in a vague manner (or, even at times are unknown), such circumstances including my temperament (be it high-strung, sanguine, or ["laid back" and] phlegmatic), my age, the season (be it summer or winter), my social status, etc. ... etc.?[195]

The answer is, as always, that this is determined by prudence, a virtue which involves careful discernment concerning our particular situation, our current duties and state of soul, our future plans, our past actions, the people who may be involved in our current situation, etc., etc., etc. ...! Sometimes, there will be multiple *correct* and non-sinful options in questions of temperance, for prudence is not always limited merely to finding the one safe path to take. It is more than a sieve filtering out bad options like stones being filtered out of a bag of flour. Prudence commands![196] Often, we can come up with many ways to behave temperately. Let's consider scenarios involving temperance in relation to several different basic matters: food, drink, clothing, sex, and knowledge. Playing out such scenarios will help to reveal the elusive character of this ever-important virtue for the Christian moral life.

The basic case of the virtue of temperance involves food. The most obvious opposed vice is gluttony, but most often people imagine that the glutton is an obese person who has a mouth full of sweet soda and two hot dogs in each hand, along with a pizza to be eaten for dinner, followed up by a pint of ice cream. However, we can go to excess with food—thus falling into sin and vice—in many ways. The sin of gluttony is committed any time that we desire and partake in food beyond the measure involved in other virtues.

For example, my wife and I love fine cheeses. As we joked when we were dating, we knew we were in love because we were sharing in this particular affection when we would visit each other—our meals were marked with our mutual love of a third thing, the wondrous taste of a well-aged blue cheese, a sharp and well-crafted cheddar, and a warm Camembert or Brie cheese topped with berries for dessert. Well, there are coronary risks involved in eating cheese with many meals. However, there also is a risk that you empty your bank account at the fromagerie. This risk has moral repercussions, for one's money is not merely to be spent endlessly on self-indulgence, even if it involves the best of all possible cheeses!

So, how does the virtue of temperance play its role here? The temperate person knows how to put off the purchasing of expensive cheeses for special events. Indeed, my wife and I try to put off visits to the cheese counter, planning such purchasing around the special events which we host at our house: Christmas, Easter, birthdays, and so forth. We try to share our own appreciation of such things with others, who may not enjoy such well-crafted food on their own or who may not be able to afford it. However, this is only possible if we do not indulge in our own love of such cheese all the time. Thus, as I joke with some cousins, we must purchase "weekday cheese" so that we might buy good cheese on shared occasions of celebration. It is like an ancient maxim: he who would have good cheese at Christmas must eat "weekday cheese" in November.

Now, our first example dealt with the case of excess. Gluttony is the most frequent sin opposed to general temperance, but it is possible to fall into deficiency as well. Aristotle seemed to think that this was quite rare—indeed, so infrequent that there really is no name for such a vice. I am reminded, however, of an example mentioned in an earlier chapter, drawn from C. S. Lewis' *Screwtape Letters*, where there is a description of a woman who strives to be "temperate" by being a bother, always asking for just enough food, but not the wrong food, not too much, of course ... This seems all very righteous because it is not gluttonous, while in fact it is quite unvirtuous! In fact, we could say that it is a kind of hidden gluttony through deficiency.[197] We could also think of the person who is far too picky with food, always causing trouble, preferring to sit sullenly without food than to eat with others. Now, while some tastes can't be changed, we nonetheless can train ourselves to have a basic appreciation for things so as to avoid being a rude guest or a boring host!

Let's turn this to the case of sobriety. I come from a family which has experienced the scourge of alcoholism. I am very sensitive to how serious this addiction is. Thus, my next example is not meant to be flippant and unaware of the great suffering that people and families experience because of addiction to alcohol (or to other substances, for that matter). Moreover, even where alcoholism is not, strictly speaking, involved, alcohol can be abused and overused. "Wine is a mocker, strong drink a brawler; and whoever is led astray by it is not wise" (Proverbs 20:1). Drunkenness is indeed a sin to be confessed. However, one of the wondrous things about Catholicism is its ability to hold together, at one and the same time, the asceticism of Lent and a true appreciation of a good drink. There is a quote that floats around on the internet attributed to G.K. Chesterton, though a digital search of his works does not turn up the words in his actual writing. Nonetheless, they cohere well with his overall worldview: "In Catholicism, the pint, the pipe, and the Cross can all fit together."

I think that we can understand the joyful side of temperance if we appreciate the fact that there are times when we can and should enjoy a properly measured amount of alcohol. The virtue of "sobriety" (understood as meaning "virtuous moderation in drinking") does not involve being a teetotaler, avoiding all alcohol at all times. Rather, the person who is "sober," in the sense of that term as used by someone like St. Thomas Aquinas, knows just when to have a drink—as a gentle "social lubricant," as a joyful and tasty cocktail, or as a way of quieting the stomach. When Saint Vincent Archabbey, a German-founded Benedictine monastery in western Pennsylvania, fought against the reigning Irish bishops (who in the nineteenth century often worked in concert with Protestant-inspired temperance movements), Blessed Pope Pius IX gave the monks official permission to brew their own beer for use at table (as they would have done in Bavaria), citing the words of St. Paul to Timothy: "No longer drink only water, but use a little wine for the sake of your stomach and your frequent ailments" (1 Timothy 5:23).[198] If the pope could be somewhat lighthearted in this regard, so can we!

The "sober" person knows how to prepare drinks to match a meal, carefully balancing the amount (and flavor) of alcohol with the food, not overspending in an inappropriate way but also knowing how to avoid being cheap when the occasion calls for celebration. If you have relatives who enjoy rye whiskey or perhaps a nice bourbon-based cocktail, then you can be quite sober if you appropriately plan such a drink into the festive meal that you host at your house. A hot summer evening with a crisp and fresh beer in hand can close off a lovely time together—all without falling into drunkenness and carousing. In the words of Chesterton, "Let a man walk ten miles steadily on a hot summer's day along a dusty English road, and he will soon discover why beer was invented."[199] Measure and balance are needed here, but there is a way that one can be too strict, not appreciating the way that, when used appropriately, wine can indeed gladden man's heart (Psalm 104:15)!

Let us turn to yet another case of temperance: modesty in dress. This topic often inflames passions. "Here it comes," we think. "He or she is going to lecture people for what they wear to Mass. 'De gustibus non est disputandum.' Taste is not subject to dispute." Well, allow me to set my sights on my own caste, the professors. Obviously, generalizations are dangerous, risking bordering on the anecdotal. However, there are two stereotypes of the professor: the tweedy professor with a bow tie and the slobby and disheveled professor who wears a T-shirt even for his or her official faculty picture. The first is potentially off-putting and the latter unprofessional, especially for someone who holds a position which involves handing on the patrimony of human knowledge to the next generation.

The general practices of dress reflect what we think about a given setting and set of social roles. The priest wears vestments in order to put on Christ, signifying that his sacramental action is, in fact, Christ's and not his own. Uniforms in a hospital help to make interactions between staff efficient. One expects someone who is giving a speech in dignified company to be dressed appropriately, lest those attending be insulted by slovenly attire which does not match the occasion. And the professor, whose expertise gives him or her a role of *teacher* in relation to *learner*, of *knower* in relation to someone who still must *come to knowledge*, should reflect this in his or her clothing. Otherwise, one might say that there is such a thing as an insult against the "truth" of the professor-student relationship.

Of course, one can overdo it. I sometimes feel that when I was in graduate school at the Catholic University of America, we overdid it a bit in the school of philosophy. A number of us prided ourselves on being better dressed than the graduate students in other departments, all of us acting very professional, not chummy "like those slobs." The error of my ways bears witness to the way that modesty and humility are interrelated: we must act in a way that befits the *truth* of who we are and the particular role that we must play. (And remember: humility is above all concerned with *living in the truth*!) The professor who insists on always playing the role of a professor, always dressed in a bow tie and tweed no matter the occasion, is guilty of immodesty by way of excess. However, the professor who slobs about, regularly wearing jeans and a T-shirt for lectures, rightly leads his or her students to wonder, "Why should I take this subject seriously, since he or she clearly doesn't think there is anything more important about this interaction than I do when going to the store?" I've known many poor professors who have their one old tweed jacket. Perhaps it is a bit too ill fitting, but at least they were aware that, given the fact that they are professionals, they should bother to attempt to dress like one.

Let those who have ears hear how this example can apply in so many ways in our own lives! It applies at work, yes! But how true it also is that we need not treat the whole world as though it were our bedroom or living room. And yes, the most important of all things in the world, the holy sacrifice of the Mass, should probably be different from going to a sporting event!

Now, let's move on to chastity. In a later chapter, we will take up the topic of contraception, which is profoundly connected to the full understanding we must have of the virtue of chastity. However, we should consider the words of Christ here, for he fulfilled the Law to the utmost: "You have heard that it was said, 'You shall not commit adultery.' But I say to you that every one who looks at a woman lustfully has already committed adultery with her in his heart" (Matthew 5:27-28). And when, on another occasion, he discussed the prohibition of divorce, his disciples responded in shock: "If such is the case of a man with his wife, it is not expedient to marry" (Matthew 19:10). Christian chastity requires a full purity of heart in sexual matters. Here we sense the great distance which separates the Christian from our broader culture in the developed world. How difficult it is for even preteens to avoid exposure to pornography, and how many marriages are endangered by the lusts to which we all are prey, the wishful thinking which so easily tempts us to think that sweeter fruit is to be found elsewhere!

There are a number of excellent resources concerning Catholic sexual ethics, and given all the intricacy (and strong feelings) involved here, I believe it best to leave such matters to other books, several of which I will cite in a note for your further reading.[200] But, no matter how many details are discussed in such texts, the basic point remains the same: there are limits in all things human, including sexuality. It is tempting today to speak of this domain of human activity as though there were no such boundaries: "It is nobody's business what I do in the bedroom!"

Now, some who say such things also express concerns about overpopulation or climate change. Obviously, we should not be rapacious consumers who are heedless of the environment. However, if need be, would such persons approve of the governmental *requirement* of contraception for married couples? Such laws would represent quite an intrusion into the bedroom and the fundamental right to raise a family. The possibility of such misuse of public authority was considered not by some conspiracy theorist in a tinfoil hat but, instead, by the last pope to wear the papal tiara, St. Paul VI, who wrote in 1968:

> Who will prevent public authorities from favoring those contraceptive methods which they consider more effective? Should they regard this as necessary, they may even impose their use on everyone. It could well happen, therefore, that when people, either individually or in family or social life, experience the inherent difficulties of the divine law and are determined to avoid them, they may give into the hands of public authorities the power to intervene in the most personal and intimate responsibility of husband and wife.[201]

Far better for the Church to preach that we should be virtuous in our spousal-sexual relationships, ever ready with the forgiveness of the confessional, than for the culture and government to treat procreation as a technical problem with a contraceptive set of limits! The Church bases all of her teaching here on the sane idea that desires are not to be followed willy-nilly. We would try to get help for someone who treats food like an unfettered good. It is insanely inconsistent not to see that this is true for sexual relations, something far more beautiful, far more interpersonal, and far more important than mere food and drink!

But, let us end with one last example, one that is perhaps more lighthearted and likely unites all people in frustration with the age in which we live. Classically, the virtue of "studiousness" is contrasted with the vices of "curiosity" and, for lack of a better term, "intellectual aloofness." The sin of "curiosity" involves striving to know things that, in fact, we are not called to know, distracting us from what is our true duty. Or, "curiosity" may involve striving to know evil and illegal things (unless, perhaps, we are called on to fight against these evils), or seeking to know things without having any care about how they relate to God and our overall worldview, or striving to know things which are beyond our powers of understanding.[202] How often, for instance, we are tempted to search "Dr. Google," convincing ourselves that we know as much as actual medical doctors!

Now, of all these various possible faults, how often indeed do we experience distraction without any real care about how the information we find fits into our overall calling as Christians? We live in an age of social media, providing endless temptations to seek out knowledge that, in fact, we have little business to know, about people whom we do not know. In fact, there is a general sin of curiosity which is ever present in our information-soaked age: using any knowledge for some end which is sinful. Thus, we look for things to stir up our anger, to make us feel self-justified, to mock others, and so forth. Social media brings all of this out in us, and how often do we all flit about online at our favorite websites, never asking ourselves, "Is this fulfilling something meaningful in my role as a saint, as a parent, as a citizen, as a professional, and so forth? Is this true recreation or mere curiosity, wasting my time on useless facts and content?" What a regular sin for the confessional! Let us all strive to make room for the knowledge that we truly must know, above all the knowledge of the Lord in the Scriptures and in the writings of his saints! Otherwise, we'll be like the person lamented in the bluegrass song "Dust on the Bible," who left the Scriptures untouched in favor of other, presumably more "interesting," books.[203]

In short, temperance is not merely concerned with putting on the brakes in view of our desires. Instead, this virtue is one more aspect of the power of grace, soaking through all of our being, through every aspect of our humanity. There are few things more beautiful than a family that lives simply but then can have a sumptuous meal on the Church's great yearly feasts. I think of my Slovak great-grandmother, who lived in incredible simplicity in an old "coal patch" house, often repeating the maxim from the Great Depression "Use it up, wear it out, make it do, or do without!" But some of my earliest memories are of her full table and house at Christmas, when in her simplicity she pulled out all the stops that she could in order to celebrate the Lord's nativity with her family. This is the sort of beauty we should look to achieve in all of our desires, and the various virtues related to temperance help us to have such spiritual and divine radiance in all the various details of life: in food, drink, dress, sex, knowledge, and, indeed, in all of our desires and enjoyments. Temperance doesn't make you a teetotaler. Rather, it helps you give a truly human (and, as a Christian, a truly divine) splendor even to these very simple and "earthy" things: "In Catholicism, the pint, the pipe, and the Cross can all fit together."

CHAPTER TWENTY-SIX

"To Love Fasting"?

In the first chapter on courage above, we used the metaphor of a charioteer steering the moral life along the racetrack of existence. The charioteer himself was prudence, the moral virtue with a ready eye to consider our own internal state as well as the circumstances surrounding our actions. The two horses were the two main categories of passions: the "passions of desire" (also known as "the concupiscible appetite") and the "passions of fear and anger" (also known as "the irascible appetite"). With its virtuous reins in hand, prudence guides us forward along the paths of morality, helping us to live the divine life of grace and the moral virtues, doing so in each and every one of our actions. The horses are not killed but, instead, are guided and used as the instruments of this forward movement. In other words, virtue does not involve us killing off our desires and emotions. Rather, virtue requires us to order these passions so that the life of human reason and, most importantly, God's own life given to us in grace might live in and through them. The horses need training!

Let us revisit here a topic only hinted at earlier when we discussed the natural law. In Catholic moral theology, there is an open discussion regarding a rather interesting and important point: when we are baptized, do we receive new, "infused" moral virtues in addition to the theological virtues of faith, hope, and love? This question divides theological schools. Some theologians, following in the line of the Franciscan Blessed John Duns Scotus, hold that we don't need to add on more character traits in addition to faith, hope, and charity. These theological virtues, along with the human virtues of prudence, justice, courage, and temperance, suffice. Faith, hope, and charity would make our justice more than human justice. End of story. No need to add on "infused Christian justice" alongside "natural human justice."

In contrast, according to the followers of St. Thomas Aquinas, drawing on a variety of sources and a different line of theological reasoning, there must be supernatural moral virtues given to us at Baptism in addition to the theological virtues. As Christians, we would need to have moral character qualities that immediately reflect our divine faith, hope, and charity. In short, even our abiding moral *character* (in addition to our particular moral *actions*) will need to be altered so that they might be in harmony with the new, divine life we now live through grace. Thus, there will be "infused moral virtues," gifts from God which are like a kind of divine dowry, supernatural versions of the natural moral virtues.[204]

Personally, I hold the Thomist position, though I've tried to keep it in the background throughout our book, for it is not a question settled by the Church. Matters of faith are one thing. Theological debates and conclusions are another. I've attempted to avoid pushing my Thomism on the reader!

Nonetheless, I do feel that the Aquinas theory presents a beautiful synthesis of nature and grace. God wishes to elevate our morality itself to the heights, so why shouldn't the *means* (our abiding moral character) measure up to the *ends* which abide in our soul (through grace and the theological virtues)? In the present case, why would not our temperance as Christians be unique in comparison with the mere temperance spoken of by Aristotle? We should have a character that readies us to find the "Christian golden mean" in all the various domains of human activity. In any case, no matter how we choose to explain it, the measure of our temperance should match up to our supernatural calling:

> Therefore, the measure imposed, for example, on the passions of concupiscence will differ when, on the one hand, we take reason's requirements as our norm and, on the other, when we temper these same passions in view of their divine rule. The rational measure will consist in abstaining so that the health of the body, the instrument of reason, as well as reason itself, may not be troubled and may attend to its superior life in peace. The supernatural measure will go so far as to "chastise his body and reduce it to servitude."[205]

The closing remark in this quote comes from St. Paul, who himself helps us to continue our race metaphor from earlier. We have spoken of the charioteer (prudence) in a way that could perhaps sound just like something spoken of by the philosophers: right and virtuous moral reasoning. Indeed, the metaphor comes from the Greek philosopher Plato, a great and profound thinker, but a non-Christian nonetheless. Should not our prudence be more? Should not our charioteer be divine? Is not his goal *heaven*? (And recall from our earliest discussion that in grace, heaven begins now! "Grace is nothing else than a beginning of Glory in us."[206]) With our minds illuminated by faith and our hearts aflame with charity, how true it is to say of our morality: "I will run in the way of your commandments *when you enlarge my understanding*!" (Psalm 119:32, emphasis added).

St. Paul uses the idea of a footrace, noting how much the athlete does in preparation to win a prize. Such a down-to-earth goal requires a great expenditure of energy! Anyone who has trained to run a race knows how much self-denial is needed even to prepare merely for a 5K course, let alone for a longer distance: hours of running, healthy eating, constant hydration, care for our muscles which risk being overexerted, and so forth. All of this is done in view of a particular, physical goal. Someone in already decent shape discovers how much such a new goal requires him or her to make lifestyle changes for the sake of dedicated training! Well, when the race is divine—something far more important, something eternal—why wouldn't we change our lives to match this goal? In St. Paul's own words,

> Do you not know that in a race all the runners compete, but only one receives the prize? So run that you may obtain it. Every athlete exercises self-control in all things. They do it to receive a perishable wreath, but we an imperishable [one]. Well, I do not run aimlessly, I do not box as one beating the air; but I pommel my body and subdue it, lest after preaching to others I myself should be disqualified. (1 Corinthians 9:24-27)

In the first chapter on courage, I mentioned the *twofold* character of the task ahead of us as we work with the virtues of courage and temperance. We must face the general weakness of human nature, for we are finite beings who are at once spirit and matter. The moral life requires a kind of spiritual conquest. However, there also are the effects of sin: original sin and the results of our own personal sins. Until the day that we die, we have a kind of underbrush in our souls, the *fomes peccati*, "tinder for sin," which we mentioned in our discussion of sin much earlier in this book. We must conquer all of this for Christ! Beyond that, however, we are also called to a superabundant righteousness. As Christ himself said, "For I tell you, unless your righteousness exceeds that of the scribes and Pharisees, you will never enter the kingdom of heaven" (Matthew 5:20).

All of these reasons lie behind the Church's traditional teaching concerning fasting and abstinence: we must conquer our weakness, we must conquer our sinfulness, and we must conquer all things on behalf of charity! We must set aside all earthly cares so that we might be attached to God with all our heart and with all our soul (Deuteronomy 4:29; Matthew 22:37). After the Second Vatican Council, the fasting practices in the Church were given much greater leeway than in the past. Many readers likely recall the fact that once upon a time all Fridays were days of abstinence from meat. In the Roman Church, this practice has been made optional, though it remains in force in the Byzantine Churches (along with the recommendation to abstain from meat on Wednesdays, as well). Prior to the council, in the Roman rite, there were also the series of "Ember Days" placed in each of the four seasons, as well as "Rogation Days" in the spring. Likewise, ancient practices during the whole of Lent were much stricter, along with fasts connected to Pentecost, the Assumption, All Saints' Day, and Christmas. In the Orthodox tradition, a number of these fasting seasons are practiced along with others, joined to quite significant abstinence from dairy products and even oil! The Byzantine Catholic Churches often straddle the Orthodox and Roman Catholic worlds, not requiring the Orthodox practices but encouraging them. The primary seminary for the Ruthenian and Melkite Catholic Churches, the Byzantine Catholic Seminary of Saints Cyril and Methodius in Pittsburgh, Pennsylvania, observes the traditional fasting for shared meals, allowing students to modify their intake as health needs see fit.

All of this goes to say that contemporary Catholic practices concerning fasting and abstinence are very mild. The traditional practices imbued the whole year with a sense of self-offering in a way that seems quite foreign to all of us who have been brought up in contemporary Catholicism. These fasts were not, as some seem to think, a kind of anti-body holdover in Catholic thought. Instead, the practices of fasting and abstinence help us to observe *in our own bodies* the love we have for God. Yes, fasting can be good for health. And, indeed, fasting can enable us to give more to the poor. These are good and noble goals. However, the true spirit of fasting must be animated by a desire to offer *our very selves* to God, even in these little details.

It is important to remember, however, what St. Paul said about his own "pommeling" of the body. He did it so that he could be available for God and for others, not so that he might stick out and seem like something special, something off-putting for those awaiting the message of salvation:

> For though I am free from all men, I have made myself a slave to all, that I might win the more. To the Jews I became as a Jew, in order to win Jews; to those under the law I became as one under the law—though not being myself under the law—that I might win those under the law. To those outside the law I became as one outside the law—not being without law toward God but under the law of Christ—that I might win those outside the law. To the weak I became weak, that I might win the weak. I have become all things to all men, that I might by all means save some. I do it all for the sake of the gospel, that I may share in its blessings. (1 Corinthians 9:19-23)

And recall, too, what Christ said about fasting. We must be humble, not showy: "And when you fast, do not look dismal, like the hypocrites, for they disfigure their faces that their fasting may be seen by men. Truly, I say to you, they have their reward. But when you fast, anoint your head and wash your face, that your fasting may not be seen by men but by your Father who is in secret; and your Father who sees in secret will reward you" (Matthew 6:16-18).

Each reader can look for a different way to reintroduce the Church's traditional practices into his or her personal calendar. A spiritual director or pastor should help guide you. The former novice master of Saint Vincent Archabbey, Fr. Sebastian Samay, OSB, whom I mentioned in an earlier chapter, would give his novice monks sane advice: choose *one thing* this Lent; build up carefully and slowly, so that you can make enduring progress each year. Otherwise, one risks getting overwhelmed by trying to do too much all at once. Reintegrating abstinence on Fridays throughout the year is a great first step. If you are a Roman Catholic, perhaps considering doing something on Wednesdays of Lent can be a way to move forward. (Byzantine Catholics already observe abstinence from meat on Wednesdays in Lent, so they can consider taking up some of the more rigorous practices of their Orthodox brethren.) The particular details can be worked out for each person, and you should never do so in an inflexible spirit, lest you risk becoming like those who wear their "holiness" on their sleeves. If you do not normally eat meat on Wednesdays throughout the year, do not burden relatives who offer you a meal, telling them, “Oh I don’t eat meat on Wednesdays.” You are breaking no Church law by sharing it with them. Make an exception. Discern if you need to do something else during the week. Or, merely humbly accept that such is life, and resume your normal course of practices the next week. Your spiritual director or pastor can help you determine what to do in such cases. But, little by little, you can build into your schedule all of these ancient Christian traditions, without, however, being self-righteous. By looking to make progress in such practices, we can each make small steps forward in listening to the advice offered by St. Benedict, who said that his monks should *love* fasting![207]

Like Qoheleth, the author of Ecclesiastes, we can say that there is a time for fasting and a time for feasting (see Ecclesiastes 3:1-8). When we celebrate the presence of Christ on the great feast days, we should indeed do so with gusto! Anyone who has celebrated Easter with an Italian “pizza rustica” filled to the brimming point with eggs, spiced meats, and cheese knows that a true Christian celebration of the paschal mystery is quite filling! However, we must also acknowledge that the bridegroom is not with us and that we await a fulfillment which still has not come (see Matthew 9:14-17). Thus, we can offer up our bodies in small ways, joining the great host of saints who embraced the practice of fasting as one aspect of their moral journey along the pathways of the divine life of grace.

CHAPTER TWENTY-SEVEN

The Church's Life-Giving Message Versus Contraception

Of all the chapters in the book, this is the one which most bears witness to the fact that the Catholic Faith is a "sign of contradiction" (see Luke 2:34). On the topic of contraception, the Church stands in marked opposition to the whole of the contemporary first world (and, increasingly, the world as a whole). The sexual revolution has left a profound imprint on society. However, it really is just the latest act in a long drama. We are riding the wave of many great changes involving years upon years of tumult and upheaval. For many centuries, European and American cultures were particularly devoted to the great call of the modern scientific and cultural revolutions, crying out, "Let us become masters and possessors of nature!" From one discovery to the next, through the great progress of industry, science, and technology, we passed from being primarily bound to the land to being a people who could soar to the moon. If we took a snapshot of technical progress every hundred years, how striking it would be to look at the pictures each century from 1569 to 1969! The world was conquered, it seems!

Yet during this time, we strove to conquer something else: the human person. This conquest was reflected in many of the great hopes giving birth to the various social sciences. In the late nineteenth century and in the early twentieth century, great expectations were voiced, hopes that were reflected, for example, in Wilsonian-Progressive dreams and also in the sweeping (and morally repugnant!) aims of the eugenics movement, looking to breed a new man. Communism had a sweeping hope too: to create "the new man," a new way of being human. And let us not be fooled. These hopes have not departed from the human heart. They have passed over into the movement known as "transhumanism," filled with the expectation that we will be able to pass beyond (*trans-*) many of the limitations imposed upon human nature. These "dreams" (or nightmares) are reflected in the striking title of the popular book by Yuval Harari: *Homo Deus*, Man-as-God.[208]

But these are big thoughts! We know very well all the tales of the "bionic man," as well as contemporary claims concerning how man and machine will come to intermesh in the near future. However, something just as explosive happened in the early 1960s: the beginning of the widespread use of oral contraceptives. Now, you may say, "Wait! Really? How are these things even comparable? Robots and humans, yes! That's truly revolutionary. But *the pill*? Come on!" I assure you that the social changes brought about by the widespread use of contraceptives have been immense. By redefining sex, making procreation a kind of "option," but not something *essential* to human nature, sexuality, and spousal fulfillment, contraception had effects which have passed through the whole of society like a kind of shock wave, though one which we often don't even notice. In this chapter, we can only touch the tiniest ripples involved in these changes, but beneath the surface-level eddies the sea is stirring![209]

In nearly all of our discussions in this book, we have been concerned with quite abstract principles. (Though, hopefully, I have managed to convince you of the beauty and life-giving character of these principles!) Here, I feel that one, frank historical observation must be made. On the topic of contraception, the Catholic Church "on the ground" did not always present a united front defending her *clear and explicit teaching concerning the moral evil of contraception*. While the popes proclaimed its intrinsic evil, many clerics, theology professors, and laity chose to look the other way, either skipping over this difficult teaching or, as sadly happens even to this day, telling the laity, "It is a question of personal conscience." This has led to a situation in which the majority of Catholics, even practicing ones, have chosen to use some form of male or female contraception, often quite unaware of the black-and-white nature of the Church's teaching on this matter. What I lay forth here, however, is something which was taught by nearly all of the Church Fathers[210] and was repeatedly taught by the popes in the twentieth century. It was taught by Pius XI in *Casti Connubii* (1930), Pius XII in his extensive "Address to Midwives" (1951), most famously by St. Paul VI in *Humanae Vitae* (1968), extensively by St. John Paul II before his pontificate (see *Love and Responsibility*, 1960) and during it (see *Evangelium Vitae*, 1995), in the new *Catechism* promulgated by St. John Paul II with the aid of Benedict XVI when the latter was Cardinal Ratzinger (see CCC 2366–2379), and in various public statements by Pope Benedict XVI and Pope Francis.

However, the Church's teaching concerning contraception is not something we must follow merely because she teaches it. No, this teaching is, in fact, a truth that belongs to the natural law—that is, to the morality that we can know merely by reflecting on what it means to be a human person, seeking to live virtuously. There are "rational" principles that make clear that the use of contraception is, in fact, a grave sin against the virtue of chastity. Let us consider these principles, for they reveal something profound about the human person. We will see just how prophetic the Church is in her teaching concerning contraception.

Marital-sexual relations have a twofold character. On the one hand, they deal with one of our most powerful and primal instincts: the desire for sexual intercourse. With his customary sanity, the Greek philosopher Aristotle noted that, really, the two basic desires that we have are for food and sex. What could be more primordial than the desire to survive, either ourselves (through adequate nutrition) or from generation to generation (through sexual reproduction)? These desires are deeply engraved in who we are, going back through millions of years of evolution.

However, marital-sexual relations are *relations*. They are not mere mutual masturbation. They are a particular way that two persons relate to each other, in a unique and very exposed way. Yes, this relationship is "mediated" through our sexual "organs." However, what human relationship is not "mediated?" We speak words by means of our mouths, through airborne vibrations, and depths of joy are expressed to another person *through* the sparkle of an eye or the upward curl of the lips in a smile. In sexual relations, we share with another person something primordial: our personality as sexual.

Notice that I did not merely say that we share "our bodies." Older language used to speak of matrimonial consent being directed to the "rights" that we exchange over each other's body for procreation (*ius in corpus in ordine ad actus per se aptos ad generationem*). From a legal perspective this is not incorrect. However, let us be careful not to think about sex as being merely about our bodies *all by themselves*. Something more profound is shared: *our very selves*, though not in any way whatsoever but, rather, *in a sexual manner*.

Sane Catholic philosophy is clear: the human person is unitedly body and spiritual soul. In fact, some Catholic thinkers have emphasized, with good reason, that body and spirit are so interrelated that our spirit is "shaped" by our bodies. There is a male way to be human and a female way to be so.[211] The Catholic philosopher Dietrich von Hildebrand expressed this very well when he wrote, "It would be incredibly superficial to consider as a mere biological difference the distinction between man and woman, which really shows us two complementary types of the spiritual person of the human species."[212] In other words, sex is not only a question of biology but, instead, shapes who we are, down to our deepest spiritual fibers.

This does not mean that human nature is somehow lacking in either man or woman. We are all equally humans. Nonetheless, our sex uniquely impacts the way that humanity is expressed in each of us. It is a kind of first-tier property which effects everything else about our persons. And each person is somewhat like Adam, who yet felt unfulfilled as all the animals of the world were given to him as companions. Ultimately, we do not find our ultimate meaning in possessions, nor in things, nor in pets, nor in any beautiful creation made by our hands and skills. Rather, we crave to look into the eyes of another person, someone who is another "small universe," a microcosm who has a unique destiny in God's providence. We wish to repeat Adam's words, "This at last is bone of my bones and flesh of my flesh" (Genesis 2:23).

Marital-sexual relations express this desire. There are many ways to be friends and a great variety of ways to share lives together. Indeed, many of these relationships are legitimate and quite fulfilling. In fact, we would be poor beggars if we did not have a number of different kinds of friends. However, in marriage we have an opportunity for a unique sort of friendship, a sharing in life and self that is actually more than a friendship, though it includes all its positive values. As a unique kind of interpersonal bond, marriage is ordered first and foremost to the procreation and education of the children begotten of the union of spouses. In fact, the union of the spouses is defined in relation to this primary end.[213] We are spousal friends first and foremost because we are *procreative spouses*. Without this, marriage loses its unique savor, and the friendship of spouses becomes just one more friendship, not a unique sharing of body and life, the founding of a family and the continuation of the great moral drama of the human species through the ages.

Of course, the Church has reserved a special place in her life for virginity "for the sake of the kingdom." This was praised by both Jesus (Matthew 19:11-12) and St. Paul (1 Corinthians 7:32-34), and it has been constantly witnessed to throughout the long history of the Church. Nonetheless, a great host of saints sings the praises of God by using the language of marriage. This very human reality has inspired the pens of many spiritual authors. Thus, the Flemish mystic Jan van Ruysbroeck wrote his *Spiritual Espousals*, St. Teresa of Avila spoke about her innermost "mansion" of the mystical life as being the place of "spiritual marriage," and the great Cistercian monk St. Bernard of Clairvaux wrote a host of sermons on the Song of Solomon, a book of Jewish love poetry found in the Old Testament. In fact, St. Bernard often would get stuck commenting on several words, spending his entire sermon on some tiny section of the text, lost in the rhapsodies of the divine love. But the base text was not a kind of disembodied, spiritualistic theological treatise. No! St. Bernard saw all of these beautiful images of the soul's love for God in a book of Scripture which is full of erotic imagery, as a bride and groom are presented to us in the midst of the great and moving drama of love.

In short, the language of spousal love goes deep. It not only goes down to the depths of who we are spiritually as human beings. It even goes so deep that the very mystery of God is expressed in terms drawn from human sexuality: Christ's ministry begins with a marriage feast (John 2:1-11), he compares the kingdom of heaven to "a king who gave a marriage feast for his son" (Matthew 22:2), the union of Christ and his Church is like the union of husband and wife (Ephesians 5:22-33), and the end of times is called the marriage feast of the Lamb (Revelation 19:7 and following). Similar lists could be drawn from the Old Testament, where God is presented as a lover scorned by Israel, whom he chose and made beautiful (Hosea; Jeremiah 2:2; Ezekiel 16). The language of spousal love is the choice vehicle for some of the most important mysteries of redemption.

Therefore, in light of all of these points of data, the Church has untiringly taught, throughout her history, that human sexuality should not be tampered with lightly. It is full of meanings. It tells us about how the generations linked together, from parent to child to child ... through the ages. And it tells us of God's own bond to us, and of us to him.

We must repeat this fundamental truth: the personal union of marriage is not just any old kind of union; it is a *sexual* union. It is a union of two enfleshed beings who share with each other one of the most primordial aspects of their life as embodied creatures: their sexuality. Part of the meaning "hidden" here is the calling to live in family and as parents. This is not the whole of sex and marriage, but it nonetheless defines its essence. It is a union which is procreative by nature. But human procreation is not merely a question of breeding. In the end, parents give their children something more profound than merely biological life. As we discussed in an earlier chapter, they give their children "the life of the soul." By being parents, we become active participants in handing on all the goods of human culture and history to our children. As Christian parents, we hand on the life of grace in the little church that is our household, the *ecclesia domestica*, the "domestic church." Marriage is a source of great fruitfulness, and the Church defends a truth which is central to the very nature of who we are as humans: contracepted sexual intercourse actively cancels this meaning. It stops it from the outset and states that its procreative character is something without real implication for the meaning of sexual relations.

I can hear a question coming, however: "What about Natural Family Planning (NFP)? Isn't that just 'Catholic contraception,' a form that is quite inexact in comparison with medically available options?" In fact, some readers may think that NFP is the same thing as the "rhythm method," which in fact is an outdated method of NFP. To dispel this rumor, I recommend that the reader consult many of the resources available to Catholic couples today, showing the great advances in NFP techniques and their highly scientific state today. I will include these resources in a footnote.[214]

The moral question is what we must focus on. In short, it is this: "How does NFP differ from contraception?" In a crystal clear set of articles which are wholly faithful to the Magisterium, the English philosopher Elizabeth

Anscombe lays out the central distinction: there is a qualitative difference between, on the one hand, actively stopping the procreative significance of marital-sexual relations and, on the other, having intercourse during an infertile period.[215] The first is contraceptive, and whether or not we explicitly think it through, it actively involves the assertion: sex does not need to have a procreative meaning. Yes, natural planning can be misused for various selfish reasons, just as so many things can be misused. However, it does not involve this active repudiation of the intertwined procreative and unitive significance of sexual intercourse in marriage. In short, it maintains the *nature of this moral action*. It does not undercut it from the start, as does the act of contraception. The contraceptive attitude says, "Sex is one more thing to be dominated, for we are 'masters and possessors of nature.'" The virtuous attitude says, "Sex is a gift, defining one of the most profound aspects of human nature—namely, the interconnection of persons and generations. It even reflects the very order of the universe which was created to include sexual dimorphism as one of its most beautiful aspects." And the Christian will add to the voice of virtue these words: "And it even can be elevated to be a symbol for supernatural realities, a metaphor for God's love for the world." What greater accolades could we think of? What sadness there is in the thought of spurning so beautiful a gift!

On more than one occasion, Christ's disciples said to him, "This teaching is difficult" (see John 6:60; Matthew 19:10). The Church's teaching concerning contraception is at great odds with the sexual liberties taken for granted throughout our culture. In fact, at its core is a claim that will strike the reader as being quite old-fashioned and, perhaps, subversive: our bodies matter for what we morally do. It is not an indifferent thing to be male or to be female. Indeed, in a separate book devoted solely to sexual ethics and bioethics, we could expand on this point to discuss many of the hot-button issues in today's culture, questions surrounding not only the quite contentious domain of LGBT-related issues[216] but also many other topics intimately connected to our embodied nature: euthanasia, palliative care, the use of experimental medication, genetic therapy, the use of stem cells, sterilization, masturbation, pornography, in vitro fertilization, and abortion.[217] However, all of these topics have a shared foundation: we are embodied creatures, and our "bodiliness" is filled with moral meaning.

The talks on the Theology of the Body delivered by St. John Paul II were primarily devoted to sexual ethics; however, even the pope noted, as he concluded his series of talks, that the Theology of the Body in fact extends to many other topics.[218]

Famously (and amusingly), the American conservative thinker William F. Buckley wrote in 1955, describing his new venture *National Review*, in the following terms: "It stands athwart history, yelling Stop, at a time when no one is inclined to do so."[219] Many think that this is what the Church is doing when it comes to contraception and many of the bioethical issues that face us in the midst of a changing world. In a sense, there is a kind of truth to this sentiment. The culture is on a different track, forging ahead in quite a different direction. Therefore, we must yell, "Stop!" However, this is only the first stage! Grace never merely says no to nature. With a merciful hand, full of the love of the Son for the brothers and sisters whom he wishes to redeem, Christ comes along and says, as in the parable of the banquet and the humble man, "Friend, go up higher" (Luke 14:10).

CONCLUDING SYNTHESIS

"Remember What You Are Called To!"

Coming now to the end of this text, let's attempt a synthesis of what we have discussed throughout all of these pages. In other words, let's try to look at the way that the primary truths of faith illuminate our divine vocation as Christian men and women. Through theological reasoning, we attempt to achieve some small *intellectus fidei*, an understanding of the Faith. In the words of St. Anselm of Canterbury, it is *faith seeking understanding*—at least to the small degree that we can understand such divine marvels, which ultimately only God himself can fully. Nonetheless, faith is a kind of knowledge, and as rational creatures we cannot help but ask, "What is the meaning of this? How do these mysteries all interrelate?" This impulse for fuller understanding is the generative source of theology as a "science"—that is, as a rational endeavor to understand what we believe.[220]

Theology is not a hodgepodge discipline, thinking "great and divine thoughts" about all sorts of things such as God, creation, morality, history, society, human work, and so forth. Sometimes, scholars study theology as though this were the case. They specialize and particularize, worrying about this or that little corner of information. They focus on the sacramental theology of St. Ambrose, the christology of St. Thomas, the spiritual theology of the Carmelite school, etc., etc., etc.! This leads to a grave temptation to miss the "big picture," forgetting to step back and see the full, divine portrait offered to us: the Triune God, giving himself to us. The Greek Fathers of the Church expressed these two great truths of theology by speaking of a distinction between *theology* and the *economy*, as we have mentioned earlier. By "theology," they meant *the study* (*-logy*) of God in himself (*theo-*). By the "economy," they meant all of God's actions in salvation history, bringing us into being and leading us back to him. These two "parts" were not separate, however, for the whole of the "economy" is founded on "theology."

The central mystery of the Faith is the mystery of the Triune God. This mystery illuminates everything in "theological science."[221] Ultimately, every theological explanation must connect back to this mystery. Nothing in theology makes *any* sense if we do not see that the "treatise on God" (or, the "theology of God") is the principal divine mystery which communicates its light to all the other mysteries. We cannot understand Christ if we do not understand the Trinity, for he is the eternal Word. Obviously, he came to reveal the Trinity of divine Persons to us. However, when we reflect theologically, it is the Trinity that gives the meaning to Christ's coming, not vice versa. The mystery of the Triune God must be present in all of the other topics of theology as well. If it is not, we will not be doing theology. We may be doing something else: sociology, history, psychology, moral philosophy, and so forth. But without a connection to the Triune God, theology ceases to be theology.

Every Sunday when we pray the Creed, in all Catholic Churches, whether Eastern or Western, we proclaim the mystery of God: the Father, the Son, and the Holy Spirit. The early Church fought for centuries to articulate in words the faith which she already lived and believed. These were the great controversies over Christ and, by implication, over the very nature of the one God in three Persons. It is so tempting to think of this "dogmatic theology" as very abstract speculation. Indeed, the person who has had a chance to study Trinitarian theology knows that it is very abstract! Theologians will argue about very obscure matters: personhood, subsistent relations, circumincession, "notional acts," "innascibility," and so forth ... All of this is necessary, and centuries of reflection have led Christian thought to a state of richness and of erudition which should make every Catholic proud of his or her intellectual inheritance.

However, the Triune God who is studied in Trinitarian theology is not merely an idea, a kind of central point around whom all of these nice and tidy terms are arrayed. The Trinity is the shared life of the three Persons of God. In God, we find the expression of the highest degree of life, so much so that God himself does not *have* life; he *is* life. We could say that the Trinitarian mystery gives life to all the other mysteries.

And what is the greatest truth of the "economy"—that is, of God's providence active in the world? It is the fact that this divine vitality has been communicated to humanity in Christ, who stands at the center of all things: "All things were made through him, and without him was not anything made that was made. In him was life, and the life was the light of men" (John 1:3-4). "In him all things were created, in heaven and on earth, visible and invisible ... all things were created through him and for him" (Colossians 1:16). In an earlier chapter, I referred to a notion drawn from christology, the "grace of union." There is no grace for the *person* of Christ. His *person* is divine. However, this person has drawn human nature to himself. He has become incarnate. And this "gift" of the Word, the second Person of the Trinity, is the greatest of all graces, the source of every other gift that would come to all of humanity. In the silence of Bethlehem and in the abandonment of the Cross, heaven has met earth so that earth might be lifted up to heaven:

> For while gentle silence enveloped all things,
> and night in its swift course was now half gone,
> your all-powerful word leaped from heaven, from the royal throne,
> into the midst of the land that was doomed,
> a stern warrior carrying the sharp sword of your authentic command,
> and stood and filled all things with death,
> and touched heaven while standing on the earth. (Wisdom 18:14-16)

> Now is the judgment of this world, now shall the ruler of this world be cast out; and I, *when I am lifted up from the earth, will draw all men to myself.* (John 12:31-32, emphasis added)

On several occasions in the opening sections of this book, we cited words from St. John which summarize all of this with succinct clarity: "And from his fulness have we all received, grace upon grace" (John 1:16). Or, as St. Paul expresses it, we have been called to be "conformed to the image of his Son, in order that he might be the first-born among many brethren" (Romans 8:29).

Moral theology attempts to articulate this new life of Christ which we are given through grace. Its emphasis is less upon *morality* than it is upon *theology*. Normally, in our language, the adjective modifies the noun. However, after all of our discussions in this book, it should now be clear that here the noun ("theology") modifies the adjective ("moral"). We do not "modify" God; rather, he modifies—no, even more, he *transforms*—us! Thus, when we say "moral theology," we should really mean "theological morality." This latter expression points us in the right direction. Some have said that the Church should be less moralizing, less tied up with telling people what is right and wrong. They call for "more spirituality, less morality!" This may seem like a noble sentiment. However, it is unacceptable, for it fails to see the true importance of the moral life, which is intimately united to the spiritual life. Therefore, it is far better for one to say, "Make your morality truly divine, truly spiritual, *truly theological*!"

Therefore, at the center of moral theology there are two very important truths: (1) our calling to beatitude, the eternal knowledge and love of God shared among the saints; and (2) the grace which makes this possible. Through grace, we are made "partakers of the divine nature" (2 Peter 1:4), and this gift is like a seed which will blossom into eternity. Just as the oak seed contains all of the vitality which will live when the tree is in its full vigor, so too does grace already contain within itself all of the life which will belong to the glory and splendor of heaven. The soul (*anima*) animates the entire life of the organism. Thus, by way of analogy, the life of heaven should animate all of our life here below. In the words of St. Thomas Aquinas cited in an earlier chapter, "Grace is nothing else than a beginning of Glory in us."[222]

The life of God never fails, but alas, we are creatures, thus meaning that we are susceptible to defect, to sin: "But we have this treasure in earthen vessels, to show that the transcendent power belongs to God and not to us" (2 Corinthians 4:7). Through venial sins, we slowly but surely cool the fire of grace in our souls. And if we fall into mortal sin, we experience a true death of soul, death in regard to the life of God given to us in grace. Blessed be God that in his great mercy he is forever ready to run out and greet us like the father of the Prodigal Son (Luke 15:11-32), and he is ready to heal our wounds like the Good Samaritan who found a man nearly dead upon the side of the road (Luke 10:30-37)! The loss of grace is like throwing away our inheritance, spitting in the face of the divine family into which we have been called. Sin leads to a kind of "degeneracy." In the most literal sense of the terms, we lose the new *regeneration*, the new birth, brought about through the gift of divine grace. You see—the stakes are quite high! To say that our morality is "theological" shows us all the more why we must grasp hold of God and strive not to sin!

The gift of grace flows over the whole of our being. Its first fruits are the theological virtues: faith, hope, and charity, all of which we discussed at length in this book. Through these "infused theological virtues," our minds are enabled to grasp revealed, supernatural truths (faith), and our wills are given a divine strength, both in supernatural assurance (hope) and, most importantly, in supernatural love (charity). The most important of these theological virtues is charity (1 Corinthians 13:13). It will last to eternity, for even now we love God with God's own love, as though we have had a kind of divine heart transplant. Moreover, just as God loves all that he has created, so too are we called to love all of our brothers and sisters with whom we walk along through the paths of life. This is the true meaning of "fraternal charity": to love all things with God's own all-consuming love.

This task will demand everything of us. Christ asks us to take up our crosses, to die with him so as to live our true life. Reread the Sermon on the Mount, and you will see this lofty and demanding calling: "Blessed are the poor in spirit ... those who mourn ... the meek ... those who hunger and thirst for righteousness ... the merciful ... the pure in heart ... the peacemakers ... those who are persecuted" (Matthew 5:3-12). Through Baptism, we die with Christ so that we might truly live his glorious life: "Do you not know that all of us who have been baptized into Christ Jesus were baptized into his death? We were buried therefore with him by baptism into death, so that as Christ was raised from the dead by the glory of the Father, we too might walk in newness of life" (Romans 6:3-4). The theological virtues will ask everything of us so that the divine life might root itself down into every nook and cranny of our being. This is why the gifts of the Holy Spirit are given to us as well, to enable us to live a truly *inspired* life, blown aloft by the divine wind itself! If we are to be moral Christians we must also be mystics—each and every one of us!

As grace refashions us, this theological life increasingly impresses itself upon all of our virtues. The pagans spoke of the "cardinal virtues": prudence, justice, courage, and temperance. What they say remains true. However, their words are only cut to the level of human nature. These virtues are concerned with human perfection. Through grace, we have a new nature, a divine nature, calling for divine perfection. Therefore, our moral virtues themselves must be stamped with the face of Christ, crucified and glorious. All of our virtue must be supernaturally excessive. Christ spoke of how we must surpass the Pharisees in holiness (Matthew 5:20). This implies, as well, that we must exceed the pagan: "For if you love those who love you, what reward have you? Do not even the tax collectors do the same? And if you salute only your brethren, what more are you doing than others? *Do not even the Gentiles do the same?*" (Matthew 5:46-47, emphasis added). All of our virtue must be transformed and elevated, to the level of divine perfection: "You, therefore, must be perfect, as your heavenly Father is perfect" (Matthew 5:48). "Whether you eat or drink, or whatever you do, do all to the glory of God" (1 Corinthians 10:31). Our justice will be loftier than human justice, filled with the self-giving love of Christ, bursting forth with mercy, which will inform all of our justice. Our courage will be inflamed by the theological virtue of hope, steeling our spines so that we may never shrink back from living our divine calling. And our temperance will turn us away from selfish acquisition and self-indulgence, so that our desire may be solely divine, always motivated by the one truly necessary thing: God and his love. The whole of our morality will reflect our divine calling.

Thus, from top to bottom, theology is concerned with the radiance of God: the Triune God, the incarnate Christ, the life of the Church and the sacraments, which are the channels of grace (and every grace will draw even those outside the fold toward the Church as toward the true garden of grace). Theology is concerned with the whole life of grace—that is, the moral life that we are called to live. Moral theology—or, again, to put it better, "theological morality"—is concerned with this lofty vocation which comes down from heaven and raises us to the knowledge and love of our glorious God. We must be transformed; we must be perfused by this divine light, so that it might radiate throughout us from top to bottom, from head to toe, in our mind and will, in our desires and fears, in all of our activities and relationships. God wants to be present in all of these places. He wants to give us the gift of being able to *truly* make this supernatural life be present throughout all of creation. By his gift, he makes us to be "fellow workers in the truth" (3 John 8).

What we have discussed in this volume is only a beginning, but it is my sincere hope that you now have some basic framework for filling out the whole building of the moral destiny to which all of us are called. Too often, we think of Christianity as "moralizing" when, in fact, it is something infinitely more than this. The life of grace is strenuous. It asks everything from us. It asks us to die to self so that Christ might live in us, giving us the divine freedom, the ability to love what we were born to love: God, who is the most lovable of all realities.

The great joy of this freedom reminds me of the words of the bluegrass song "I Don't Want My Golden Slippers."[223] Or, as would be more appropriate for a book of theology, let us close with the words of Scripture, which express the task, the freedom, and the joy of our calling as Christians: "For freedom Christ has set us free; stand fast therefore, and do not submit again to a yoke of slavery ... For you were called to freedom, brethren; only do not use your freedom as an opportunity for the flesh, but through love be servants of one another" (Galatians 5:1, 13). And in the words of our beloved Savior: "These things I have spoken to you, *that my joy may be in you, and that your joy may be full*" (John 15:11, emphasis added).

NOTES

1. Benedict of Nursia, *RB 1980: The Rule of St. Benedict; in Latin and English with Notes*, ed. Timothy Fry et al. (Collegeville, MN: Liturgical Press, 1981), 72 (pp. 293–295, slightly modified).

2. Augustine, *Confessions* 11.4 (my translation).

3. I owe this short formulation to scholarly work by Fr. William Wallace, OP, *The Role of Demonstration in Moral Theology* (Washington, DC: Thomist Press, 1962), 149–152.

4. See Charles Journet, *Entretiens sur la charité* (Paris: Parole et Silence, 1999), 29. (Unless otherwise noted, all quotes from Cardinal Journet that I will use in this book are my own translation.)

5. See Ambroise Gardeil, *La vraie vie chrétienne*, ed. H.-D. Gardeil (Paris: Desclée de Brouwer, 1935), 185. (Unless otherwise noted, all quotes from Fr. Gardeil that I will use in this book are my own translation.)

6. John Chrysostom, *Homilies on Matthew*, in *Nicene and Post-Nicene Fathers*, First Series, vol. 10, ed. Philip Schaff, trans. George Prevost and M. B. Riddle (Buffalo, NY: Christian Literature, 1888), 15.11, revised and ed. Kevin Knight, https://www.newadvent.org/fathers/200115.htm.

7. For a beautiful reflection on the love of God, see the work of the great Cistercian monk William of St. Thierry, *The Nature and Dignity of Love*, trans. Thomas X. Davis (Kalamazoo, MI: Cistercian, 1981); and "On Contemplating God," in *On Contemplating God, Prayer, Meditations*, trans. Sister Penelope (Kalamazoo, MI: Cistercian, 1977), 36–64.

8. John Chrysostom, *Homilies on Matthew* 15.11.

9. For a beautiful reflection on this theme, see C. S. Lewis, "Sweeter Than Honey," in *Reflections on the Psalms* (San Diego: Harcourt Brace Jovanovich, 1958), 54–65.

10. Aquinas, *Summa Theologica* II-II.120.1.1.

11. See Aquinas, I-II.98–105.

12. See Aquinas, I.60.5.

13. *The Divine Comedy of Dante Alighieri: Paradiso*, trans. Allen Mandelbaum (New York: Bantam Books, 1986), 303 (canto 33).

14. See Jacques Maritain, *The Sin of the Angel*, trans. William L. Rossner (Westminster, MD: Newman, 1959), 22–23.

15. See Jean-Hervé Nicolas, *Les profondeurs de la grâce* (Paris: Beauchesne, 1969), 282.

16. The language of "image" and "likeness" is understood differently by different figures throughout Church history. A good example of this can be found in a text like Thomas Aquinas's *Summa Theologica* I.93.9, where St. Thomas attempts to reconcile several different usages of the Fathers regarding this terminology. Although St. Irenaeus of Lyon (130–202) is often cited as being careful to distinguish these two terms, St. John of Damascus (675–749) will come to clearly distinguish between *image* and *likeness* so that *image* will, for him, refer to our intellect and free will, whereas *likeness* will apply to our life of virtue (see *Exposition on the Orthodox Faith* II.12). Thus, the *image* would be the goodness of nature that remains after the Fall (especially referring to our spiritual faculties, the intellect and the will), whereas the *likeness* would reflect our sanctification (or lack thereof). Nonetheless, even after the Fall, we can be said to be created "in the likeness of God" insofar as we are all called *to be remade in Christ*, to be remade in the likeness of the new Adam (see Romans 5:12-20). In the language of classical Western theology, God "antecedently" wills all to be saved and therefore does not deprive us of the grace of redemption and divinization, so long as we do not resist this gift.

    On this topic, the reader might consult Norman Russell, *The Doctrine of Deification in the Greek Patristic Tradition* (Oxford: Oxford University Press, 2009), 103, 107, 127, 135, 202–203, 210, 246, 299, and 328; and Tomáš Cardinal Špidlík, *The Spirituality of the Christian East*, trans. Anthony P. Gythiel (Collegeville, MN: Liturgical Press, 1986), 55–62. What we must maintain is that the image and likeness are not fatally destroyed, a position held by certain classical Protestant thinkers, often referred to as theories of "total depravity." For a beautiful Western reflection on this, see *The Mystical Evolution in the Development and Vitality of the Church*, trans. Jordan Aumann (St. Louis, MO: B. Herder, 1949), 62. Bearing in mind certain differences between Catholics and Orthodox thinkers when it comes to explaining original sin, this passage may be compared profitably with what is written by the Orthodox author Panayiotis Nellas in *Deification in Christ: Orthodox Perspectives on the Nature of the Human Person*, trans. Normal Russell (Yonkers, NY: St. Vladimir's Seminary Press, 1987), 23–42.

17. See Gardeil, *La vraie vie chrétienne*, 12.

18. For a beautiful reflection on this theme of salvation history, see John Saward, *Redeemer in the Womb* (San Francisco: Ignatius, 1993).

19. Council of Trent, *Decree on Justification*, 7 (Denzinger, 1529, slightly altered with emphasis added).

20. This paragraph is but a nontechnical commentary on Aquinas, *Summa Theologica* III.8.5. See Benoît-Dominique de la Soujeole, *Introduction to the Mystery of the Church*, trans. Michael J. Miller (Washington, DC: Catholic University of America Press, 2014), 99–111.

21. See Benedict, *RB 1980*, 158–159. This translation opts for the weaker phrase "the light that comes from God." It is sometimes translated merely as "divine light." However, the editors of *RB 1980* note the need for a stronger expression, and I personally remember the very wise and linguistically learned Fr. Sebastian Samay, OSB, the former novice master at Saint Vincent Archabbey, insisting that we must read this word's suffix as etymologically coming from *facere* (=to do or make). Therefore, I opt for the translation which he preferred: "the God-making / God-fashioning / God-forming light."

22. Aquinas, *Summa Theologica* II-II.24.3.2.

23. Gardeil, *La vraie vie chrétienne*, 86.

24. For beautiful homilies written on this topic, see Brian E. Daley, trans., *Light on the Mountain: Greek Patristic and Byzantine Homilies on the Transfiguration of the Lord* (Yonkers, NY: St. Vladimir's Seminary Press, 2013).

25. See Jacques Maritain, *St. Thomas and the Problem of Evil* (Milwaukee: Marquette University Press, 1942); Jacques Maritain, *God and the Permission of Evil*, trans. Joseph W. Evans (Milwaukee: Bruce, 1966); Réginald Garrigou-Lagrange, *Predestination*, trans. Bede Rose (St. Louis: B. Herder, 1939); Réginald Garrigou-Lagrange, *Providence*, trans. Bede Rose (St. Louis: B. Herder, 1937); and Charles Journet, *The Meaning of Evil* (Providence, RI: Cluny Media, 2020).

26. See John Paul II, *Veritatis Splendor* (August 6, 1993), 65–68.

27. For help in preparing for confession, many useful resources are available, including Fr. Joshua Johnson and Fr. Mike Schmitz's *Pocket Guide to the Sacrament of Reconciliation* (West Chester, PA: Ascension, 2021).

28. "The Gods of the Copybook Headings," in *Kipling: Poems*, ed. Peter Washington (New York: Alfred A. Knopf, 2007), 233.

29. Journet, *Entretiens sur la charité*, 72.

30. Gardeil, *La vraie vie chrétienne*, 98.

31. Gregory of Nyssa, *The Life of Moses*, trans. Abraham J. Malherbe and Everett Ferguson (New York: Paulist Press, 1978), 227.

32. I have slightly edited this quotation for clarity in printed form, given that it was originally in spoken form. Fr. Sebastian has died, so I cannot get his approval for this rendition, though my changes were minor. He was a great man, whom I had the privilege of living with for three years during my years discerning a potential vocation to the Benedictine life.

33. See Gregory of Nyssa, *Life of Moses*, 239.

34. Anonymous, "Just a Closer Walk with Thee," Hymnary.org, accessed August 19, 2020, https://hymnary.org/text/i_am_weak_but_thou_art_strong.

35. For a beautiful reflection on this theme, read the first book of St. Augustine's *Confessions*.

36. For a beautiful reflection on the "philosophical psychology" presupposed for this chapter, see Pierre-Marie Emonet, *The Greatest Marvel of Nature: An Introduction to the Philosophy of the Human Person*, trans. Robert R. Barr (New York: Crossroad, 2000).

37. See Gardeil, *La vraie vie chrétienne*, 27.

38. Aquinas, *Summa Theologica* II-II.23.1.

39. For a beautiful reflection on faith as a human phenomenon, see Josef Pieper, "On Faith," trans. Richard and Clara Winston, in *Faith, Hope, Love* (San Francisco: Ignatius, 2012), 15–84.

40. Obviously, this does not mean that supernatural faith is impossible outside of membership in the Church. The Church and her theologians have a rich history of discussions concerning how faith can be had in such circumstances. However, the Church remains the "true home of grace," and Christ's own desire, quite clearly emphasized in his own words, is that all be gathered into one flock (John 10:1-18, 17:21-26).

41. Aquinas, *De veritate* 27.1.

42. On this point, I am *not* following the RSV translation of the Scriptures. The text of the RSV presents this text in a way that has been ably critiqued by Pope Benedict XVI in nos. 7–9 of his encyclical *Spe Salvi* (November 30, 2007).

43. See commentary on stanza 12 of *The Spiritual Canticle*, by John of the Cross, in *The Collected Works of St. John of the Cross*, rev. ed., trans. Kieran Kavanaugh and Otilio Rodriguez (Washington, DC: ICS, 1991), 516–519.

44. Gardeil, *La vraie vie chrétienne*, 268.

45. For important and profound technical precisions on this topic, see Dominic Legge, "Like Splendor Flowing from the Sun: The Holy Spirit and Christ's Grace," in *The Trinitarian Christology of St. Thomas Aquinas* (Oxford: Oxford University Press, 2017), 131–171.

46. *Lumen Gentium* (November 21, 1964), 48.

47. See Ambroise Gardeil, *Christ-Consciousness*, trans. Preacheress of Carisbrook (London: Blackfriars, 1954), 12–17. (Note especially p. 13.)

48. See the index entry for *hesed* in John Bergsma and Brant Pitre, *A Catholic Introduction to the Bible*, vol. 1, *The Old Testament* (San Francisco: Ignatius, 2018).

49. Roy Acuff, "This World Can't Stand Long," Musixmatch.com, accessed August 19, 2020, https://www.musixmatch.com/lyrics/Roy-Acuff/This-World-Can-t-Stand-Long.

50. *Dies Irae*, Preces-latinae.org, accessed August 19, 2020, http://www.preces-latinae.org/thesaurus/Hymni/DiesIrae.html (emphasis added).

51. "Funeral for a Layman in a Church: Hymns of St. John Damascene," in *The Office of Christian Burial According to the Byzantine Rite* (Pittsburgh, PA: Byzantine Seminary Press, 2001), 83.

52. For beautiful reflections on this theme, see Pope Benedict XVI, *Spe Salvi*.

53. Jennie Wilson, "Hold to God's Unchanging Hand," Hymnary.org, accessed August 19, 2020, https://hymnary.org/text/time_is_filled_with_swift_transition (emphasis added).

54. See Jacques Maritain, *The Degrees of Knowledge*, ed. Ralph McInerny, trans. Gerald Phelan et al. (Notre Dame, IN: Notre Dame University Press, 2002), 257–258.

55. See Journet, *Entretiens sur la charité*, 25–37.

56. The Vagabonds, "When It's Lamplighting Time in the Valley," Bluegrasslyrics.com, accessed August 14, 2020, https://www.bluegrasslyrics.com/song/when-its-lamplighting-time-in-the-valley/.

57. Journet, *Entretiens sur la charité*, 29–30.

58. A beautiful collection of patristic texts related to this theme can be found in Daniel A. Keating, *Deification and Grace* (Naples, FL: Sapientia Press of Ave Maria University, 2007), 11–38.

59. "O Lord, I Am Not Worthy," Hymnary.org, accessed October 2, 2020, https://hymnary.org/text/o_lord_i_am_not_worthy.

60. John Henry Newman, "Praise to the Holiest in the Height," Hymnary.org, accessed October 2, 2020, https://hymnary.org/text/praise_to_the_holiest_in_the_height.

61. Gardeil, *La vraie vie chrétienne*, 31.

62. Gregory the Great, *Life and Miracles of St. Benedict: Book Two of the Dialogues*, trans. Odo J. Zimmermann and Benedict R. Avery (Collegeville, MN: Liturgical Press, 1949), 67–69.

63. See Augustine, *Homilies on the First Epistle of John*, in *Nicene and Post-Nicene Fathers,* First Series, vol. 7, ed. Philip Schaff, trans. H. Browne (Buffalo, NY: Christian Literature, 1888), 7.8, revised and ed. Kevin Knight, https://www.newadvent.org/fathers/170207.htm: "Once for all, then, a short precept is given you: Love, and do what you will: whether you hold your peace, through love hold your peace; whether you cry out, through love cry out; whether you correct, through love correct; whether you spare, through love do you spare: let the root of love be within, of this root can nothing spring but what is good."

64. "Preface I of Saints," IBreviaryWeb, accessed October 2, 2020, http://www.ibreviary.com/m2/messale.php?s=prefazio&id=504.

65. See Matt Hadro, "How to Not Be a 'Beige Catholic,' According to Bishop Barron," *Catholic News Agency*, June 26, 2016, https://www.catholicnewsagency.com/news/34095/how-to-not-be-a-beige-catholic-according-to-bishop-barron.

66. "O Holy Spirit, Mighty Defender," English translation of "Carju nebesnyj, Bože mohučij" by Fr. William Levkulic, in *A Proposed Hymnal for the Byzantine Catholic Metropolitan Church of Pittsburgh,* May 25, 2020, Metropolitan Cantor Institute, Byzantine Catholic Archeparchy of Pittsburgh, https://mci.archpitt.org/songs/Hymnal_draft_2020-05.pdf (emphasis added). See William Levkulic, *The Divine Liturgy: A Book of Prayer* (Pittsburgh: Byzantine Seminary Press, 1978), 152.

67. *Lumen Gentium*, 41.

68. See Aquinas, *Summa Theologica* I-II.68. For several very good Thomistic reflections on the gifts of the Holy Spirit, see Walter Farrell, "The Breath of Happiness," in *A Companion to the Summa*, vol. 2, *The Pursuit of Happiness* (New York: Sheed

and Ward, 1945); Walter Farrell and Dominic Hughes, *Swift Victory: Essays on the Gifts of the Holy Spirit* (New York: Sheed and Ward, 1955); Ambroise Gardeil, *The Holy Spirit in Christian Life*, trans. anon. (London: Blackfriars Publications, 1953); and Ambroise Gardeil, *The Gifts of the Holy Spirit in the Dominican Saints*, trans. Anselm M. Townsend (Providence, RI: Cluny Media, 2016).

69. *Veni, Sancte Spiritus*, Preces-latinae.org, accessed August 24, 2020, http://www.preces-latinae.org/thesaurus/Hymni/VSS-2.html.

70. In this chapter, I am in particular indebted to the thought of Fr. Jean-Hervé Nicolas, OP, Fr. Emmanuel Doronzo, OMI, and to a lesser extent Fr. Édouard Hugon, OP. In particular, see Jean-Hervé Nicolas, *Synthèse dogmatique* (Fribourg: Éditions Universitaires, 1985), §§608–766.

71. *Lumen Gentium*, 8.

72. In my discussion of "sacramental causality," I am clearly simplifying the issues at hand, drawing on the Thomist *theological* school at times for my rhetoric, though striving to remain within the more general lines of what the Church requires *de fide* for belief in sacramental causality. The Church has not definitively pronounced on behalf of this or that school of theology, except where the basic truths defined, for example, by Trent have been put in danger.

73. This is to be understood in a very general sense, though I personally adhere to the Thomist school's theological position concerning the "motive of the Incarnation," especially as elaborated by someone like Fr. Réginald Garrigou-Lagrange in *Christ the Savior: A Commentary on the Third Part of St. Thomas' Theological Summa*, trans. Bede Rose (St. Louis: B. Herder, 1950), 10–107.

74. Charles Wesley, "Hail the Day That Sees Him Rise," Hymnary.org, accessed August 17, 2020, https://hymnary.org/text/hail_the_day_that_sees_him_rise.

75. Aquinas, *Summa Theologica* III.62.5. The theme of Christ's humanity as the "conjoined instrument" of his divinity is ancient, going back to the Fathers. A classic study on it can be found in the French translation of the work of Theophil Tschipke, *L'humanité du Christ comme instrument de salut de la divinité*, trans. Philibert Secrétan (Fribourg: Academic Press, 2003).

76. See "The Sacraments: Christ's Acts," in A.-M. Roguet, *Christ Acts Through the Sacraments*, trans. Carisbrooke Dominicans (Collegeville, MN: Liturgical Press, 1954), 11–17. As regards the ministers of the sacraments, we are setting aside here the question of Matrimony, where the spouses play a special role in the ministering of the sacrament.

77. *Lumen Gentium*, 11.

78. Congregation of Rites, instruction, *Eucharisticum mysterium*, 6, quoted in CCC 1325.

79. *Planned Parenthood of Southeastern Pa. v. Casey*, 505 U.S. 833, 851 (1992) (emphasis added).

80. *Roe v. Wade*, 410 U.S. 113 (1973).

81. For a very good and accessible overview of what is discussed in this paragraph, see Emonet, *The Greatest Marvel of Nature*.

82. In addition to Fr. Emonet's excellent text, the more advanced reader likely will benefit from the somewhat eclectic but ever-fruitful reflections of the broad-souled Fr. Norris Clarke, SJ, in *Person and Being* (Milwaukee: Marquette University Press, 1993). Even more advanced, but incredibly powerful philosophically, is Anton Pegis, *At the Origins of the Thomistic Notion of Man* (New York: MacMillan, 1963).

83. A witty example of this kind of intemperance can be found in chapter 17 of C. S. Lewis' *The Screwtape Letters* (New York: Touchstone, 1996).

84. For some reflection on the use of natural law language by the early Church Fathers, see Stanley S. Harakas, "Eastern Orthodox Perspectives on Natural Law," *Selected Papers from the Annual Meeting (American Society of Christian Ethics)* (1977): 41–56. For a good, if somewhat dated, text on the history and theory of the natural law, see Heinrich Rommen, *The Natural Law: A Study in Legal and Social History and Philosophy*, trans. Thomas R. Hanley (Indianapolis: Liberty Fund, 1998).

85. See Réginald Garrigou-Lagrange, *De revelatione per ecclesiam catholicam proposita*, 5th ed. (Rome: Desclée et Socii, 1950), 1.2.12.5.

86. For some introduction to these themes, see Gerard M. Verschuuren, *The Myth of an Anti-Science Church: Galileo, Darwin, Teilhard, Hawking, Dawkins* (Brooklyn, NY: Angelico, 2019); James Hannam, *The Genesis of Science: How the Christian Middle Ages Launched the Scientific Revolution* (Washington, DC: Regnery, 2011); and Aidan Nichols, *The Conversation of Faith and Reason: Modern Catholic Thought from Hermes to Benedict XVI* (Chicago: Hillenbrand Books, 2011).

87. See Rommen, *The Natural Law*. The original German title was *Die ewige Wiederkehr des Naturrechts*, meaning "The Eternal Return of the Natural Law."

88. See G. K. Chesterton, "The Paradoxes of Christianity," in *Orthodoxy* (Project Gutenberg), accessed April 23, 2021, http://www.gkc.org.uk/gkc/books/ortho14.txt.

89. Cicero, *Rep.* III, 22, 33, quoted in CCC 1956.

90. For an informative theological study on the vice of acedia, see Jean-Charles Nault, *The Noonday Devil: Acedia, the Unnamed Evil of Our Times*, trans. Michael J. Miller (San Francisco: Ignatius, 2015). For contemporary spiritual reflections on the vice of acedia, see R. J. Snell, *Acedia and Its Discontents: Metaphysical Boredom in an Empire of Desire* (Kettering, OH: Angelico, 2015); and Kathleen Norris, *Acedia and Me: A Marriage, Monks, and a Writer's Life* (New York: Riverhead Books, 2008).

91. Evagrius Ponticus, *Praktikos*, trans. Luke Dysinger, 12, accessed September 3, 2020, http://www.ldysinger.com/Evagrius/01_Prak/00a_start.htm.

92. See Aquinas, *Summa Theologica* II-II.35.

93. Evagrius Ponticus, *Praktikos*, 14.

94. See Journet, *The Meaning of Evil.*

95. "The Exsultet: The Proclamation of Easter," https://www.usccb.org/prayer-and-worship/liturgical-year-and-calendar/easter/easter-proclamation-exsultet.

96. For further reflection on how to apply St. Benedict's recommendations on humility in the day-to-day life of lay Christians, see J. Augustine Wetta, *Humility Rules: Saint Benedict's Twelve-Step Guide to Genuine Self-Esteem* (San Francisco: Ignatius, 2018); and Michael Casey, *A Guide to Living in the Truth: St. Benedict's Teaching on Humility* (Liguori, MO: Liguori/Triumph, 2001).

97. Benedict, *RB 1980*, 7.9 (p. 193).

98. See Daley, *Light on the Mountain*; Andreas Andreopoulos, *This Is My Beloved Son: The Transfiguration of Christ* (Brewster, MA: Paraclete Press, 2012); and Robert Barron, "Transfiguration and Deification," Word on Fire (website), August 6, 2017, https://www.wordonfire.org/resources/homily/transfiguration-and-deification/5544/.

99. Benedicta Ward, trans., *The Desert Fathers: Sayings of the Early Christian Monks* (New York: Penguin Books, 2003), 7.1 (p. 60, emphasis added). See Nault, *The Noonday Devil*, 39–40.

100. See Aquinas, *Summa Theologica* II-II.81.2.2.

101. See Benedict, *RB 1980*, 7.55 (p. 201).

102. G.K. Chesterton, "On Certain Modern Writers and the Institution of the Family," in *Heretics* (New York: John Lane, 1919; Project Gutenberg, 1996), http://www.gkc.org.uk/gkc/books/heret12.txt (emphasis added).

103. See Benedict, *RB 1980*, 7.67–69 (p. 201–203).

104. Gardeil, *La vraie vie chrétienne*, 69.

105. See Aquinas, *Summa Theologica* II-II.161.1.

106. See the story related in Joseph Cardinal Ratzinger, "Conscience and Truth," in *On Conscience: Two Essays by Joseph Ratzinger* (San Francisco: Ignatius; Philadelphia: National Catholic Bioethics Center, 2007), 13–14.

107. The "technical" tale of the relationship between the terms *conscience* and *prudence* is more nuanced. For some details, see my introductory notes in Benedict Merkelbach, "Where Should We Place the Treatise on Conscience in Moral Theology?" *Nova et Vetera* 18, no. 3 (2020): 1017–1037, available online at https://stpaulcenter.com/12-nv-18-3-merkelbach/.

108. For the reader who is interested in more details on this topic, see Réginald Garrigou-Lagrange, "Prudence's Place in the Organism of the Virtues," in Matthew K. Minerd, ed. and trans., *Philosophizing in Faith: Essays on the Beginning and End of Wisdom* (Providence, RI: Cluny Media, 2019), 153–170. The more advanced reader can consult the quite excellent second main chapter in Fr. Ambroise Gardeil's *La vraie vie chrétienne*, cited already on a number of occasions. This text is scheduled for publication by the Catholic University of America Press in 2021.

109. Charles Dickens, *A Christmas Carol* (New York: Airmont Books, 1963), 32.

110. *Veni, Creator Spiritus*, Preces-latinae.org, accessed August 4, 2020, http://www.preces-latinae.org/thesaurus/Hymni/VeniCreator.html. Drawn from an anonymous translation.

111. On the problem of "situation ethics," a topic which is somewhat dated *as regards its name* but nonetheless just as current today as it was when Pope Pius XII spoke out against it vociferously, see Dietrich von Hildebrand and Alice von Hildebrand, *Morality and Situation Ethics*, new ed. (Steubenville, OH: Hildebrand Press, 2019).

112. G.K. Chesterton, "The Suicide of Thought," in *Orthodoxy* (Project Gutenberg), accessed October 2, 2020, http://www.gkc.org.uk/gkc/books/ortho14.txt. On this important and nuanced topic, the more advanced reader may benefit from consulting Réginald Garrigou-Lagrange, "The Instability of the Acquired Moral Virtues in the State of Mortal Sin," in *Philosophizing in Faith*, 171–182.

113. John Paul II, *Veritatis Splendor* (August 6, 1993), 65–70.

114. Joseph Cardinal Ratzinger, "Conscience and Truth," in *On Conscience*, 13–14.

115. See Réginald Garrigou-Lagrange, *The Order of Things: The Realism of the Principle of Finality*, trans. Matthew K. Minerd (Steubenville, OH: Emmaus Academic, 2020), 132n24.

116. See Michel Labourdette, *"Grand cours" de théologie morale*, vol. 2, *Les actes humains* (Paris: Parole et Silence, 2016), 204–245.

117. For everything discussed in the second half of this chapter, the advanced reader will benefit from the excellent insights concerning this topic found in Steven Long, *The Teleological Grammar of the Moral Act*, 2nd ed. (Naples, FL: Sapientia Press of Ave Maria University, 2015).

118. See Gardeil, *La vraie vie chrétienne*, 101–189.

119. Aquinas, *Summa Theologica* I.21.4.

120. *The Autobiography of G. K. Chesterton* (San Francisco: Ignatius, 2006), 99 (emphasis added).

121. See Gardeil, *La vraie vie chrétienne*, 291–300.

122. G.K. Chesterton, "The Age of the Crusades," in *A Short History of England* (1917), accessed October 2, 2020, http://www.gkc.org.uk/gkc/books/history.txt.

123. See Bede, *Bede's Ecclesiastical History of England*, trans. A. M. Sellar (London: George Bell and Sons, 1907), 117 (chapter 13).

124. See Abraham Joshua Heschel, *God in Search of Man: A Philosophy of Judaism* (New York: Farrar, Straus and Giroux, 1983).

125. For related reflections, see Josef Pieper, *Justice*, in *The Four Cardinal Virtues*, trans. Daniel F. Coogan (Notre Dame, IN: University of Notre Dame Press, 1965), 43–116.

126. See Aquinas, *Summa Theologica* II-II.57–122.

127. Aristotle, *Politics* 3.16.

128. Hippolyte Taine, *Les Origines de la France contemporaine*, vol. 2, *Le régime moderne*, 118–119, cited in Garrigou-Lagrange, *The Order of Things*, 304.

129. Though based on the basic insights expressed by St. Thomas Aquinas, this chapter is indebted in a particular way to the work by Fr. Ambroise Gardeil, OP, which I have already cited on many occasions. See Gardeil, *La vraie vie chrétienne*, 192–358.

130. Ovid, *Metamorphoses* 1.84–86; see Ambroise Gardeil, "Vie humaine et vie divine," *Revue des Jeunes* (April 10, 1927): 5–17.

131. Gardeil, *La vraie vie chrétienne*, 69.

132. For a germane reflection on this topic, see James V. Schall, *The Order of Things* (San Francisco: Ignatius, 2007).

133. See Aquinas, *Summa Theologica* III.73.3; and Benedict XVI, *Sacramentum Caritatis* (February 22, 2007), vatican.va.

134. See Abraham Joshua Heschel, *The Sabbath: Its Meaning for Modern Man* (New York: Farrar, Straus and Giroux, 2005).

135. Then, for a Catholic account of the Sabbath and the role of worship in human life, see St. John Paul II's apostolic letter *Dies Domini* (May 31, 1998), http://www.vatican.va/content/john-paul-ii/en/apost_letters/1998/documents/hf_jp-ii_apl_05071998_dies-domini.html. Also, you may consider reading Josef Pieper, *In Search of the Sacred*, trans. Lothar Krauth (San Francisco: Ignatius, 1988); and Josef Pieper, *Leisure: The Basis of Culture*, trans. Alexander Dru (San Francisco: Ignatius, 2009).

136. See "O Sacrum Convivium," Preces-latinae.org, accessed August 10, 2020, http://www.preces-latinae.org/thesaurus/Euch/SacrumConv.html.

137. Aristotle, *Nicomachean Ethics*, in *The Complete Works of Aristotle*, ed. Jonathan Barnes, trans. W.D. Ross, vol. 2 (Princeton, NJ: Princeton University Press, 1995), 9.1 (1164b3–6, slightly altered and emphasis added).

138. Leon R. Kass, "The Ten Commandments," in *Leading a Worthy Life: Finding Meaning in Modern Times* (New York: Encounter Books, 2017), 367 ("contraceived" changed to "contracept" for clarity).

139. Kass, 367.

140. See Aquinas, *Summa Theologica* I-II.100.6.

141. See Aquinas, II-II.101.1.

142. See Jonah Goldberg, "Human Nature: Our Inner Tribesman," in *Suicide of the West* (New York: Crown Forum, 2018), 23–46.

143. See Kass, *Leading a Worthy Life*, 365.

144. See David S. Crawford, ed., *The Body as Anticipatory Sign: Commemorating the Anniversaries of "Humanae Vitae" and "Veritatis Splendor,"* ed. David S. Crawford (Washington, DC: Humanum Academic, 2021).

145. See Aquinas, *Summa Theologica* II-II.101.

146. However, for very technical theological reasons, I follow others in holding that we must see Mary's predestination to the divine maternity as being the source of all of her other prerogatives. See Réginald Garrigou-Lagrange, *The Mother of the Saviour and Our Interior Life*, trans. Bernard J. Kelly (St. Louis, MO: B. Herder, 1949), 17–44.

147. For example, see Cliff Hess, "Blue Ridge Mountain Blues," Bluegrasslyrics.com, accessed September 8, 2020, https://www.bluegrasslyrics.com/song/blue-ridge-mountain-blues/.

148. See Matthew K. Minerd, "Giving Nature Its Due—Even in Sacramental Matrimony," *Homiletic and Pastoral Review*, September 9, 2017, https://www.hprweb.com/2017/09/giving-nature-its-due-even-in-sacramental-matrimony/.

149. Pius XI, *Casti Connubii* (December 31, 1930), 13; see John Paul II, *Familiaris Consortio* (November 22, 1981), 38–39.

150. There are some arguments among Catholics about the nature of the common good. Many of these disagreements seem to be more over words than over realities. For a sampling of various parties who are all safe and faithful Catholic thinkers, see Yves R. Simon, *A General Theory of Authority* (Notre Dame, IN: University of Notre Dame Press, 1980); Yves R. Simon, *Philosophy of Democratic Government* (Notre Dame, IN: University of Notre Dame Press, 1993); Jacques Maritain, *The Person and the Common Good*, trans. John J. Fitzgerald (Notre Dame, IN: University of Notre Dame Press, 2009); and Charles De Koninck, *The Primacy of the Common Good Against the Personalists*, in *The Writings of Charles De Koninck*, ed. and trans. Ralph McInerny (Notre Dame, IN: University of Notre Dame Press, 2009), 2:63–164.

151. Dickens, *A Christmas Carol*, 17–18 (emphasis added).

152. Congregation for the Doctrine of the Faith, *Libertatis Conscientia* (1986), 94, https://www.vatican.va/roman_curia/congregations/cfaith/documents/rc_con_cfaith_doc_19860322_freedom-liberation_en.html. The document, promulgated by St. John Paul II, here cites the Second Vatican Council's declaration *Gravissimum Educationis* (3 and 6), Pius XI's encyclical *Divini Illius Magistri* (28, 38, and 66), and article 5 of the 1983 "Charter of the Rights of the Family" promulgated by the Pontifical Council for the Family.

153. See Aristotle, *Nicomachean Ethics* 1.2.

154. For an outline of this teaching in its classical form, see Réginald Garrigou-Lagrange, "The Divine Requirements of the Final End in Political Matters," in *Philosophizing in Faith*, 205–218.

155. Garrigou-Lagrange, "Truth and Indifferentism," in *Philosophizing in Faith*, 234.

156. *Dignitatis Humanae* (December 7, 1965), 1.

157. For a practical guide, see *Clear Conscience: A Catholic Guide to Voting* (West Chester, PA: Ascension, 2020).

158. For example, see Robert P. George, *Conscience and Its Enemies: Confronting the Dogmas of Liberal Secularism* (Wilmington, DE: ISI Books, 2016).

159. See Raymond-Léopold Bruckberger, *God and Politics*, trans. Eleanor Levieux (Chicago: J. Philip O'Hara, 1971), 45–52.

160. Immanuel Kant, "Idea for a Universal History with a Cosmopolitan Aim," trans. Allen W. Wood, in *Anthropology, History, and Education*, ed. Günter Zöller and Robert B. Louden (Cambridge: Cambridge University Press, 2008), 8:23 (slightly modified).

161. See Aquinas, *Summa Theologica* II-II.26.8.

162. Aquinas, II-II.101.1.

163. See the beautiful little text by Fr. Pierre-Marie Emonet, *The Greatest Marvel of Nature.*

164. Gardeil, "Vie humaine et vie divine," 5.

165. Gardeil, 17.

166. See Réginald Garrigou-Lagrange, "The Subordination of the State to the Perfection of the Human Person According to St. Thomas," in *Philosophizing in Faith*, 201–202; Maritain, *The Person and the Common Good*, 20; and Aquinas, *Summa Theologica* I.54.4 (along with John of St. Thomas' commentary on this text).

167. Blaise Pascal, *Pensées*, in *Pensées and Other Writings*, ed. Anthony Levi, trans. Honor Levi (Oxford: Oxford University Press, 2008), 237.

168. Tertullian, *Apologeticum* 9.8, quoted in Congregation for the Doctrine of the Faith, "Declaration on Procured Abortion" (November 18, 1974), 6, http://www.vatican.va/roman_curia/congregations/cfaith/documents/rc_con_cfaith_doc_19741118_declaration-abortion_en.html. Admittedly, Tertullian is a slightly problematic figure, given that he died outside of union with the Church. Nonetheless, the Magisterium did not hesitate to cite him, and he is an important authority in the early Western Church concerning a number of topics.

169. See Congregation for the Doctrine of the Faith, "Declaration on Procured Abortion," 6–8.

170. The National Catholic Bioethics Center provides a helpful summary. See "Maternal-Fetal Conflicts," February 2015, National Catholic Bioethics Center, https://www.ncbcenter.org/resources-and-statements-cms/summary-maternal-fetal-conflicts. See also chapter 2 of Janet E. Smith and Christopher Kaczor, *Life Issues, Medical Choices: Questions and Answers for Catholics* (Cincinnati, OH: Servant, 2016).

171. For an accessible introduction see Smith and Kaczor, *Life Issues, Medical Choices*.

172. For a recent, challenging discussion of Catholicism and the problems involved in living in a consumeristic society, see David Cloutier, *The Vice of Luxury: Economic Excess in a Consumer Age* (Washington, DC: Georgetown University Press, 2015). For Patristic reflections on this chapter's topic, see St. John Chrysostom, *On Wealth and Poverty*, trans. Catharine P. Roth (Crestwood, NY: St. Vladimir's Seminary Press, 1999); and St. Basil the Great, *On Social Justice*, trans. C. Paul Schroeder (Yonkers, NY: St. Vladimir's Seminary Press, 2009).

173. Thomas Hobbes, *Leviathan*, ed. Richard Tuck, rev. ed. (Cambridge: Cambridge University Press, 1999), 174 (chapter 24).

174. Aristotle, *Politics* 1.9 (trans. Ross, slightly altered).

175. The classic text on this topic is Josef Pieper's *Leisure: The Basis of Culture*. Also, see Matthew Minerd, "Leisure: The Basis of Everything?," *Homiletic and Pastoral Review* (January 2017), https://www.hprweb.com/2017/01/leisure-the-basis-of-everything/.

176. See *Lumen Gentium*, 5. This famous chapter of the conciliar document was prepared for by many profound discussions in the nineteenth and twentieth centuries.

177. A recent, very large tome on this topic might be of interest. See Eugene McCarraher, *The Enchantments of Mammon: How Capitalism Became the Religion of Modernity* (Cambridge, MA: Belknap, 2019); and lest one think that the answer is socialism or Marxism (both errors which have been condemned by the Church), see Jacques Maritain's reflections on how Marxism is merely the flip side of classical liberalism, in *Integral Humanism: Temporal and Spiritual Problems of a New Christendom*, trans. Joseph W. Evans (New York: Charles Scribner's Sons, 1968), 35–94.

178. For a recent study, see Thomas C. Behr, *Social Justice and Subsidiarity: Luigi Taparelli and the Origins of Modern Catholic Social Thought* (Washington, DC: Catholic University of America Press, 2019).

179. Letter attributed to Barnabas, in International Commission on English in the Liturgy, *The Liturgy of the Hours: According to the Roman Rite*, vol. 4, *Ordinary Time: Weeks 18–34* (New York: Catholic Book Publishing, 1975), 71–72 (quotation marks added).

180. See Servais Pinckaers, *Passions and Virtue*, trans. Benedict M. Guevin (Washington, DC: Catholic University of America Press, 2015); Nicholas E. Lombardo, *The Logic of Desire: Aquinas on Emotion* (Washington, DC: Catholic University of America Press, 2011); and Robert Miner, *Thomas Aquinas on the Passions: A Study of Summa Theologiae; Ia2ae 22–48* (Cambridge: Cambridge University Press, 2011).

181. Epictetus, *Discourses and Selected Writings*, trans. and ed. Robert Dobbin (New York: Penguin Classics, 2008); and Marcus Aurelius, *Meditations*, trans. Gregory Hays (New York: Modern Library, 2003).

182. See Ward, *The Desert Fathers*.

183. Gardeil, *La vraie vie chrétienne*, 115–116.

184. For a lovely reflection on this topic, see Pieper, "Fortitude Must Not Trust Itself," in *The Four Cardinal Virtues*, 122–125.

185. Fr. Réginald Garrigou-Lagrange wrote an excellent, though brief, reflection on the role of prudence in justice in contrast to its role in the virtues of courage and temperance. See Garrigou-Lagrange, *The Order of Things*, 282–284.

186. There are many such "Enlightenments," some of which are darker than certain pro-Enlightenment apologists like Steven Pinker might wish to admit.

187. "Christian Persecution 'At Near Genocide Levels,'" News, BBC.com, May 3, 2019, https://www.bbc.com/news/uk-48146305.

188. I have in mind here, in particular, the work of the Orthodox author Rod Dreher, *Live Not by Lies: A Manual for Christian Dissidents* (New York: Sentinel, 2020).

189. See CCC 2425; Leo XIII, *Rerum Novarum* (May 15, 1891), 4, 5, 14, 15, and 17; Pius XI, *Quadragesimo Anno* (May 15, 1931), 111–128; and John Paul II, *Centesimus Annus* (May 1, 1991), 12–21. The Church has also condemned unfettered capitalism, but as some American commentators have joked, we would need to look far and wide to find the supposed rule of libertarians in the United States, whose "capitalism" is quite far from being completely unregulated.

190. See Ryan T. Anderson, *When Harry Became Sally: Responding to the Transgender Moment* (New York: Encounter Books, 2018). In fact, during the editing of this book, Dr. Anderson's text was indeed "cancelled," as Amazon removed it from its listings. See Joan Desmond, "Amazon Erases 'When Harry Became Sally,' Ryan Anderson's Book About Transgenderism," *National Catholic Register*, February 24, 2021, https://www.ncregister.com/blog/amazon-erases-when-sally-became-harry.

191. Kipling, "If—" in *Poems*, 171.

192. Aquinas, *Summa Theologica* II-II.123.6.

193. "From a Letter to Diognetus," 5–6, Vatican.va, accessed April 20, 2021, http://www.vatican.va/spirit/documents/spirit_20010522_diogneto_en.html.

194. There are other virtues attached to temperance, as one can see by reading the treatise on temperance in Thomas Aquinas' *Summa Theologica* (II-II.141–170). However, we are here only presenting an overview.

195. Garrigou-Lagrange, *The Order of Things*, 274–275.

196. See Gardeil, *La vraie vie chrétienne*, 110.

197. See chapter 17 of C. S. Lewis' *The Screwtape Letters*.

198. For a brief accounting of this, see Jerome Oetgen, *Mission to America: A History of Saint Vincent Archabbey, the First Benedictine Monastery in the United States* (Washington, DC: Catholic University of America Press, 2000), 78–79.

199. G. K. Chesterton, "Wine When It Is Red," in *All Things Considered* (1915; Project Gutenberg, 2004), http://www.gkc.org.uk/gkc/books/All_Things_Considered.html.

200. See Karol Wojtyla, *Love and Responsibility*, trans. H. T. Willetts (San Francisco: Ignatius, 1993); Christopher West, *Good News About Sex and Marriage,* rev. ed. (Cincinnati, OH: Servant, 2004); and John S. Grabowski, *Sex and Virtue: An Introduction to Sexual Ethics* (Washington, DC: Catholic University of America Press, 2003).

201. Paul VI, *Humanae Vitae* (July 25, 1968), 17.

202. See Aquinas, *Summa Theologica* II-II.167.

203. Johnnie Bailes and Walter Bailes, "Dust on the Bible," BluegrassNet (website), accessed October 2, 2020, https://www.bluegrassnet.com/lyrics/the-dust-on-the-bible.

204. However, even Thomist theologians and philosophers debate how the natural moral virtues and the infused moral virtues relate to each other: do they coexist, or does grace "replace" the natural moral virtues with the infused moral virtues? These debates become highly technical. For my part, joining many traditional Thomistic commentators, I hold the "coexistence" position. The technical details are not appropriate for a text like this. A summary of an argument I agree with on this topic can be found in Romanus Cessario, "What Causes the Moral Virtues to Develop?," in *The Moral Virtues and Theological Ethics* (Notre Dame, IN: University of Notre Dame Press, 1991), 94–125.

205. Gardeil, *La vraie vie chrétienne*, 129–130.

206. Aquinas, *Summa Theologica* II-II.24.3.2.

207. On this topic, see Adalbert de Vogüé, *To Love Fasting: The Monastic Experience* (Petersham, MA: St. Bede's, 1989).

208. See Yuval Harari, *Homo Deus: A Brief History of Tomorrow* (New York: Harper, 2017). A helpful response to Harari's outlook can be found in the work of the great Jewish bioethicist Leon Kass, *Leading a Worthy Life*.

209. Mary Eberstadt has presented this in a number of very informative books. See Mary Eberstadt, *Adam and Eve After the Pill: Paradoxes of the Sexual Revolution* (San Francisco: Ignatius, 2013); *How the West Really Lost God: A New Theory of Secularization* (West Conshohocken, PA: Templeton, 2013); and *Primal Screams: How the Sexual Revolution Created Identity Politics* (West Conshohocken, PA: Templeton, 2019).

210. This was shown very convincingly in a now-difficult-to-find paper once given by Tikhon Alexander Pino, "Contraception and the Orthodox Church: Contemporary Theology and the Sources of Tradition." At the time of the writing of this book, it seems that the author has removed it from public view because of planned publication in the Orthodox periodical *The Orthodox Word*.

211. For an outline of how this idea is presented by the Thomist philosopher Jacques Maritain, see Matthew K. Minerd, "Maritain and the Metaphysics of Sexual Differentiation," in *The Things That Matter: Essays Inspired by the Later Work of Jacques Maritain*, ed. Heidi Giebel (Washington, DC: Catholic University of America Press, 2018), 150–167.

212. Dietrich von Hildebrand, *Marriage: The Mystery of Faithful Love* (Manchester, NH: Sophia Institute, 1997), 13.

213. I defend and discuss this slightly older theological language in a popular article, "Giving Nature Its Due—Even in Sacramental Matrimony."

214. See Saint Paul VI Institute, https://popepaulvi.com; Couple to Couple League, https://ccli.org; Marquette Method Natural Family Planning Services, https://www.mmnfp.com; FCCA: FertilityCare Centers of America, https://fertilitycare.org; BOMA-USA: Billings Ovulation Method Association, https://www.boma-usa.org; and Natural Womanhood, https://naturalwomanhood.org. I would like to thank my wife, Courtney, for helping to gather this information, as well as Fr. Deacon Gregory Gath and his wife, Beth.

215. See G. E. M. Anscombe, "Contraception and Chastity" and "On *Humanae Vitae*," in *Faith in a Hard Ground: Essays on Religion, Philosophy and Ethics by G. E. M. Anscombe*, ed. Mary Geach and Luke Gormally (Charlottesville, VA: Imprint Academic, 2008), 170–198.

216. On these contentious issues, I would recommend that the faithful Catholic begin with the following texts: Janet Smith and Paul Check, eds., *Living the Truth in Love: Pastoral Approaches to Same-Sex Attraction* (San Francisco: Ignatius, 2015); and Anderson, *When Harry Became Sally*.

217. For a clear and faithful account of these issues see Smith and Kaczor, *Life Issues, Medical Choices*.

218. I am deeply indebted to Fr. Deacon Jonathan Deane of the Byzantine Catholic Eparchy of Phoenix for this insight and reference.

219. William F. Buckley Jr., "Our Mission Statement," *National Review*, November 19, 1955, https://www.nationalreview.com/1955/11/our-mission-statement-william-f-buckley-jr/.

220. My presentation of theology is indebted to the Thomist school. See Matthew K. Minerd, "Wisdom Be Attentive: The Noetic Structure of Sapiential Knowledge," *Nova et Vetera* (English ed.) 18, no. 4 (Fall 2020): 1103–1146.

221. I have written a lengthy article slightly critiquing this traditional vocabulary, which, however, has merit. See my article cited above, "Wisdom Be Attentive: The Noetic Structure of Sapiential Knowledge."

222. Aquinas, *Summa Theologica* II-II.24.3.2.

223. Tom T. Hall, "I Don't Want My Golden Slippers," Classic Country Lyrics (website), accessed August 14, 2020, https://www.classic-country-song-lyrics.com/idontwantmygoldenslipperslyricschords.html.